ON RELIGION

KARL MARX and FRIEDRICH ENGELS

ON RELIGION

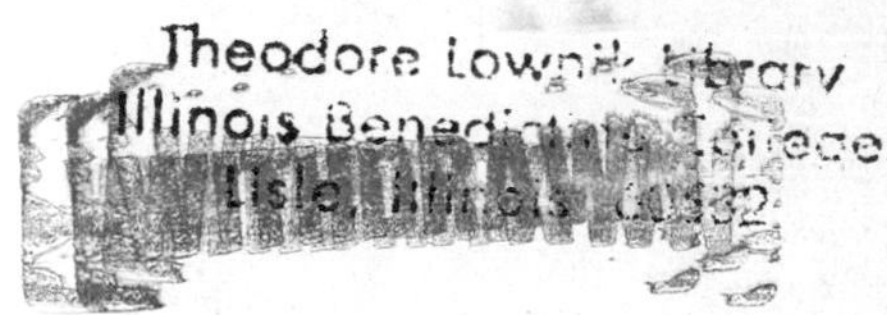

INTRODUCTION BY REINHOLD NIEBUHR

SCHOCKEN BOOKS • NEW YORK

Third Printing, 1969

This volume is reprinted from
the edition of 1957 published by
The Foreign Languages Publishing House, Moscow.

Library of Congress Catalog Card No. 64-15219
Manufactured in the United States of America

CONTENTS

INTRODUCTION

"In Germany the criticism of religion is the premise of all criticism,"[1] declared Marx in a classical phrase which gives a key to many of the observations on religion by the two men whose writings are gathered in this volume. In religion we have the final claim to absolute truth; Marx and Engels are social scientists, interested empirically in the way that the claim of the absolute is used as a screen for particular competitive historical interests.

Much of what Marx and Engels observed has become the object of attention of all social and cultural historians, if indeed it has not always been the true object of history. When Engels reviews the transmutation of Christianity from a little eschatalogical sect to an imperial religion, or from Augustine's rigorous separation of the "City of God" and the "city of this world" to the structure of papal power over political affairs constructed by Gregory VII in the Middle Ages, or when he analyses the social forces and influences which made the Reformation radical in the sense that it used Biblical authority to undermine ecclesiastical authority, and reactionary in the sense that it made the church subservient to the princes and ruthlessly opposed the Anabaptists, he is making observations on historical sequences which are the usual preoccupation of historians of culture and of political life.

It could be said that the observations of Marx and Engels validate the Marxist thesis that "the criticism of religion is the premise of all criticism" because the absolute claim is used as a weapon for various historically relative, and usually established, social and political forces. Yet, their appreciation of the

---

[1] Marx and Engels: *On Religion,* "Contribution to the Critique of Hegel's Philosophy of Right," p. 41.

socially radical peasants of the sixteenth century under Anabaptist religious leadership, revealed particularly in Engels' article on the Peasant Wars, is not quite in agreement with Marxism's central thesis that religion is a weapon always used by the established social forces. Later Marxists, Bernstein particularly, regarded the radical sects of the Cromwellian Revolution in the seventeenth century, rightly, as forerunners of the Marxist movement.[2] The radical sectarians appropriated Messianism to make of it an instrument of social revolt, while the more conservative religious forces used otherworldly hopes to beguile men from injustices in history. Nevertheless, it must be realized that, with the exception of this polemical quirk, the general order of Marxist observations on the relation of the claim to the absolute to the relative forces of history are unexceptionable. They would be accepted by any historian, religious or irreligious, who has an empirical grasp of historical facts.

I have said that these writings of Marx and Engels on religion reveal the passion for empirical observation and analysis, shared by them with many moderns; moreover, here too are clues to that remarkable development of which many students have been made aware: of an irreligion transmuted into a new political religion, canonized precisely in the writings of Marx (and the later Lenin) as sacred scripture, and preached in notoriously practical and opportune ways as the principles for a revolutionary reformation of the social order according to an immutable dogma.

One of the most significant clues to the mystery of this ironic transmutation is provided in these early writings. It consists in the vagueness of both Marx and Engels about the problem of knowledge, and their consequent tendency to equate the epistemology of empiricism with the metaphysical theory of materialism. This tendency is revealed in Marx's attitude toward the medieval philosopher Duns Scotus. Marx

[2] Eduard Bernstein: *Cromwell and Communism,* Schocken 1963.

made this observation about Duns Scotus: "Materialism is the native son of Great Britain. Even Britain's Scholastic Duns wondered 'can matter think?' In order to bring about that miracle, he had recourse to God's omnipotence, i.e., he forced theology to preach materialism. In addition he was a nominalist. Nominalism is the main component of British materialism, and in general the first expression of materialism. The real founder of English materialism and of all modern experimental science was Bacon."[3]

Thus nominalism, the first form of empiricism, and the whole empirical tradition is equated with the metaphysical position of materialism. The reason for this identification is obvious. Marx rightly observes that idealism in epistemology leads to metaphysical idealism which leads to "theological prejudice." About Locke and Condillac, Marx observes: "Locke's immediate follower, Condillac, who also translated him into French, once opposed Locke's sensualism to seventeenth century metaphysics. He proved that the French had opposed metaphysics as a mere bungling fancy and theological prejudice."[4] It is clear that the ex-Hegelian and anti-Hegelian Marx rightly equates metaphysical idealism with religion. But he wrongly equates empiricism, an epistemological theory, with materialism as metaphysical doctrine. We know, of course, that empiricism in epistemology and naturalism in metaphysics, outside the orbit of Marxism are akin. But non-Marxist empiricism abhors all dogmas, while Marx's metaphysics without a solution of the epistemological problem, the problem of knowledge, becomes the basis of a great religio-political dogma.

The path which is traveled becomes clear in Engels' essay on "Feuerbach and the End of German Classical Philosophy." Engels agrees with Feuerbach in their common anti-Hegelianism. He asserts that the young Hegelians were driven back

---

[3] Marx and Engels: "The Holy Family, or Critique of Critical Criticism," p. 63.

[4] Ibid., p. 66.

by the practical necessities of their fight against positive religion, to Anglo-French materialism. "This brought them into conflict with their school system. While materialism conceives nature as the sole reality, nature in the Hegelian system represents merely the 'alienation' of the absolute idea, so to say, a degradation of the idea. At all events thinking and its thought product, the idea, is here the primary, nature the derivative, which only exists by condescension of the idea. In this contradiction they floundered as well or ill as they could. . . . Then came Feuerbach's *Essence of Christianity*. With one blow it pulverized the contradiction in that it placed, without circumlocutions, materialism on the throne again."[5]

The logic of the Marxist viewpoint is clear. Any theory which takes the problem of knowledge seriously enough to distinguish between the self as object and the self as knower is potentially idealism; it ends by giving primacy to the theoretical "copies of reality" rather than to reality itself. An empirical approach to epistemology on the other hand is identified with "materialism," that is, a philosophical naturalism and a vaguely conceived epistemology which guarantees the primacy of "reality vis à vis the fanciful copies of reality." Thus we arrive at absolute truth in the name of science against absolute pretensions in the name of religion and idealism.

Marx distinguishes between two forms of French materialism. He affirms that Cartesian materialism merges into natural science. But the other branch, concerned with historical problems, "leads directly to socialism and communism." He then proceeds to prove deductively, not empirically, how this comes about. He writes, in *The Holy Family, or Critique of Critical Criticism:* "There is no need of any great penetration to see from the teaching of materialism on the original goodness and equal intellectual endowment of men, the omnipotence of experience, habit, and education, and the influence of environment on man, the great significance of industry, the justification

[5] Ibid., "Feuerbach and the End of Classical German Philosophy," p. 223.

of enjoyment, etc., how necessarily materialism is connected with communism and socialism. If man draws all his knowledge, sensation, etc., from the world of the senses and the experience gained in it, the empirical world must be arranged so that in it man experiences and gets used to what is really human and that he becomes aware of himself as a man. If correctly understood, interest is the principle of all morals, man's private interests must be made to coincide with the interest of humanity. If man is unfree in the materialist sense, i.e., free not through the negative power to avoid this or that, but through the positive power to assert his true individuality, crime must not be punished in the individual, but the antisocial source of crime must be destroyed, and each man must be given social scope for the vital manifestation of his being."[6]

In this breathtaking series of propositions, Marx, the revolutionary humanist, pretends to draw self-evident deductions from the mere presupposition of metaphysical materialism—which for Marx meant essentially Lockean empiricism. All the propositions, dear to a revolutionary and apocalyptic idealist—universalism, collectivism, humanism, and socialism—are drawn, like so many rabbits, out of the hat of materialism.

If one remembers that for Marx materialism and empiricism are practically identical, and realizes that all his criticisms of either orthodox religion or Hegelian idealism and all his refutations of their pretensions to "eternal" validity avail themselves of empirical analyses of their claims, one can only regard this passage, and similar passages, as the ladders on which the empirical critic of the status quo climbed up to the heaven and haven of a new religious apocalypse which made him the revered prophet of a new world religion, as potent in the twentieth century as was Islam in the seventh.

In his climb up the ladder Marx obviously left behind his passion for empirical observation and analysis. His humanism was taken from the humanistic tradition of the West, but his

[6] Ibid, "Holy Family," pp. 67-68.

collectivism, the assignment of a messianic role to the "proletariat," and his doctrine of a climactic revolution in which the kingdom of universal justice would be ushered in as a heaven on earth were all highly speculative, even more so than all historical generalizations usually are. Marx deduces these doctrines from "materialism" without bothering to establish them by refuting the democratic and individualistic doctrines of his fellow empiricist, John Locke, or the political absolutism of his fellow materialist, Thomas Hobbes. The latter's political absolutism, incidentally, had strong affinities with the doctrines of Hegel, whom Marx, with the aid of Feuerbach, had summarily dismissed.

Evidently even a scrupulous empirical method fails to achieve common conclusions in the complex field of historical causation, in which causal sequences on many different levels intertwine. Marx, as an empiricist, would have been just another learned man. As an apocalyptic dogmatist, he became the founder of a new religion, whose writings would be quoted as parts of a new sacred canon.

The most interesting portion of this transformation of an empirical observer into a religious prophet who appropriated the messianic visions of Jewish and Christian faith, was that from the beginning the common humanism was subordinated in Marx's vision to the purposes of a revolutionist who wanted, not so much to understand the world, as to remake it. In his *Theses on Feuerbach,* Marx makes this criticism of previous materialism: "The chief defect of hitherto existing materialism, that of Feuerbach included, is that the thing, reality, sensuousness, is made the object of contemplation (*Anschauung*), but not the human sensuous activity, practice."[7] Reality must be studied for the sake of transforming it. Here speaks the revolutionist and religious prophet, rather than the scientist and philosopher.

A modern school of post-Marxist Marxism is celebrating

[7] Ibid, "Theses on Feuerbach," p. 69.

Marx's "early humanism" as if it were an original purity which has since been corrupted by political polemics. But the historic evidence reveals this humanism to have always been a subordinate part of his political revolutionary propaganda. Thus the theme of the "alienation" or "estrangement" of the worker from his humanity transmutes the Hegelian idea of alienation to make it mean that modern industry, by treating the worker as a commodity, has alienated him from his humanity. Marx writes: "We have considered the act of estranging practical human activity, labor, in two of its aspects: 1) the relation of the worker to the product of his labor as an alien object exercising power over him, and, 2) the relation of the worker to the act of producing in the labor process. This relation of the worker to his own activity is an alien activity, not belonging to him. It is activity as suffering, strength as weakness, begetting as emasculating the worker's own physical and mental energy, his personal life, or what is life other than activity, which is turned against him and neither depends on nor belongs to him. Here we have self-estrangement, as we previously had estrangement from the thing."[8]

This indictment of the dehumanizing effect of modern industry is indeed an expression of Marx's humanism, but the argument about man is strictly subordinated to the polemical purpose of an anti-bourgeois revolutionist. The words and the dialectic mode of thought remind one of Hegel, rather than Locke, whose empiricism Marx frequently cites but whose convictions he never quotes. Thus the anti-Hegelian materialist speaks in terms of Hegelian dialectic to project a materialistic version of an even more traditional religious apocalypse.

What is lacking is a discriminate and truly empirical analysis of the effects of modern technical civilization on the humanity of the working person, so as to determine to what degree the deleterious effects are inherent in the technical

---

[8] Karl Marx: *Economic and Philosophic Manuscripts of 1844*, Foreign Languages Publishing House, Moscow, pp. 73-74.

process itself and to what degree these effects are due to the profit motive in modern industry. Undoubtedly the indictment was relevant to the historic facts of early nineteenth century European industrialism. This relevance made the Marxist dogma effective in the nineteenth century but implausible in twentieth century European culture where an open society had taken innumerable steps to guard the rights and the essential humanity of the person.

Insofar as some of the dehumanizing effects are inherent in the technical process itself, they are, of course, symptomatic of the rapid process of industrialization throughout the world in which a communist and capitalist bloc of nations are ironically competing. Unfortunately Marx's celebrated humanism, belatedly discovered by certain intellectuals and allegedly purged of Leninist and Stalinist corruptions, does not serve us in making the necessary empirical distinctions about the effects of industrialism, whether inherent in the technical process or in a social order.

It was from the very beginning too indiscriminate, too lacking in empirical precision, too much the weapon of the "class struggle" and the instrument of the revolutionary prophet who had transmuted atheism into a new religion. The priests of this religion are now the priest-kings of an empire based on utopian illusions, of a culture in which materialism has become the canonized philosophy. The vaunted affinity between empiricism and materialism has been transmuted into a new dogma.

The irony of these developments is complete. But preoccupation with the irony of these developments cannot obscure either the original humanistic passion of Marx's enterprise or the dogmatic uses to which it was put and the dogmatic atrophy in which it has now been enmeshed. That atrophy was not a corruption, introduced by later Marxists, whether Lenin or Stalin. It was inherent in Marx's transmutation of empiricism to materialism to revolutionary religious apocalypse.

REINHOLD NIEBUHR

Union Theological Seminary
New York, October 1963

KARL MARX

FOREWORD TO THESIS: *THE DIFFERENCE BETWEEN THE NATURAL PHILOSOPHY OF DEMOCRITUS AND THE NATURAL PHILOSOPHY OF EPICURUS*

The form of this treatise would be more strictly scientific, on the one hand, and less pedantic in some points, on the other, had it not been originally intended as a doctor's thesis. However, I am obliged through external causes to have it printed in its present form. Besides, I believe that in it I have solved a hitherto unsolved problem in the history of Greek philosophy.

Experts know that there are no preliminary works which could be useful in any way for the subject of this treatise. Up to this time there has been nothing but repetition of Cicero's and Plutarch's rigmarole. Gassendi, who freed Epicurus from the interdict laid on him by the Fathers of the Church and the whole of the Middle Ages—that age of materialized irrationalism—provides but one interesting point in his observations.[1] He tries to conciliate his Catholic conscience with his heathen knowledge and Epicurus with the Church—an obviously futile effort. It is like throwing the habit of a Christian nun over the exuberant body of the Greek Lais. It is more a case of Gassendi learning philosophy from Epicurus than being able to teach us about Epicurus's philosophy.

This treatise should be considered as a precursor to a larger work in which I shall expound in detail the cycle of the Epicurean, stoic and sceptic philosophies in their connection with the whole of Greek speculation.[2] The shortcomings of this treatise as to form and the like will be remedied in that work.

Hegel, on the whole, correctly defined the general features of the above-mentioned systems. But in the admirably extensive and daring plan of his *History of Philosophy*, from which we can date all history of philosophy, it was impossible, for one thing, to go into details, and, for another, the great thinker's view of what he called speculation *par excellence* prevented him from acknowledging the higher importance of those systems for the history of Greek philosophy and for the Greek mind in general. These systems are the key to the true history of Greek philosophy. A more profound indication of their relation to Greek life is to be found in my friend Köppen's *Friedrich der Grosse und seine Widersacher (Frederick the Great and His Opponents)*.

If a criticism of Plutarch's polemic against Epicurus's theology is added as an appendix, it is because that polemic is not unique, but is representative of an *espèce* in that it very aptly shows the attitude of theologizing reason to philosophy.

The criticism makes no mention of the falseness of Plutarch's standpoint in general when he cites philosophy before the forum of religion. On this point a passage from David Hume will do as well as any kind of discussion:

" 'Tis certainly a kind of indignity to philosophy, whose *sovereign authority* ought everywhere to be acknowledged, to oblige her on every occasion to make apologies for her conclusions, and justify herself to every particular art and science which may be offended at her. *This puts one in mind of a king arraigned for high treason against his subjects.*"[3]

As long as philosophy still has a drop of blood left in its world-conquering, absolutely free heart, it will not cease to call to its opponents with Epicurus: "ἀσβὴζ δὲ οὐχ ὁ τοὺζ τῶυ πολλῶυ θεοὺζ ἀναιρῶν, ἀλλ' ὁ τὰς τῶν παλλῶν δόξας θεοῖς προσάπτων."*

Philosophy makes no secret of it. Prometheus's admission:

ἁπλῶ λόγω τοὺς πάντας ἐχθαίρω θεοὺς**

is its own admission, its own motto against all gods, heavenly and earthly, who do not acknowledge the consciousness of man as the supreme divinity. There must be no god on a level with it.

And to the wretched March hares who exult over the apparent deterioration of philosophy's social position it again answers, as Prometheus did to Hermes, the messenger of the gods:

τῆς σῆς λαυαείας τὴν ἐμὴν δυσπραξίαν,
σαφῶς ἐπίστασ', οὐκ ἄν ἀλλάξαιμ' ἐγώ.
κρεῖσσον γὰρ οἶμαι τῇδε λατρεύειν πετρᾳ
ἢ πατρὶ φῦναι Ζηνὶ πιστὸν ἄγγελον.***

Prometheus is the noblest of saints and martyrs in the calendar of philosophy.

Berlin, March 1841

---

* Not he who rejects the gods of the crowd is impious, but he who embraces the crowd's opinion of the gods. (From Epicurus's letter to Menokeus on the tenth book of Diogenes Laertius.)—*Ed.*

** In sooth all gods I hate. (From *Prometheus Bound* by Aeschylus.)—*Ed.*

*** I shall never exchange my fetters for slavish servility. 'Tis better to be chained to the rock than bound to the service of Zeus. (*Ibid.*)—*Ed.*

KARL MARX

THE LEADING ARTICLE OF No. 179 OF *KÖLNISCHE ZEITUNG*[4]

Hitherto we credited *Kölnische Zeitung* with being, if not the "paper of Rhineland intellectuals," at least the Rhineland "Advertiser."* We saw above all in its political leaders a means, as wise as it was select, of disgusting the reader with politics so that he would turn all the more eagerly to the luxuriant, industriously pulsating and often charmingly witty domain of advertisement, so that here too the motto would be *per aspera ad astra*,** through politics to oysters. But the fair proportion that *Kölnische Zeitung* so far managed to maintain between politics and advertisements has been upset of late by what could be called "political industry advertisements." In the initial uncertainty where the new variety should be inserted, it happened that an advert was transformed into a leading article and the leading article into an advert of the kind that is called in political language a denunciation but which, if paid for, is merely called an advertisement.***

---

* Marx here makes a pun on "Blatt der Intelligenz"—newspaper of the intellectuals—and "Intelligenzblatt"—Advertiser.—*Ed.*

** A pun on the similarity in sound between the Latin *astra*, stars, and the German *Austern*, oysters.—*Ed.*

*** *Anzeige* in German may mean advertisement or denunciation. —*Ed.*

It is a custom in the north to treat guests to exquisite liqueurs before meagre meals. We are all the more willing to follow that custom in regard to our northern guests and give them spirits before the meal, as in the meal itself, the "ailing"* article in No. 179 of *Kölnische Zeitung*, we find no spirits at all. So first we treat the reader to a scene from Lucian's *Dialogues of the Gods* in a translation accessible to all,[5] for among our readers there will be at least *one* who is no Hellene.

Lucian's *Dialogues of the Gods*

XXIV. COMPLAINTS OF HERMES

Hermes, Maia

Hermes. Is there, dear mother, in the whole heavens, a God more harassed than I?

Maia. Speak not so, my son.

Hermes. Why should I not? I, who have a multitude of affairs to attend to, must always work alone and submit to so many slavish duties? I must rise in the small hours of the morning and clean out the dining hall, arrange the couches in the Council Room, and when everything is in order attend on Jupiter, running errands all day as his messenger. Hardly am I back, covered with dust, when I must serve the ambrosia. And what is most annoying, I am the only one to whom no peace is granted even at night, for then I must escort the souls of the dead to Pluto and act as attendant at their judgment. It is not enough for me to work during the day, I must attend the

* Pun on *leitender Artikel*—leading article—and *leidender Artikel* —weak, sickly, article.—*Ed.*

> *gymnastics*, act the *herald* at the assemblies of the people, and help the popular orators to learn their speeches. No, I, who am torn asunder by so many matters, must over and above attend to the *whole business of the dead.*

Since his expulsion from the Olympus Hermes has been going on by force of habit with his "slavish duties" and the whole business of the dead.

Whether it was Hermes himself or his son Pan, the caprine god, who wrote the ailing article in No. 179, we shall leave the reader to decide remembering that Hermes of the Greeks was the god of eloquence and logic.

"To spread philosophical and religious views by means of the newspapers or to combat them in newspapers seem to us equally inadmissible."

As the old man chattered away it was easy for me to note that he* was bent on a tedious litany of oracles, but I calmed my impatience, for why should I not believe the sensible man who is so impartial as to speak out his opinion quite frankly in his own house, and I read on. But lo and behold! This article, which cannot be reproached with a single philosophical view, has at least a tendency to combat philosophical views and spread religious ones.

Of what use to us is an article which disputes its own right to exist, which introduces itself by a declaration of its own incompetence. The loquacious author will answer us. He explains how his bombastic articles are to be read. He confines himself to giving fragments whose "concatenation and interconnection" he leaves to "the ingenuity of his reader" to discover—the most appropriate method for the kind of advertisement that he deals with. So we shall "concatenate and interconnect" and it is not our fault if the rosary does not become a string of pearls.

---

* Hermes, editor of *Kölnische Zeitung.—Ed.*

The author states:

"A party which makes use of these means" (spreading and combating philosophical and religious views in newspapers) "thereby shows, in *our* opinion, that its intentions *are not honourable* and that it is less interested in teaching and enlightening the people than in attaining *ulterior aims*."

This being *his* opinion, the article can have nothing else in view than the attainment of ulterior aims. These "ulterior aims" will not remain concealed.

The state, the author says, has not only the right, but also the duty "to silence *non-professional* praters." He means the *opponents* of his views, for he has long agreed with himself that he is a *professional* prater.

It is a question, therefore, of a further tightening of censorship in religious matters, a new police measure against the press which has hardly begun to breathe freely.

"In our opinion, the state can be reproached with undue forbearance rather than with excessive rigour."

But the author of the leading article thinks better of it: it is dangerous to reproach the state; so he addresses himself to the authorities, his accusation against freedom of the press becomes an accusation against the censors; he accuses the censors of applying too "little censorship."

"A blameworthy forbearance has been shown so far, *not, admittedly, by the state,* but by '*individual authorities*,' in allowing the new philosophical school to permit itself the most unseemly attacks upon Christianity in public papers and other printed works not intended exclusively for scientific readers."

The author pauses again and thinks better of it again: not eight days ago he found that with freedom of censorship there was too little freedom of the press; he now finds that with compulsion of censors there is too little compulsion by the censorship.

That must be set right again.

"As long as censorship exists it is its most urgent duty to cut out such repulsive excrescences of boyish insolence as have repeatedly offended our eyes in recent days."

Weak eyes! Weak eyes! And the "weakest eye will be offended by an expression which can only be intended for the powers of comprehension of the broad masses."

If relaxed censorship allows repulsive excrescences to appear, what can be expected of freedom of the press? If our eyes are too weak to bear the "insolence" [*Übermut*] of what has been censored, how can they be strong enough to bear the "audacity" [*Mut*] of the free press?

"As long as censorship exists it is its most urgent duty to. . . ." And once it no longer exists? The sentence must be interpreted: It is the most urgent duty of the censorship to exist as long as possible.

And again the author thinks better of it:

"It is not our function to act as *public* prosecutor and therefore we refrain from any more precise specification."

What heavenly kindness the man has! He refrains from more precise "specification" whereas only by quite precise, quite distinct signs could he prove and show what *his* view aims at; he utters but vague, half-whispered words of suspicion; it is not his function to act as *public* prosecutor: his function is to be a *concealed accuser*.

For the last time the wretched man thinks better of it: his function is to write liberal leading articles, to play the "loyal supporter of freedom of the press." He therefore springs to his last position:

"We could not refrain from protesting against a procedure which, if it is not a result of casual negligence, can have no other aim than to discredit a freer press movement in the public eye and to give the game to its opponents who fear to lose by playing fair."

The censorship, says this champion of freedom of the press, who is as daring as he is penetrating, if it is not merely the English leopard with the inscription, "I sleep, wake me not!", has engaged in this "godless" procedure in order to discredit a freer press movement in the public eye.

Is there still any need to discredit a press movement which draws the censorship's attention to "*casual negligences*" and which expects to get its renown in the public eye from the "*censor's penknife*"?

This movement can be called "free" only to the extent that the licence of shamelessness is sometimes called "free." And is it not the shamelessness of absurdity and hypocrisy to try to pass as a champion of the freer press movement and at the same time to teach that the press will fall into the gutter the moment two gendarmes stop holding its arms.

What do we need the censorship for, what do we need this leading article for when the philosophical press discredits itself in the public eye? The author, of course, does not want to limit in any way "*the freedom of scientific research.*"

"In our day, *scientific research* is rightly allowed the widest and most boundless scope."

But the following pronouncement will show what a conception this gentleman has of scientific research:

"A sharp distinction must be made between what is required by the freedom of scientific research, which can but benefit Christianity itself, and what is beyond the bounds of scientific research."

Who should decide on the bounds of scientific research if not scientific research itself! According to the leading article bounds should be prescribed to scientific research. The leading article, therefore, knows an "*official reason*" which does not learn from scientific research but teaches it and which, like a learned providence, prescribes the length every hair should have to transform a scientific beard into one of world significance. The leading article believes in the scientific inspiration of the censorship.

Before further pursuing these "silly" explanations of the leading article on "scientific research," let us regale ourselves a while on Mr. H.'s* *"philosophy of religion,"* his "own science"!

"Religion is the foundation of the state, as it is the most necessary condition for every social association not aimed merely at attaining some ulterior aim."

Proof: "In its crudest form as *childish fetishism* it raises man to a certain extent above sensuous appetites, which, if he lets himself be dominated exclusively by them, *debase him to an animal* and make him incapable of fulfilling any more elevated purpose."

The leading article calls fetishism[6] the "*crudest* form" of religion. It therefore admits something which is recognized as established by all men of "scientific research" even without his consensus, that "*animal worship*" is a *higher* religious form than fetishism, but does not animal worship debase man below the animal, does it not make the animal man's god?

Now this talk about "fetishism"! Real pfenning magazine learning! Fetishism is so far from raising man *above* the appetites that it is on the contrary "the *religion of sensuous appetites*." The fantasy of the appetites tricks the fetish worshipper into believing that an "inanimate object" will give up its natural character to gratify his desires. The crude appetite of the fetish worshipper therefore *smashes* the fetish when the latter ceases to be its most devoted servant.

"In those nations which attained a higher historic significance, the prime of national life coincides with the highest

* Hermes.—*Ed.*

development of their sense of religion, and the decline of their greatness and power coincides with the decline of their religious culture."

The truth will be obtained by exactly reversing the assertion of the author; he has turned history upside down. Greece and Rome are certainly the countries of the highest "historical culture" among the peoples of antiquity. The peak of Greece's greatest internal progress coincides with the time of Pericles, its external zenith with the time of Alexander. In Pericles' time the sophists, Socrates, who may be called philosophy incarnate, art and rhetoric had superseded religion. Alexander's time was the time of Aristotle, who rejected the eternity of the "individual" spirit and the god of the positive religions. And then Rome! Read Cicero! Epicurean, stoic[7] or sceptic[8] philosophy was the religion of the Romans of culture when Rome reached the zenith of its career. If with the downfall of the old states the religions of the old states disappear, this needs no further explanation than that the "true religion" of the peoples of antiquity was the cult of "their nationality," of their "state." It was not the downfall of the old religions that brought the downfall of the old states, but the downfall of the old states that brought the downfall of the old religions. And ignorance like that of the leading article proclaims itself the "legislator of scientific research" and writes "decrees" for philosophy.

"The whole ancient world was bound to collapse because the progress that the peoples made in their scientific development necessarily involved the discovery of the errors on which their religious views were based."

So, according to the leading article, the whole ancient world perished because scientific research disclosed the errors of the antique religions. Would the ancient world not have perished if research had passed over in silence the errors of the religions, if the author of the leading article had recommended to the Roman authorities to cut out Lucretius's and Lucian's works?

For the rest, we take the liberty of adding to Mr. H.'s erudition by means of a note.

Just as the downfall of the ancient world was approaching there arose the *school of Alexandria*, which strove to prove by force "the eternal truth" of Greek mythology and its thorough agreement "with the data of scientific research." The Emperor Julian also belonged to that trend, which thought it would cause the new spirit of the times that was asserting itself to disappear if it kept its eyes closed so as not to see it. But let us keep to Mr. H.'s results! In the religions of antiquity "the faint notions of the divine were veiled in the deepest night of error" and could therefore not resist scientific research. With Christianity the situation is reversed, as any thinking machine will conclude. Indeed, Mr. H.'s says:

"The best conclusions of scientific research have so far served only to confirm the truths of the Christian religion."

Apart from the fact that every philosophy of the past without exception was accused by the theologians of apostasy, not excepting even the pious Malebranche and the inspired Jakob Böhme, that Leibniz was accused by the Brunswick peasants of being a "*Löwenix*" (*Glaubenichts*—one who believes in nothing) and by the Englishman Clarke and Newton's other followers of being an atheist; apart from the fact that Christianity, as the most capable and consistent of the Protestant theologians affirm, cannot agree with reason because "worldly" and "religious" reason contradict each other, which Tertullian classically expressed: "*verum est, quia absurdum est*"; apart from all this, how can the agreement of scientific research with religion be proved except by forcing research to resolve itself into religion by letting it follow its own course. The least we can say is that further compulsion is no proof.

If, of course, you acknowledge beforehand as scientific research only what conforms to your own view, it is not difficult for you to make prophecies; but then what advantage has your assertion over that of the Indian Brahmin who proves the holiness of the Vedas[9] by reserving for himself alone the right to read it!

Yes, says H.'s, "scientific research." But any research that contradicts Christianity "stops half-way" or "takes a wrong road." Can one make the argument easier for oneself?

Once scientific research "has '*made clear*' to itself the content of what it has found, it will never clash with the truths of Christianity" but at the same time the state must ensure that this "*making clear*" is impossible, for research must never appeal to the powers of comprehension of the masses, i.e., must never become popular and clear *to itself*. Even if it is attacked by all the unscientific papers of the monarchy it must be modest and keep silence.

Christianity precludes the possibility of "any new decadence," but the police must be on its guard so that the philosophizing newspaper writers do not lead to decadence; it must keep an extremely strict guard. Error will be recognized as such of itself in the struggle with truth, without any need for suppression by external force; but the state must make the struggle of truth easier by depriving the champions of "error" not indeed of internal freedom, which it cannot take away from them, but of the possibility of that freedom, the possibility of existence.

Christianity is sure of victory, but according to Mr. H.'s it is not so sure of victory that it can scorn the help of the police.

If from the outset everything which contradicts your faith is error and must be dealt with as such, what is there to distinguish your claims from those of the Mohammedans, from the claims of any other religion? Must philosophy adopt different principles for every country, according to the saying "different countries, different customs," in order not to contradict the basic truths of dogma? Must it believe in one country that $3 \times 1 = 1$, in another that women have no soul and in yet another that beer is drunk in heaven? Is there not a *universal human* nature just as there is a universal nature of plants and heavenly bodies? Philosophy asks what is true, not what is acknowledged as such, what is true for all men, not what is true for individuals: philosophy's metaphysical truths do not know the boundaries of political geography; its political truths know too well where the "boundaries" begin to confuse the illusory horizon of particular world and national outlooks with the true horizon of the human mind. H.'s is the weakest of all the champions of Christianity.

His only proof in favour of Christianity is Christianity's *long existence*. Has not philosophy also existed from Thales down to our time and has it not precisely now, according to H.'s himself, greater claims and a greater opinion of its own importance than ever?

How, finally, does H.'s prove that the state is a "Christian" state, that instead of being a free association of moral human beings it is an association of believers, that its purpose, instead of being to make freedom a reality is to make dogma a reality? "Our European states all have Christianity as their foundation."

The *French* state too? The *Charte*,[10] Article 3, says not that "every Christian" or "only the Christian" but "*tous les Français* are equally eligible for civil and military posts."

The Prussian *Landrecht* also says, Part II, Section XIII: "The *primary* duty of the Supreme Head of the State is to maintain both internal and external peace and security and to safeguard each and every one in what is his from violence and interference."

But according to § 1 the Supreme Head of the State combines in his person all "duties and rights of the State,"

It does not say that the primary duty of the state is the suppression of heretical errors and bliss in the other world.

If, however, some European states are in fact founded upon Christianity, do those states conform to their conception, is the "pure existence" of a condition the right of that condition?

In the view of our H.'s it is so, for he reminds the supporters of Young Hegelianism "that according to the laws in force in the greater part of the state *marriage not consecrated by the Church* is declared *concubinage* and as such is punished by the *police* courts."

If, therefore, "marriage not consecrated by the Church" is considered on the Rhine according to the Napoleonic Code as "marriage" and on the Spree according to the Prussian *Landrecht* as "concubinage," the "police court" punishment must be an argument for the philosophers that what is right in one place is wrong in another, that not the Napoleonic Code, but the *Landrecht* has the scientific and moral, the reasonable conception of marriage. This "philosophy of police court punishment" may be convincing in other places, it is not convincing in *Prussia.* For the rest, how little inclined the Prussian *Landrecht* is to "holy" marriage is shown by § 12, Part II, Section 1.

"However, a marriage which is allowed by the laws of the *Land* loses none of its *civil* validity by the fact that the dispensation of the spiritual authorities has not been requested or has been refused."

Here in Prussia, too, marriage is partly emancipated from the "spiritual authorities" and its "civil" validity is distinct from its "ecclesiastical."

It goes without saying that our great Christian state-philosopher has not a very "high" view of the state.

"Since our states are not only *associations based on right*, but at the same time true *educational institutions* with the only difference that they extend their care to a *broader* field than the institutions intended for the education of youth," etc., "all public education" is based "on the foundation of Christianity."

The education of our school children is based just as much on the classics of old and on science in general as on the Catechism.

The state, according to H.'s, is distinguished from a children's home not by content but by size—it extends its "care" to a broader field.

But the true "public education" of the state is rather the reasonable and public being of the state; the state itself educates its members by making them members of the state, by changing the aims of the individual into general aims, coarse urge into moral inclination, natural independence into spiritual freedom, by the individual finding his delight in the life of the whole and the whole in the disposition of the individual.

The leading article, on the other hand, makes the state not an association of free human beings mutually educating one another, but a crowd of adults whose destiny is to be educated from above and to pass from the "narrow" schoolroom to the "broader" one.

This theory of education and guardianship is here brought forward by a supporter of freedom of the press who, in his love for this belle, notes the "negligences of the censorship," who knows how to depict the "powers of comprehension of the masses" in the appropriate place (perhaps the powers of comprehension of the masses have seemed so precarious to *Kölnische Zeitung of late* because the masses have forgotten how to appreciate the superiorities of the "unphilosophical newspaper"?) and who advises scientists to have one view for the stage and another one for the backstage!

As the leading article showed us its "*short*" view of the

state it will now expound to us its *low view* "*of Christianity*."

"All the newspaper articles in the world will never convince a population that feels on the whole well and happy that it is in a wretched predicament."

We should think not! The *material* feeling of well-being and happiness is more proof against newspaper articles than the bliss-giving and all-conquering assurance of faith! H.'s does not sing "Our God is a strong fortress." The truly believing heart of the "masses" is probably more exposed to the rust of doubt than the refined worldly culture of the "few."

H.'s fears "even incitement to insurrection in a *well-ordered* state" less than in a "well-ordered church," although the latter may besides be led by the "spirit of God" to all truth. A fine believer, and the grounds he has! Political articles are within the comprehension of the masses, he says, but philosophical articles are beyond it!

If, finally, we contrast the leading article's hint: "the *half*-measures that have been taken recently against Young Hegelianism have had the consequences half-measures usually have," to the *ingenuous* wish that the last steps of the Hegelians might pass over "without *too unfavourable* consequences for them" we can understand Cornwall's words in *King Lear*:

He cannot flatter, he!—
An honest man and plain,—he must speak truth:
An' they will take it, so; if not, he's plain.
These kind of knaves I know, which in their plainness
Harbour more craft, and more corrupter ends,
Than twenty silly ducking observants,
That stretch their duties nicely.

We would think we were insulting the readers of *Rheinische Zeitung*[11] if we fancied they would be satisfied with the comical rather than serious show of a *ci-devant* liberal, "a young man of days gone by,"[12] being sent back to where he belongs; we wish to say a few words about "*the matter itself*." As long as we were engaged in a polemic with the ailing article it would not have been right to interrupt it in the process of its self-annihilation.

First the question is raised: "Should philosophy discuss religious matters also in newspaper articles?"

This question can be answered only by criticizing it.

Philosophy, above all German philosophy, has a propensity to solitude, to systematical seclusion, to dispassionate self-contemplation which opposes it from the outset in its estrangement to the quick-witted and alive-to-events newspapers whose only delight is in information. Philosophy, taken in its systematic development, is unpopular; its secret weaving within itself seems to the layman to be an occupation as overstrained as it is unpractical; it is considered as a professor of magic whose incantations sound pompous because they are unintelligible.

Philosophy, in accordance with its character, has never made the first step towards replacing the ascetic priestly vestments by the light conventional garb of the newspapers. But philosophers do not grow out of the soil like mushrooms, they are the product of their time and of their people, whose most subtle, precious and invisible sap circulates in philosophical ideas. The same spirit that builds railways by the hands of the workers builds philosophical systems in the brain of the philosophers. Philosophy does not stand outside the world any more than man's brain is outside of him because it is not in his stomach; but, of course, philosophy is in the world with its brain before it stands on the earth with its feet, whereas many another human sphere has long been rooted in the earth by its feet and plucks the fruits of the world with its hands before it has any idea that the "head" also belongs to the world or that this world is the world of the head.

Because every true philosophy is the spiritual quintessence of its time, the time must come when philosophy not only internally by its content but externally by its appearance comes into contact and mutual reaction with the real contemporary world. Philosophy then ceases to be a definite system in presence of other definite systems, it becomes philosophy generally, in presence of the world, it becomes the philosophy of the world of the present. The formal features which attest that philosophy has achieved that importance, that it is the living soul of culture, that philosophy is becoming worldly and the world philosophical, were the same in all times: any history book will show, repeated with stereotyped fidelity, the simplest rituals which unmistakably mark philosophy's introduction into drawing-rooms and priests' studies, the editorial offices of newspapers and the antichambers of courts, into the hatred and the love of the people of the time. Philosophy is introduced into the world by the clamour of its enemies who betray their internal infection by their desperate appeals for help against the blaze of ideas. These cries of its enemies mean as much for philosophy as the first cry of a child for the anxious ear of the mother, they are the cry of life of the ideas which have burst open the orderly hieroglyphic husk of the system and become citizens of the world. The Corybantes and Cabiri,[13] who with the roll of drums announce to the world the birth of baby Zeus, first turn against the religious section of the philosophers, partly because their inquisitorial instinct can secure a firmer hold on this sentimental side of the public, partly because the public, to which the opponents of philosophy also belong, can feel the ideal sphere of philosophy only with its ideal feelers, and the only field of ideas in the value of which the public believes almost as much as in the system of material needs is that of religious ideas, and, finally, because religion polemizes not against a definite system of philosophy but against the philosophy generally of the definite systems.

The true philosophy of the present does not differ as far as this fate is concerned from the true philosophies of the past. Indeed, this fate is a proof that history owed to the truth of philosophy.

And for six years the German papers have been drumming against the religious trend in philosophy, calumniating it, distorting it, bowdlerizing it.[14] *Allgemeine Augsburger* sang bravuras, nearly every overture played the theme that philosophy was not worthy of being discussed by the lady sage, that it was the idle bragging of youth, a fashion for blasé coteries. But in spite of all that it could not be got rid of and there was more drumming, for in its anti-philosophical caterwauling the *Augsburger* plays but one instrument, the monotonous kettle-drum. All German papers, from *Berliner politisches Wochenblatt*[15] and *Hamburger Correspondent*[16] to the obscure local papers, down to *Kölnische Zeitung* blared out about Hegel and Schelling, Feuerbach and Bauer, *Deutsche Jahrbücher*,[17] etc.—Finally the curiosity of the public was aroused and it wanted to see the Leviathan with its own eyes, all the more as semi-official articles threatened philosophy that it would have a legal syllabus officially prescribed for it. And that was when philosophy appeared in the papers. Long had it kept silence before the self-complacent superficiality which boasted in a few stale newspaper phrases that it could blow away like soap-bubbles years of study of genius, the hard-won fruits of self-sacrificing solitude, the results of that invisible but slowly extenuating struggle of contemplation; philosophy had even *protested against the newspapers* as being an inappropriate field, but in the end it had to break its silence, it became a newspaper correspondent and—unheard-of diversion!—it suddenly occurred to the garrulous newspaper purveyors that philosophy is no food for the newspaper public and they could not refrain from drawing the attention of the governments to the dishonesty of bringing questions of philosophy and religion into the sphere of the newspapers not to enlighten the public but to attain ulterior aims.

What is there so bad that philosophy could say about religion or about itself that your newspaper clamour had not long ago imputed to it in far worse and more frivolous terms? It only needs to repeat what you unphilosophical Capuchins have preached about it in thousands and thousands of polemics, and it has said the worst.

But philosophy speaks differently of religious and philosophical objects than you have. You speak without having studied them, it speaks after study; you appeal to the emotions, it appeals to reason; you curse, it teaches; you promise heaven and earth, it promises nothing but truth; you demand faith in your faith, it demands not faith in its results but the test of doubt; you frighten, it calms. And truly, philosophy is world-wise enough to know that its results flatter the desire for pleasure or the egoism neither of the heavenly nor of the earthly world; but the public that loves truth and knowledge for their own sakes will be able to measure itself in judgment and morality with ignorant, servile, inconsistent and mercenary scribes.

Admittedly somebody or other, by reason of the worthlessness of his intellect or views, may misinterpret philosophy, but do not you Protestants believe that the Catholics misinterpret Christianity, do you not reproach the Christian religion with the disgraceful times of the eighth and ninth centuries, the night of St. Bartholomew[18] and the Inquisition? There are conclusive proofs that the hatred of the Protestant theology for philosophers arises largely out of philosophy's tolerance towards the particular confession as such. Feuerbach and Strauss were reproached more for maintaining that Catholic dogmas were Christian than for stating that the dogmas of Christianity were not dogmas of reason.

But if occasional individuals cannot digest modern philosophy and die of philosophical indigestion, that proves no more against philosophy than the occasional blowing up of a few passengers by the bursting of a boiler proves against mechanics.

The question whether philosophical and religious matters should be discussed in newspapers resolves itself in its own emptiness.

If such questions already have an interest for the public as *newspaper questions*, they have become *questions of the day*; then the point is not whether they should be discussed but where and how they should be discussed, whether within the bounds of the family and the hotels, of the schools and the churches, but not by the press; by the opponents of philosophy, but not by the philosophers; whether in the obscure language of private opinion but not in the clarifying language of public reason. Then the point is whether what lives in reality belongs to the realm of the press; it is no longer a question of a particular content of the press, the question is the general one whether the press must be really the press, i.e., a free press.

From the first question we completely separate the second: "Should politics be dealt with philosophically by the newspapers in a so-called Christian state?"

If religion becomes a political quality, an object of politics, there seems to be hardly any need to mention that the newspapers not only may, but must, discuss political objects. It seems from the start that the wisdom of this world, philosophy, has more right to bother about the kingdom of this world, about the state, than the wisdom of the other world, religion. The point here is not whether the state should be philosophized about, but whether it should be philosophized about well or badly, philosophically or unphilosophically, with prejudice or without, with consciousness or without, consistently or inconsistently, in a completely rational or half rational way. If you make religion a theory of state right, then you make religion itself a kind of philosophy.

Was it not Christianity before anything else that separated church and state?

Read Saint Augustine's *De Civitate Dei*, study the Fathers of the Church and the spirit of Christianity and then come back and tell us which is the "Christian State," the church or the state! Does not every minute of your practical life give the lie to your theory? Do you consider it wrong to appeal to the courts when you are cheated? But the apostle writes that that is wrong. Do you offer your right cheek when you are struck upon the left, or do you not institute proceedings for assault? Yet the Gospel forbids that. Do you not claim your reasonable right in this world? Do you not grumble at the slightest raising of a duty? Are you not furious at the slightest infringement of your personal liberty? But you have been told that the sufferings of this life are not to be compared with the bliss of the future, that suffering in patience and the bliss of hope are cardinal virtues.

Are not most of your court proceedings and the majority of civil laws concerned with property? But you have been told that your treasure is not of this world. If you base yourselves on giving to Caesar the things which are Caesar's and to God the things which are God's, do not consider the mammon of gold alone but at least just as much free reason as the Caesar of this world, and the "action of free reason" is what we call philosophizing.

When in the Holy Alliance at first a quasi-religious alliance of states was to be formed and religion was to be the state motto of Europe, *the Pope* showed profound sense and perfect consistence in refusing to join it, for in his view the universal Christian link between nations was the Church and not diplomacy, not a worldly alliance of states.

The truly religious state is the theocratic state; the prince of such states must be either the God of religion, Jehovah himself, as in the Jewish state, God's representative, the Dalai Lama, as in Tibet, or finally, as Görres correctly demands of Christian states in his last work, they must all submit to a church which is an "infallible church." For if, as in Protestantism, there is no supreme head of the church, the domination of religion is nothing but the religion of domination, the cult of the will of the government.

Once a state includes several confessions with equal rights it cannot be a religious state without violating particular confessions; it cannot be a church which condemns adherents of another confession as heretics, which makes every piece of bread dependent on faith, which makes dogma the link between separate individuals and existence as citizens of the state. Ask the Catholic inhabitants of "poor green Erin," ask the Huguenots[19] before the French Revolution: they did not appeal to religion, for their religion was not the religion of the state; they appealed to the "Rights of Humanity" and philosophy interprets the Rights of Humanity and demands that the state be the state of human nature.

But the half, the limited, rationalism, which is as unbelieving as it is theological, says that the universal Christian spirit, irrespective of confessional differences, must be the spirit of the state! It is the greatest irreligiousness, the wantonness of worldly reason, to separate the general spirit of religion from the positive religion; this separation of religion from its dogmas and institutions is equal to asserting that the universal spirit of right must reign in the state irrespective of the definite laws and the positive institutions of right.

If you presume to stand so high above religion as to have the right to separate the general spirit of religion from its positive definitions, what reproach have you to make to the philosophers if they want to make the separation complete and not a half-way one, if they proclaim not the Christian, but the human spirit, the universal spirit of religion?

Christians live in states with differing constitutions, some in a republic, some in an absolute, some again in a constitutional monarchy. Christianity does not decide on the *correctness* of the constitutions, for it knows no distinction between constitutions, it teaches, as religion must: Submit to the authority, for *all authority* is ordained by God. The correctness of state constitutions is, therefore, to be judged not according to Christianity, not according to the nature, the essence of the state itself, not according to the nature of Christian society, but according to the nature of human society.

The Byzantine state was the properly religious state, for there dogmas were matters of state, but the Byzantine state was the worst of all states. The states of the *ancien régime* were the most Christian states, nonetheless they were states of "the will of court."

There is a dilemma that "sound" common sense cannot solve. Either the Christian state corresponds to the concept of the state as a realization of rational freedom, and then nothing else can be demanded for it to be a Christian state than that it be a reasonable state; then it is enough to develop the state out of the reason of human relations, a work accomplished by philosophy. Or the state of rational freedom cannot be developed out of Christianity: then you will yourselves concede that this development does not lie in the tendency of Christianity, for Christianity does not wish for a bad state, and any state which is not the embodiment of rational freedom is a bad state.

Answer the dilemma as you like, you will have to concede that the state is not to be constituted from religion but from the reason of freedom. Only the crassest ignorance can assert that the theory of making the state-concept independent is a passing whim of modern philosophers.

Philosophy has done nothing in politics that physics, mathematics, medicine, every science, has not done within its own sphere. Bacon of Verulam declared theological physics to be a virgin vowed to God and barren; he emancipated physics from theology and she became fruitful. You have no more to ask the politician if he has faith than the doctor. Immediately before and after the time of Copernicus's great discoveries on the true solar system the law of gravitation of the state was discovered: the centre of gravity of the state was found within the state itself. As various European governments tried to apply this result with the initial superficiality of practice to the system of equilibrium of states, similarly Macchiavelli and Campanella began before them and Hobbes, Spinoza, and Hugo Grotius afterwards down to Rousseau, Fichte and Hegel, to consider the state with the eye of man and to develop its natural laws from reason and experience, not from theology, any more than Copernicus let himself be influenced by Joshua's supposed command to the sun to stand still over Gideon and the moon over the vale of Ajalon. Modern philosophy has only continued a work already started by Heraclitus and Aristotle. So it is not the reason of modern philosophy that you are polemizing against, but the ever modern philosophy of reason. Naturally, the ignorance that yesterday or perhaps the day before discovered in *Rheinische* or *Königsberger Zeitung*[20] the age-old ideas on the state considers the ideas of history as notions which occurred overnight to certain individuals because they appear new to it and came to it overnight; it forgets that it has assumed the old role of the doctor of Sorbonne who considered it his duty to accuse Montesquieu in public because the latter was frivolous enough to maintain that the political quality, not the virtue of the Church, was the highest quality in the state; it forgets that it has assumed the role of Joachim Lange, who denounced Wolf because his doctrine of predestination would lead to desertion among soldiers and thereby to a relaxation of military discipline and finally to the collapse of the state; lastly it forgets that the Prussian *Landrecht* comes from the very school of philosophy of "that Wolf" and the Napoleonic Code comes not from the Old Testament but from the school of ideas of Voltaire, Rousseau, Condorcet, Mirabeau and Montesquieu and from the French Revolution. Ignorance is a demon and we are afraid it will yet play us more than one tragedy; the greatest Greek poets were right when they represented it in the terrible dramas of the royal houses of Mycenae and Thebes as tragic fate.

Whereas the earlier teachers of state law construed the state out of ambition or sociability, or even reason, though not out of the reason of society but rather out of the reason of the individual, the more ideal and profound view of modern philosophy construes it out of the idea of the whole. It considers the state as the great organism in which freedom of right, of morals and of politics has to be implemented and in which in the laws of the state the individual citizen merely obeys the natural laws of his own reason, human reason. *Sapienti sat.**

We shall conclude with a further philosophical farewell to *Kölnische Zeitung*. It was reasonable of it to take to itself a liberal "of times gone by." One can most comfortably be both liberal and reactionary at the same time, if only

* Sufficient for the wise man.—*Ed.*

one is always skilful enough to address only liberals of the recent past who know no other dilemma than that of Vidocq—"prisoner or gaoler." It was still more reasonable that the liberal of the recent past combated the liberals of the present. Without parties there is no development, without a parting there is no progress. We hope that with the leading article of No. 179 *Kölnische Zeitung* has begun a new era, the era of character.

KARL MARX

CONTRIBUTION TO THE CRITIQUE OF HEGEL'S PHILOSOPHY OF RIGHT

INTRODUCTION

For Germany the *criticism of religion* is in the main complete, and criticism of religion is the premise of all criticism.

The *profane* existence of error is discredited after its *heavenly oratio pro aris et focis** has been rejected. Man, who looked for a superman in the fantastic reality of heaven and found nothing there but the *reflexion* of himself, will no longer be disposed to find but the *semblance* of himself, the non-human [*Unmensch*] where he seeks and must seek his true reality.

The basis of irreligious criticism is: *Man makes religion*, religion does not make man. In other words, religion is the self-consciousness and self-feeling of man who has either not yet found himself or has already lost himself again. But *man* is no abstract being squatting outside the world. Man is *the world of man*, the state, society. This state, this society, produce religion, *a reversed world-consciousness*, because they are *a reversed world*. Religion is the general theory of that world, its encyclopaedic compendium, its logic in a popular form, its spiritualistic *point d'honneur*, its enthusiasm, its moral sanction, its solemn completion, its universal ground for consolation and justification. It is *the fantastic realization* of the human essence because the

* Speech for the altars and hearths.—*Ed.*

human essence has no true reality. The struggle against religion is therefore mediately the fight against *the other world*, of which religion is the spiritual *aroma.*

Religious distress is at the same time the *expression* of real distress and the *protest* against real distress. Religion is the sigh of the oppressed creature, the heart of a heartless world, just as it is the spirit of a spiritless situation. It is the *opium* of the people.

The abolition of religion as the *illusory* happiness of the people is required for their *real* happiness. The demand to give up the illusions about its condition is the *demand to give up a condition which needs illusions*. The criticism of religion is therefore *in embryo the criticism of the vale of woe*, the *halo* of which is religion.

Criticism has plucked the imaginary flowers from the chain not so that man will wear the chain without any fantasy or consolation but so that he will shake off the chain and cull the living flower. The criticism of religion disillusions man to make him think and act and shape his reality like a man who has been disillusioned and has come to reason, so that he will revolve round himself and therefore round his true sun. Religion is only the illusory sun which revolves round man as long as he does not revolve round himself.

The task of history, therefore, once the *world beyond the truth* has disappeared, is to establish the *truth of this world.* The immediate *task of philosophy*, which is at the service of history, once the *saintly form* of human self-alienation has been unmasked, is to unmask self-alienation in its *unholy forms*. Thus the criticism of heaven turns into the criticism of the earth, the *criticism of religion* into the *criticism of right* and the *criticism of theology* into the *criticism of politics*.

The following exposition—a contribution to that work—bears immediately not on the original, but on a copy, the

German *philosophy* of state and of right, for the single reason that it is writen in *Germany*.

If one wanted to proceed from the *status quo* itself in Germany, even in the only appropriate way, i.e., negatively, the result would still be an *anachronism*. Even the negation of our political present is already covered with dust in the historical lumber-room of modern nations. If I negate the powdered pigtail, I still have an unpowdered pigtail. If I negate the German state of affairs in 1843, then, according to the French computation of time, I am hardly in the year 1789, and still less in the focus of the present.

Yes, German history flatters itself with a movement which no people in the heaven of history went through before it or will go through after it. For we shared the restorations of the modern nations although we had not shared their revolutions. We were restored, first because other nations dared to carry out a revolution and second because other nations suffered a counter-revolution, the first time because our rulers were afraid, and the second because our rulers were not afraid. Led by our shepherds, we never found ourselves in the company of freedom except once—on the *day of its burial.*

A school which legalizes the baseness of today by the baseness of yesterday, a school that declares rebellious every cry of the serf against the knout once that knout is a time-honoured, ancestral, historical one, a school to which history only shows its *a posteriori* as the God of Israel did to his servant Moses—the *historical school of right*[21]—would hence have discovered German history had it not been a discovery of German history itself. Shylock, but Shylock the servant, it swears on its bond, its historical bond, its Christian-Germanic bond, to have every pound of flesh cut from the heart of the people.

Good-natured enthusiasts, Germanomaniacs by extraction and free-thinkers by reflexion, on the contrary, seek our history of freedom beyond our history in the ancient Teutonic forests. But what difference is there between the history of our freedom and the history of the boar's freedom if it can be found only in the forests? Besides, it is common knowledge that the forest echoes back what you shout into it. So peace to the ancient Teutonic forests!

War on the German state of affairs! By all means! They are *below the level of history*, they are *beneath any criticism*, but they are still an object of criticism like the criminal who is below the level of humanity but still an object for the *executioner*. In the struggle against that state of affairs criticism is no passion of the head, it is the head of passion. It is not a lancet, it is a weapon. Its object is its *enemy*, which it wants not to refute but to *exterminate*. For the spirit of that state of affairs is refuted. In itself it is no object *worthy of thought*, it is an *existence* which is as despicable as it is despised. Criticism does not need to make things clear to itself as regards this object, for it has already settled accounts with it. It no longer assumes the quality of an *end in itself*, but only of a *means*. Its essential pathos is *indignation*, its essential work is *denunciation*.

It is a case of describing the dull reciprocal pressure of all social spheres one on another, a general inactive ill-humour, a limitedness which recognizes itself as much as it mistakes itself, within the frame of a government system which, living on the preservation of all wretchedness, is itself nothing but *wretchedness in office*.

What a sight! This infinitely proceeding division of society into the most manifold races opposed to one another by petty antipathies, uneasy consciences and brutal mediocrity, and which, precisely because of their reciprocal ambiguous and distrustful attitude, are all, without exception although with various formalities, treated by their *rulers* as *conceded existences*. And they must recognize and acknowledge as a *concession of heaven* the very fact that they are *mastered, ruled, possessed*! And on the other side are the rulers themselves, whose greatness is in inverse proportion to their number!

Criticism dealing with this content is criticism in a *hand-to-hand fight*, and in such a fight the point is not whether the opponent is a noble, equal, *interesting* opponent, the point is to *strike* him. The point is not to let the Germans have a minute for self-deception and resignation. The actual pressure must be made more pressing by adding to it consciousness of pressure, the shame must be made more shameful by publicizing it. Every sphere of German society must be shown as the *partie honteuse* of German society; these petrified relations must be forced to dance by singing their own tune to them! The people must be taught to be *terrified* at itself in order to give it *courage*. This will be fulfilling an imperative need of the German nation, and the needs of the nations are in themselves the ultimate reason for their satisfaction.

This struggle against the limited content of the German *status quo* cannot be without interest even for the *modern* nations, for the German *status quo* is the *open completion of the ancien régime* and the *ancien régime* is the *concealed deficiency of the modern state*. The struggle against the German political present is the struggle against the past of the modern nations, and they are still burdened with reminders of that past. It is instructive for them to see the *ancien régime*, which has been through its *tragedy* with them, playing its *comedy* as a German *revenant*. *Tragic* indeed was the history of the *ancien régime* so long as it was the pre-existing power of the world, and freedom, on the other hand, was a personal notion; in short, as long as it believed and had to believe in its own justification. As long as the *ancien régime*, as an existing world order, struggled against a world that was only coming into being, there was on its side a historical error, not a personal one. That is why its downfall was tragic.

On the other hand, the present German régime, an anachronism, a flagrant contradiction of generally recognized axioms, the nothingness of the *ancien régime* exhibited to the world, only imagines that it believes in itself and demands that the world should imagine the same thing. If it believed in its own *essence*, would it try to hide that essence under the *semblance* of an alien essence and seek refuge in hypocrisy and sophism? The modern *ancien régime* is rather only the *comedian* of a world order whose *true heroes* are dead. History is thorough and goes through many phases when carrying an old form to the grave. The last phase of a world-historical form is its *comedy*. The gods of Greece, already tragically wounded to death in Aeschylus's *Prometheus Bound*, had to re-die a comic death in Lucian's *Dialogues*. Why this course of history? So that humanity should part with its past *cheerfully*. This *cheerful* historical destiny is what we vindicate for the political authorities of Germany.

Meanwhile, once *modern* politico-social reality itself is subjected to criticism, once criticism rises to truly human problems, it finds itself outside the German *status quo* or else it would reach out for its object *below* its object. An example. The relation of industry, of the world of wealth generally, to the political world is one of the major problems of modern times. In what form is this problem beginning to engage the attention of the Germans? In the form of *protective duties*, of the *prohibitive system*, of *national economy*. Germanomania has passed out of man into matter, and thus one morning our cotton barons and iron heroes saw themselves turned into patriots. People are therefore beginning in Germany to acknowledge the sovereignty of monopoly on the inside through lending it *sovereignty on the outside*. People are therefore now about to begin in Germany with what people in France and England are about to end. The old corrupt condition against which these countries are revolting in theory and which they only bear as one bears chains is greeted in Germany as the dawn of a beautiful future which still hardly dares to pass from *crafty* theory to the most ruthless practice. Whereas the problem in France and England is: *Political economy* or *the rule of society over wealth*, in Germany it is: *National economy* or *the mastery of private property over nationality*. In France and England, then, it is a case of abolishing monopoly that has proceeded to its last consequences; in Germany it is a case of proceeding to the last consequences of monopoly. There it is a case of solution, here as yet a case of collision. This is an adequate example of the *German* form of modern problems, an example of how our history, like a clumsy recruit, still has to do extra drill on things that are old and hackneyed in history.

If therefore the *whole* German development did not exceed the German *political* development, a German could at the most have the share in the problems of the present that a *Russian* has. But, when the separate individual is not bound by the limitations of the nation, the nation as a whole is still less liberated by the liberation of one individual. The fact that Greece had a Scythian[22] among its philosophers did not help the Scythians to make a single step towards Greek culture.

Luckily we Germans are not Scythians.

As the ancient peoples went through their pre-history in imagination, in *mythology*, so we Germans have gone through our post-history in thought, in *philosophy*. We are *philosophical* contemporaries of the present without being its *historical* contemporaries. German philosophy is the *ideal prolongation* of German history. If therefore, instead of the *oeuvres incomplètes* of our real history, we criticize the *oeuvres posthumes* of our ideal history, *philos-*

ophy, our criticism is in the midst of the questions of which the present says: *that is the question*. What in progressive nations is a *practical* break with modern state conditions is in Germany, where even those conditions do not yet exist, at first a *critical* break with the philosophical reflexion of those conditions.

German philosophy of right and state is the only *German history* which is *al pari** with the *official* modern present. The German nation must therefore join this its dream-history to its present conditions and subject to criticism not only these existing conditions, but at the same time their abstract continuation. Its future cannot be *limited* either to the immediate negation of its real conditions of state and right or to the immediate implementation of its ideal state and right conditions, for it has the immediate negation of its real conditions in its ideal conditions, and it has almost *outlived* the immediate implementation of its ideal conditions in the contemplation of neighbouring nations. Hence it is with good reason that the *practical* political party in Germany demands the *negation of philosophy*. It is wrong, not in its demand, but in stopping at the demand, which it neither seriously implements nor can implement. It believes that it implements that negation by turning its back to philosophy and its head away from it and muttering a few trite and angry phrases about it. Owing to the limitation of its outlook it does not include philosophy in the circle of *German* reality or it even fancies it is *beneath* German practice and the theories that serve it. You demand that *real life embryos* be made the starting-point but you forget that the real life embryo of the German nation has grown so far only inside its *cranium*. In a word—*You cannot abolish philosophy without making it a reality*.

The same mistake, but with the factors *reversed*, was

* On a level.—*Ed.*

made by the *theoretical* party originating from philosophy.

In the present struggle it saw *only the critical struggle of philosophy against the German world*; it did not give a thought to the fact that *philosophy up to the present* itself belongs to this world and is its *completion*, although an ideal one. Critical towards its counterpart, it was uncritical towards itself when, proceeding from the *premises* of philosophy, it either stopped at the results given by philosophy or passed off demands and results from somewhere else as immediate demands and results of philosophy, although these, provided they are justified, can be obtained only by the *negation of philosophy up to the present*, of philosophy as such. We reserve ourselves the right to a more detailed description of this section. Its basic deficiency may be reduced to the following: *It thought it could make philosophy a reality without abolishing it.*

The criticism of *the German philosophy of state and right*, which attained its most consistent, richest and last formulation through *Hegel*, is both a critical analysis of the modern state and of the reality connected with it, and the resolute negation of the whole *manner of the German consciousness in politics and right* as practised hereto, the most distinguished, most universal expression of which, raised to the level of a *science*, is the *speculative philosophy of right* itself. If the speculative philosophy of right, that abstract extravagant *thinking* on the modern state, the reality of which remains a thing of the beyond, if only beyond the Rhine, was possible only in Germany, inversely the *German* thought-image of the modern state which makes abstraction of *real man* was possible only because and insofar as the modern state itself makes abstraction of *real man* or satisfies *the whole* of man only in imagination. In politics the Germans *thought* what other nations *did*. Germany was their *theoretical conscience*. The abstraction and presumption of its thought was always in step with the one-sidedness and lowliness of its reality. If therefore the *status quo* of *German statehood* expresses *the completion of the ancien régime*, the completion of the thorn in the flesh of the modern state, the *status quo of German state science* expresses the *incompletion of the modern state*, the defectiveness of its flesh itself.

Already as the resolute opponent of the previous form of *German* political consciousness the criticism of speculative philosophy of right strays, not into itself, but into *problems* which there is only one means of solving—*practice*.

It is asked: can Germany attain a practice *à la hauteur des principes*, i.e., a *revolution* which will raise it not only to the *official level* of the modern nations but to the *height of humanity* which will be the near future of those nations?

The weapon of criticism cannot, of course, replace criticism of the weapon, material force must be overthrown by material force; but theory also becomes a material force as soon as it has gripped the masses. Theory is capable of gripping the masses as soon as it demonstrates *ad hominem*, and it demonstrates *ad hominem* as soon as it becomes radical. To be radical is to grasp the root of the matter. But for man the root is man himself. The evident proof of the radicalism of German theory, and hence of its practical energy, is that it proceeds from a resolute *positive* abolition of religion. The criticism of religion ends with the teaching that *man is the highest essence for man*, hence with the *categoric imperative to overthrow all relations* in which man is a debased, enslaved, abandoned, despicable essence, relations which cannot be better described than by the cry of a Frenchman when it was planned to introduce a tax on dogs: Poor dogs! They want to treat you as human beings!

Even historically, theoretical emancipation has specific practical significance for Germany. For Germany's *revolutionary* past is theoretical, it is the *Reformation*. As the revolution then began in the brain of the *monk*, so now it begins in the brain of the *philosopher*.

Luther, we grant, overcame bondage out of *devotion* by replacing it by bondage out of *conviction*. He shattered faith in authority because he restored the authority of faith. He turned priests into laymen because he turned laymen into priests. He freed man from outer religiosity because he made religiosity the inner man. He freed the body from chains because he enchained the heart.

But if Protestantism was not the true solution of the problem it was at least the true setting of it. It was no longer a case of the layman's struggle against the *priest outside himself* but of his struggle against *his own priest inside himself*, his *priestly nature*. And if the Protestant transformation of the German laymen into priests emancipated the lay popes, the *princes*, with the whole of their priestly clique, the privileged and philistines, the philosophical transformation of priestly Germans into men will emancipate the *people*. But *secularization* will not stop at the *confiscation of church estates* set in motion mainly by hypocritical Prussia any more than emancipation stops at princes. The Peasant War, the most radical fact of German history, came to grief because of theology. Today, when theology itself has come to grief, the most unfree fact of German history, our *status quo*, will be shattered against philosophy. On the eve of the Reformation official Germany was the most unconditional slave of Rome. On the eve of its revolution it is the unconditional slave of less than Rome, of Prussia and Austria, of country junkers and philistines.

Meanwhile, a major difficulty seems to stand in the way of a *radical* German revolution.

For revolutions require a *passive* element, a *material* basis. Theory is fulfilled in a people only insofar as it is the fulfilment of the needs of that people. But will the monstrous discrepancy between the demands of German thought and the answers of German reality find a corresponding discrepancy between civil society and the state and between civil society and itself? Will the theoretical needs be immediate practical needs? It is not enough for thought to strive for realization, reality must itself strive towards thought.

But Germany did not rise to the intermediary stage of political emancipation at the same time as the modern nations. It has not yet reached in practice the stages which it has surpassed in theory. How can it do a *somersault*, not only over its own limitations, but at the same time over the limitations of the modern nations, over limitations which it must in reality feel and strive for as for emancipation from its real limitations? Only a revolution of radical needs can be a radical revolution and it seems that precisely the preconditions and ground for such needs are lacking.

If Germany has accompanied the development of the modern nations only with the abstract activity of thought without taking an effective share in the real struggle of that development, it has, on the other hand, shared the *sufferings* of that development, without sharing in its enjoyment or its partial satisfaction. To the abstract activity on the one hand corresponds the abstract suffering on the other. That is why Germany will one day find itself on the level of European decadence before ever having been on the level of European emancipation. It will be comparable to a *fetish worshipper* pining away with the diseases of Christianity.

If we now consider the *German governments* we find that because of the circumstances of the time, because of Germany's condition, because of the standpoint of German education and finally under the impulse of its own fortunate instinct, they are driven to combine the *civilized shortcomings of the modern state world*, the advantages of which we do not enjoy, with the *barbaric deficiencies of the ancien régime,* which we enjoy in full; hence Germany must share more and more, if not in the reasonableness, at least in the unreasonableness of those state formations which are beyond the bounds of its *status quo.* Is there in the world, for example, a country which shares so naively in all the illusions of constitutional statehood without sharing in its realities as so-called constitutional Germany? And was it not perforce the notion of a German government to combine the tortures of censorship with the tortures of the French September laws[23] which provide for freedom of the press? As you could find the *gods* of all nations in the Roman Pantheon, so you will find in the Germans' Holy Roman Empire all the *sins* of all state forms. That this eclecticism will reach a so far unprecedented height is guaranteed in particular by the *political-aesthetic gourmanderie* of a German king* who intended to play all the roles of monarchy, whether feudal or bureaucratic, absolute or constitutional, autocratic or democratic, if not in the person of the people, at least in his *own* person, and if not for the people, at least for *himself. Germany, as the deficiency of the political present constituted as a world of its own,* will not be able to throw down the specific German limitations without throwing down the general limitation of the political present.

It is not the *radical* revolution, not the *general human* emancipation which is a utopian dream for Germany, but rather the partial, the *merely* political revolution, the revolution which leaves the pillars of the house standing. On what is a partial, a merely political revolution based? On *part of civil society emancipating* itself and attaining *general* domination; on a definite class, proceeding from its *particular situation,* undertaking the general emancipation

* Frederick William IV.—*Ed.*

of society. This class emancipates the whole of society but only provided the whole of society is in the same situation as this class, e.g., possesses money and education or can acquire them at will.

No class of civil society can play this role without arousing a moment of enthusiasm in itself and in the masses, a moment in which it fraternizes and merges with society in general, becomes confused with it and is perceived and acknowledged as its *general representative*, a moment in which its claims and rights are truly the claims and rights of society itself, a moment in which it is truly the social head and the social heart. Only in the name of the general rights of society can a particular class vindicate for itself general domination. For the storming of this emancipatory position, and hence for the political exploitation of all sections of society in the interests of its own section, revolutionary energy and spiritual self-feeling alone are not sufficient. For the *revolution of a nation* and the *emancipation of a particular class* of civil society to coincide, for *one* estate to be acknowledged as the estate of the whole society, all the defects of society must conversely be concentrated in another class, a particular estate must be the estate of the general stumbling-block, the incorporation of the general limitation, a particular social sphere must be recognized as the *notorious crime* of the whole of society, so that liberation from that sphere appears as general self-liberation. For *one* estate to be *par excellence* the estate of liberation, another estate must conversely be the obvious estate of oppression. The negative general significance of the French nobility and the French clergy determined the positive general significance of the nearest neighbouring and opposed class of the *bourgeoisie*.

But no particular class in Germany has the consistency, the penetration, the courage or the ruthlessness that could mark it out as the negative representative of society. No more has any estate the breadth of soul that identifies itself, even for a moment, with the soul of the nation, the geniality that inspires material might to political violence, or that revolutionary daring which flings at the adversary the defiant words: *I am nothing but I must be everything.* The main stem of German morals and honesty, of the classes as well as of individuals, is rather that *modest egoism* which asserts its limitcdness and allows it to be asserted against itself. The relation of the various sections of German society is therefore not dramatic but epic. Each of them begins to be aware of itself and begins to camp beside the others with all its particular claims not as soon as it is oppressed, but as soon as the circumstances of the time relations, without the section's own participation, create a social substratum on which it can in turn exert pressure. Even the *moral self-feeling of the German middle class* rests only on the consciousness that it is the common representative of the philistine mediocrity of all the other classes. It is therefore not only the German kings who accede to the throne *mal a propos*, it is every section of civil society which goes through a defeat before it celebrates victory and develops its own limitations before it overcomes the limitations facing it, asserts its narrow-hearted essence before it has been able to assert its magnanimous essence; thus the very opportunity of a great role has passed away before it is to hand, and every class, once it begins the struggle against the class opposed to it, is involved in the struggle against the class below it. Hence the higher nobility is struggling against the monarchy, the bureaucrat against the nobility, and the bourgeois against them all, while the proletariat is already beginning to find itself struggling against the bourgeoisie. The middle class hardly dares to grasp the thought of emancipation from its own standpoint when the development of the social conditions and the progress of political theory already declare that standpoint antiquated or at least problematic.

In France it is enough for somebody to be something for him to want to be everything; in Germany nobody can be anything if he is not prepared to renounce everything. In France partial emancipation is the basis of universal emancipation; in Germany universal emancipation is the *conditio sine qua non* of any partial emancipation. In France it is the reality of gradual liberation that must give birth to complete freedom, in Germany the impossibility of gradual liberation. In France every class of the nation is a *political idealist* and becomes aware of itself at first not as a particular class but as a representative of social requirements generally. The role of *emancipator* therefore passes in dramatic motion to the various classes of the French nation one after the other until it finally comes to the class which implements social freedom no longer with the provision of certain conditions lying outside man and yet created by human society, but rather organizes all conditions of human existence on the premises of social freedom. On the contrary, in Germany, where practical life is as spiritless as spiritual life is unpractical, no class in civil society has any need or capacity for general emancipation until it is forced by its *immediate* condition, by *material* necessity, by its *very chains*.

Where, then, is the *positive* possibility of a German emancipation?

Answer: In the formation of a class with *radical chains*, a class of civil society which is not a class of civil society, an estate which is the dissolution of all estates, a sphere which has a universal character by its universal suffering and claims no *particular right* because no *particular wrong* but *wrong generally* is perpetrated against it; which can invoke no *historical* but only its *human* title, which does not stand in any one-sided antithesis to the consequences but in all-round antithesis to the premises of German statehood; a sphere, finally, which cannot emancipate itself without emancipating itself from all other spheres of society and thereby emancipating all other spheres of society, which, in a word, is the *complete loss* of man and hence can win itself only through the *complete re-winning of man.* This dissolution of society as a particular estate is the *proletariat.*

The proletariat is beginning to appear in Germany as a result of the rising *industrial* movement. For it is not the *naturally arising* poor but the *artificially impoverished,* not the human masses mechanically oppressed by the gravity of society but the masses resulting from the *drastic dissolution* of society, mainly of the middle estate, that form the proletariat, although, as is easily understood, the naturally arising poor and the Christian-Germanic serfs gradually join its ranks.

By heralding the *dissolution of the hereto existing world order* the proletariat merely proclaims the *secret of its own existence*, for it is the *factual* dissolution of that world order. By demanding the *negation of private property,* the proletariat merely raises to the rank of a *principle of society* what society has raised to the rank of *its* principle, what is already incorporated in *it* as the negative result of society without its own participation. The proletarian then finds himself possessing the same right in regard to the world which is coming into being as the *German king* in regard to the world which has come into being when he calls the people *his* people as he calls the horse *his* horse. By declaring the people his private property the king merely proclaims that the private owner is king.

As philosophy finds its *material* weapon in the proletariat, so the proletariat finds its *spiritual* weapon in philosophy. And once the lightning of thought has squarely struck this ingenuous soil of the people the emancipation of the *Germans* into *men* will be accomplished.

Let us sum up the result:

The only *practically* possible liberation of Germany is liberation from the point of view of *the* theory which proclaims man to be the highest essence of man. In Germany emancipation from the *Middle Ages* is possible only as emancipation from the *partial* victories over the Middle Ages as well. In Germany *no* kind of bondage can be shattered without *every* kind of bondage being shattered. The *fundamental* Germany cannot revolutionize without revolutionizing *from the foundation. The emancipation of the German* is *the emancipation of man.* The *head* of this emancipation is *philosophy*, its *heart* is the *proletariat.* Philosophy cannot be made a reality without the abolition of the proletariat, the proletariat cannot be abolished without philosophy being made a reality.

When all inner requisites are fulfilled the *day of German resurrection* will be proclaimed by the *crowing of the cock of Gaul.*

KARL MARX AND FREDERICK ENGELS

THE HOLY FAMILY, OR CRITIQUE OF CRITICAL CRITICISM

AGAINST BRUNO BAUER AND CO.

(Extract from Chapter VI)

D) CRITICAL BATTLE AGAINST FRENCH MATERIALISM

"*Spinozism* dominated the eighteenth century in its later French variety which made matter into substance, as well as in deism, which conferred on matter a more spiritual name. . . . *Spinoza's French school* and the supporters of deism were but two sects disputing over the true meaning of *his system*. . . . The simple fate of this Enlightenment was its sinking into *romanticism* after being obliged to surrender to the reaction which began after the French movement."

That is what *Criticism* says.

To the critical history of French materialism we shall oppose a brief outline of its profane, voluminous history We shall admit with due respect the abyss between history as it really happened and history as it happened according to the decree of "*Absolute Criticism*," the creator equally of the old and of the new. And finally, obeying the prescriptions of *Criticism*, we shall make the "Why?", "Whence?" and "Whither?" of Critical history the "objects of a persevering study."

"Speaking *exactly* and in the *prosaic* sense," the French Enlightenment of the eighteenth century, in particular *French materialism*, was not only a struggle against the existing political institutions and the existing religion and theology; it was just as much an *open* struggle against *metaphysics*[24] of the *seventeenth century*, and against all metaphysics, in particular that of *Descartes, Malebranche, Spinoza and Leibniz. Philosophy* was opposed to *metaphysics* as *Feuerbach*, in his first decisive attack on *Hegel* opposed *sober philosophy* to *drunken speculation.* Seventeenth-century *metaphysics*, beaten off the field by the French Enlightenment, to be precise, by *French materialism* of the eighteenth century, was given a *victorious and solid restoration* in *German philosophy*, particularly, in *speculative German philosophy* of the nineteenth century. After *Hegel* linked it in so masterly a fashion with all subsequent metaphysics and with German idealism and founded a metaphysical universal kingdom, the attack on *speculative metaphysics* and *metaphysics in general* again corresponded, as in the eighteenth century, to the attack on theology. It will be defeated for ever by *materialism* which has now been perfected by the work of *speculation* itself and coincides with *humanism.* As *Feuerbach* represented *materialism* in the *theoretical* domain, French and English *socialism* and *communism* in the *practical* field represented *materialism* which *coincided* with *humanism.*

"Speaking *exactly* and in the *prosaic* sense," there are *two trends in French materialism*; one traces its origin to *Descartes*, the other to *Locke*. The latter is *mainly* a *French* development and leads direct to *socialism.* The former, *mechanical* materialism, merges with what is properly French *natural science.* The two trends cross in the course of development. We have no need here to go deep into French materialism, which comes direct from *Descartes*, any more than into the French *Newton* school or the development of French natural science in general.

We shall therefore just note the following:

Descartes in his *physics* endowed *matter* with self-creative power and conceived *mechanical* motion as the act of its life. He completely separated his *physics* from his *metaphysics*. *Within* his physics *matter* is the only *substance*, the only basis of being and of knowledge.

Mechanical French materialism followed *Descartes' physics* in opposition to his metaphysics. His followers were by profession *anti-metaphysicists*, i.e., *physicists*.

The school begins with the *physician Leroy*, reaches its zenith with the physician *Cabanis*, and the physician *Lamettrie* is its centre. Descartes was still living when Leroy, like Lamettrie in the eighteenth century, transposed the Cartesian structure of *animals* to the human soul and affirmed that the soul is a *modus of the body* and *ideas are mechanical motions*. Leroy even thought Descartes had kept his real opinion secret. Descartes protested. At the end of the eighteenth century *Cabanis* perfected Cartesian materialism in his treatise: *Rapport du physique et du moral de l'homme.*

Cartesian materialism still exists today in France. It had great success in *mechanical natural science* which, "speaking *exactly* and in the *prosaic* sense" will be least of all reproached with *romanticism*.

Metaphysics of the seventeenth century, represented in France by *Descartes*, had *materialism* as its *antagonist* from its very birth. It personally opposed Descartes in *Gassendi*, the restorer of *Epicurean* materialism. French and English materialism was always closely related to *Democritus* and *Epicurus*. Cartesian metaphysics had another opponent in the *English* materialist *Hobbes*. Gassendi and Hobbes were victorious over their opponent long after their death when metaphysics was already officially dominant in all French schools.

Voltaire observed that the indifference of Frenchmen to the disputes between Jesuits and Jansenists[25] in the eighteenth century was due less to philosophy than to *Law's* financial speculation. And, in fact, the downfall of seventeenth-century metaphysics can be explained by the materialistic theory of the eighteenth century only as far as that theoretical movement itself is explained by the practical nature of French life at the time. That life was turned to the immediate present, worldly enjoyment and worldly interests, the *earthly* world. Its anti-theological, anti-metaphysical and materialistic practice demanded corresponding anti-theological, anti-metaphysical and materialistic theories. Metaphysics had *in practice* lost all credit. Here we have only to indicate briefly the *theoretical* process.

In the seventeenth century metaphysics (cf. Descartes, Leibniz, and others) still had an element of *positive*, profane content. It made discoveries in mathematics, physics and other exact sciences which seemed to come within its pale. This appearance was done away with as early as the beginning of the eighteenth century. The positive sciences broke off from it and determined their own separate fields. The whole wealth of metaphysics was reduced to beings of thought and heavenly things, although this was the very time when real beings and earthly things began to be the centre of all interest. Metaphysics had gone stale. In the very year in which Malebranche and Arnauld, the last great French metaphysicians of the seventeenth century, died, *Helvétius* and *Condillac* were born.

The man who deprived seventeenth-century metaphysics of all *credit* in the domain of *theory* was *Pierre Bayle*. His weapon was *scepticism*, which he forged out of metaphysics' own magic formulae. He at first proceeded from Cartesian metaphysics. As *Feuerbach* was driven by the fight against speculative theology to the fight against *speculative philosophy* precisely because he recognized in speculation the last prop of theology, because he had to force theology to turn back from pretended science to *coarse*, repulsive *faith*, so Bayle too was driven by religious doubt to doubt about metaphysics which was the support of that faith. He therefore critically investigated metaphysics from its very origin. He became its historian in order to write the history of its death. He mainly refuted *Spinoza* and *Leibniz*.

Pierre Bayle did not only prepare the reception of materialism and the philosophy of common sense in France by shattering metaphysics with his scepticism. He heralded *atheistic society*, which was soon to come to existence, by *proving* that a society consisting only of atheists is *possible*, that an atheist *can* be a respectable man and that it is not by atheism but by superstition and idolatry that man debases himself.

To quote the expression of a French writer, *Pierre Bayle* was "*the last metaphysician in the seventeenth-century sense of the word and the first philosopher in the sense of the eighteenth century*."

Besides the negative refutation of seventeenth-century theology and metaphysics, a *positive, anti-metaphysical* system was required. A book was needed which would systematize and theoretically justify the practice of life of the time. *Locke's* treatise on the origin of human reason came from across the Channel as if in answer to a call. It was welcomed enthusiastically like a long-awaited guest.

To the question: Was *Locke* perchance a follower of *Spinoza*? "Profane" history may answer:

Materialism is the native son *of Great Britain*. Even Britain's scholastic *Duns Scotus* wondered: "*Can matter think?*"

In order to bring about that miracle he had recourse to God's omnipotence, i.e., he forced *theology* itself to preach *materialism*. In addition he was a *nominalist*.[26] Nominalism is a main component of *English* materialism and is in general the *first expression of materialism*.

The real founder of *English materialism* and all *modern experimental* science was *Bacon*. For him natural science was true science and *physics* based on perception was the most excellent part of natural science. *Anaxagoras* with his *homoeomeria* and *Democritus* with his atoms are often the authorities he refers to. According to his teaching the *senses* are infallible and are the *source* of all knowledge. Science is *experimental* and consists in applying a *rational method* to the data provided by the senses. Induction, analysis, comparison, observation and experiment are the principal requisites of rational method. The first and most important of the inherent qualities of *matter* is *motion*, not only *mechanical* and *mathematical* movement, but still more *impulse*, *vital life-spirit*, *tension*, or, to use Jacob Böhme's expression, the *throes* [*Qual*] of matter. The primary forms of matter are the living, individualizing *forces of being* inherent in it and producing the distinctions between the species.

In *Bacon*, its first creator, materialism contained latent and still in a naive way the germs of all-round development. Matter smiled at man with poetical sensuous brightness. The aphoristic doctrine itself, on the other hand, was full of the inconsistencies of theology.

In its further development materialism became *one-sided*. *Hobbes* was the one who *systematized Bacon's* materialism. Sensuousness lost its bloom and became the abstract sensuousness of the *geometrician*. *Physical* motion was sacrificed to the *mechanical* or *mathematical*, *geometry* was proclaimed the principal science. Materialism became *hostile to humanity*. In order to overcome the *anti-human incorporeal* spirit in its own field, materialism itself was obliged to mortify its flesh and become an *ascetic*. It appeared as a *being of reason*, but it also developed the implacable logic of reason.

If man's senses are the source of all his knowledge, Hobbes argues, proceeding from Bacon, then conception, thought, imagination, etc., are nothing but phantoms of the material world more or less divested of its sensuous form. Science can only give a name to these phantoms. One name can be applied to several phantoms. There can even be names of names. But it would be a contradiction to say, on the one hand, that all ideas have their origin in the world of the senses and to maintain, on the other hand, that a word is more than a word, that besides the beings represented, which are always individual, there exist also general beings. An *incorporeal substance* is just as much a contradiction as an *incorporeal body*. *Body*, *being*, *substance* are one and the same *real* idea. One cannot separate the thought from matter *which* thinks. Matter is the subject of all changes. The word *infinite* is *meaningless* unless it means the capacity of our mind to go on adding without end. Since only what is material is perceptible, knowable, *nothing* is known of the existence of God. I am sure only of my own existence. Every human passion is a mechanical motion ending or beginning. The objects of impulses are what is called good. Man is subject to the same laws as nature; might and freedom are identical.

Hobbes systematized Bacon, but did not give a more precise proof of his basic principle that our knowledge and our ideas have their source in the world of the senses.

Locke proved the principle of Bacon and Hobbes in his essay on the origin of human reason.

Just as Hobbes did away with the *theistic*[27] prejudices in Bacon's materialism, so Collins, Dodwall, Coward, Hartley, Priestley and others broke down the last bounds of Locke's sensualism. For materialists, at least, deism[28] is no more than a convenient and easy way of getting rid of religion.

We have already mentioned how opportune Locke's work was for the French. Locke founded the philosophy of *bon sens*, of common sense; i.e., he said indirectly that no philosopher can be at variance with the healthy human senses and reason based on them.

Locke's *immediate* follower, *Condillac*, who also translated him into *French*, at once opposed Locke's sensualism to seventeenth-century *metaphysics*. He proved that the French had quite rightly rejected metaphysics as the mere bungling of fancy and theological prejudice. He published a refutation of the systems of *Descartes, Spinoza, Leibniz* and *Malebranche*.

In his *Essai sur l'origine des connaissances humaines* he expounded Locke's ideas and proved that not only the soul, but the senses too, not only the art of creating ideas, but also the art of sensuous perception are matters of *experience* and *habit*. The whole development of man therefore depends on *education* and *environment*. It was only by *eclectic* philosophy that Condillac was ousted from the French schools.

The difference between *French* and *English* materialism follows from the difference between the two nations. The French imparted to English materialism wit, flesh and blood, and eloquence. They gave it the temperament and grace that it lacked. They *civilized* it.

In *Helvétius*, who also based himself on Locke, materialism became really French. Helvétius conceived it immediately in its application to social life, (Helvétius, *De l'homme, de ses facultés intellectuelles et de son éducation*). Sensuous qualities and self-love, enjoyment and correctly understood personal interests are the bases of moral. The natural equality of human intelligence, the unity of progress of reason and progress of industry, the natural goodness of man and the omnipotence of education are the main points in his system.

In *Lamettrie's* works we find a combination of Descartes' system and English materialism. He makes use of Descartes' physics in detail. His "*Man Machine*" is a treatise after the model of Descartes' beast-machine. The physical part of Holbach's *Système de la nature, ou des lois du monde physique et du monde moral* is also a result of the combination of French and English materialism, while the moral part is based substantially on the moral of Helvétius. *Robinet* (*De la Nature*), the French materialist who had the most connection with metaphysics and was therefore praised by Hegel, refers explicitly to *Leibniz*.

We need not dwell on Volney, Dupuis, Diderot and others any more than on the physiocrats, having already proved the dual origin of French materialism from Descartes' physics and English materialism and the opposition of French materialism to seventeenth-century *metaphysics* and to the metaphysics of Descartes, Spinoza, Malebranche, and Leibniz. The Germans could not see this opposition before they came into the same opposition with *speculative metaphysics*.

As *Cartesian* materialism merges into *natural science proper*, the other branch of French materialism leads direct to *socialism* and *communism*.

There is no need of any great penetration to see from the teaching of materialism on the original goodness and equal intellectual endowment of men, the omnipotence of experience, habit and education, and the influence of environment on man, the great significance of industry, the justification of enjoyment, etc., how necessarily materialism is connected with communism and socialism. If man draws all his knowledge, sensation, etc., from the world of the senses and the experience gained in it, the empirical world must be arranged so that in it man experiences and gets used to what is really human and that he becomes aware of himself as man. If correctly understood interest is the principle of all moral, man's private interest must be made to coincide with the interest of humanity. If man is unfree in the materialist sense, i.e., is free not through the negative power to avoid this or that, but through the positive power to assert his true individuality, crime must not be punished in the individual, but the anti-social source of crime must be destroyed, and each man must be given social scope for the vital manifestation of his being. If man is shaped by his surroundings, his surroundings must be made human. If man is social by nature, he will develop his true nature only in society, and the power of his nature must be measured not by the power of separate individuals but by the power of society.

This and similar propositions are to be found almost literally even in the oldest French materialists. This is not the place to assess them. *Fable of the Bees, or Private Vices Made Public Benefits*, by *Mandeville*, one of the early English followers of Locke, is typical of the social tendencies of materialism. He proves that in *modern* society vice is *indispensable* and *useful.* This was by no means an apology of modern society.

Fourier proceeds immediately from the teaching of the French materialists. The *Babouvists* were coarse, uncivilized materialists, but mature communism too comes *directly* from *French materialism.* The latter returned to its mother-country, *England,* in the form *Helvétius* gave it. *Bentham* based his system of *correctly understood interest* on Helvétius's moral, and *Owen* proceeded from *Bentham's* system to found English communism. Exiled to England, the Frenchman *Cabet* came under the influence of communist ideas there and on his return to France became the most popular, although the most superficial, representative of communism. Like Owen, the more scientific French communists, *Dezamy, Gay* and others, developed the teaching of *materialism* as the teaching of *real humanism* and the *logical* basis of *communism.* . . .

KARL MARX

THESES ON FEUERBACH

I

The chief defect of all hitherto existing materialism—that of Feuerbach included—is that the thing [*Gegenstand*], reality, sensuousness, is conceived only in the form of the *object* [*Objekt*] or of *contemplation* [*Anschauung*], but not as *human sensuous activity, practice*, not subjectively. Hence it happened that the *active* side, in contradistinction to materialism, was developed by idealism—but only abstractly, since, of course, idealism does not know real, sensuous activity as such. Feuerbach wants sensuous objects, really differentiated from the thought-objects, but he does not conceive human activity itself as *objective* [*gegenständliche*] activity. Hence, in the *Essence of Christianity*, he regards the theoretical attitude as the only genuinely human attitude, while practice is conceived and fixed only in its dirty-judaical form of appearance. Hence he does not grasp the significance of "revolutionary," of "practical-critical," activity.

II

The question whether objective [*gegenständliche*] truth can be attributed to human thinking is not a question of theory but a *practical* question. In practice man must prove the truth, that is, the reality and power, the this-sidedness

[*Diesseitigkeit*] of his thinking. The dispute over the reality or non-reality of thinking which is isolated from practice is a purely *scholastic* question.

III

The materialist doctrine that men are products of circumstances and upbringing, and that, therefore, changed men are products of other circumstances and changed upbringing, forgets that it is men that change circumstances and that the educator himself needs educating. Hence, this doctrine necessarily arrives at dividing society into two parts, of which one is superior to society (in Robert Owen, for example).

The coincidence of the changing of circumstances and of human activity can be conceived and rationally understood only as *revolutionizing practice.*

IV

Feuerbach starts out from the fact of religious self-alienation, the duplication of the world into a religious, imaginary world and a real one. His work consists in the dissolution of the religious world into its secular basis. He overlooks the fact that after this work is completed the chief thing still remains to be done. For the fact that the secular foundation detaches itself from itself and establishes itself in the clouds as an independent realm is really only to be explained by the self-cleavage and self-contradictoriness of this secular basis. The latter must itself, therefore, first be understood in its contradiction, and then revolutionized in practice by the removal of the contradiction. Thus, for instance, once the earthly family is discovered to be the secret of the holy family, the former must then itself be criticized in theory and revolutionized in practice.

V

Feuerbach, not satisfied with *abstract thinking*, appeals to *sensuous contemplation*; but he does not conceive sensuousness as *practical*, human-sensuous activity.

VI

Feuerbach resolves the religious essence into the *human* essence. But the human essence is no abstraction inherent in each single individual. In its reality it is the ensemble of the social relations.

Feuerbach, who does not enter upon a criticism of this real essence, is consequently compelled:

1. To abstract from the historical process and to fix the religious sentiment [*Gemüt*] as something by itself and to presuppose an abstract—*isolated*—human individual.

2. The human essence, therefore, can with him be comprehended only as "genus," as an internal, dumb generality which merely *naturally* unites the many individuals.

VII

Feuerbach, consequently, does not see that the "religious sentiment" is itself a *social product*, and that the abstract individual whom he analyzes belongs in reality to a particular form of society.

VIII

Social life is essentially *practical*. All mysteries which mislead theory to mysticism find their rational solution in human practice and in the comprehension of this practice.

IX

The highest point attained by *contemplative* materialism, that is, materialism which does not understand sensuousness as practical activity, is the contemplation of single individuals in "civil society."

X

The standpoint of the old materialism is "civil" society; the standpoint of the new is *human* society, or socialized humanity.

XI

The philosophers have only *interpreted* the world, in various ways; the point, however, is to *change* it.

KARL MARX AND FREDERICK ENGELS

GERMAN IDEOLOGY

(From Chapter I)

...The fact is, therefore: definite persons who are productively active in definite ways enter into definite social and political relations. Empiric observation must in every single case reveal the connection of the social and political organization with production, empirically and without any mystification or speculation. The social organization and the state constantly arise from the life-process of definite individuals, of those individuals not as they or other people imagine them to be, but as they are *really*, i.e., as they act, as they materially produce, consequently as they are active under definite material limitations, provisions and conditions which do not depend on their free will.*

The production of notions, ideas and consciousness is from the beginning directly interwoven with the material

* In the manuscript the following is crossed out: "The ideas that these individuals have are ideas either of their relation to nature or of their relation to one another or of their own constitution. It is clear that in all these cases these ideas are the conscious expression—true or illusory—of their real relations and activity, of their production, their intercourse, their social and political organization. The opposite assumption is possible only when besides the spirit of the real materially determined individuals another spirit apart is presupposed. If the conscious expression of the real relations of these individuals is illusory, if in their ideas they turn reality upside down, this again is a result of their limited material activity and their consequent limited social relations."—*Ed.*

activity and the material intercourse of human beings, the language of real life. The production of men's ideas, thinking, their spiritual intercourse, here appear as the direct efflux of their material condition. The same applies to spiritual production as represented in the language of politics, laws, morals, religion, metaphysics, etc. of a people. The producers of men's ideas, notions, etc., are men, but real active men as determined by a definite development of their productive forces and the intercourse corresponding to those productive forces up to its remotest form. Consciousness [*das Bewußtsein*] can never be anything else but conscious being [*das bewußte Sein*], and the being of men is their real life-process. If in the whole of ideology men and their relations appear upside down as in a *camera obscura* this is due as much to their historical life-process as the inversion of objects on the retina is due to their immediate physical life-process.

In direct opposition to German philosophy, which comes down from heaven to earth, here there is ascension from earth to heaven. That means that we proceed not from what men say, fancy or imagine, nor from men as they are spoken of, thought, fancied, imagined in order to arrive from them at men of flesh and blood; we proceed from the really active men and see the development of the ideological reflexes and echoes of their real life-process as proceeding from that life-process. Even the nebulous images in the brain of men are necessary sublimates of their material, empirically observable, materially preconditioned, life-process. Thus, morals, religion, metaphysics and other forms of ideology and the forms of consciousness corresponding to them no longer retain their apparent independence. They have no history, they have no development, but men, developing their material production and their material intercourse, with this, their reality, their thinking and the products of their thinking also change. It is not consciousness that determines life, but life that determines consciousness. In the first view one proceeds from consciousness as from the living individual; in the second, in conformity with real life, from the real living individuals themselves, considering consciousness only as *their* consciousness. . . .

* * *

Consciousness is therefore from the start a product of society, and it remains such as long as men exist at all. At the beginning consciousness is of course only consciousness of the *immediate* sensuous surroundings and consciousness of the limited connection with other persons and things outside the individual becoming conscious of itself; at the same time it is consciousness of nature, which at the beginning confronts man as a completely alien, almighty and unassailable power to which man's attitude is a purely animal one and to which he submits like a beast; it is therefore a purely animal consciousness of nature (nature worship).

It is immediately obvious that this nature worship or this definite attitude to nature is determined by the form of society and conversely. Here as everywhere the identity of man and nature is so apparent that the limited attitude of men towards nature conditions their limited attitude to one another and their limited attitude to one another determines their limited attitude towards nature for the very reason that nature has yet hardly been modified by history; on the other hand, consciousness of the necessity of intercourse with surrounding individuals is the beginning of consciousness of living in society at all. This beginning is as animal-like as social life itself at this stage; it is mere herd consciousness, and man is distinguished from the sheep only by his consciousness taking the place of instinct or by his instinct being a conscious one. This sheep or stock consciousness receives further development and education by increased productivity, the multiplication of needs and the multiplication of the population underlying both the former. At the same time division of labour develops, being originally nothing else than the division of labour in the sexual act, then division of labour which took place of itself or "naturally" as a result of natural aptitudes (e.g. bodily strength), needs, coincidence, etc., etc. The division of labour becomes real division only from the instant when the division of material and spiritual labour takes place.* From this instant consciousness *can* really fancy that it is something else than consciousness of existing practice, that it *really* imagines something without imagining anything real; from this instant consciousness is able to emancipate itself from the world and to go on to the forming of "pure" theory, theology, philosophy, morals, etc. But even if this theory, theology, philosophy, morals, etc., enter into contradiction with the existing relations, this can happen only because the existing social relations have entered into contradiction with the existing production forces. This, by the way, may also happen in a definite national sphere of relations because the contradiction lies not within that national sphere but between that national consciousness and the practice of other nations,** i.e., between the national and the universal consciousness of a nation (as is the case in Germany today).

For the rest, it makes no difference what consciousness undertakes by itself: out of all this rubbish we retain only one result: that these three factors—the production forces, the social condition and consciousness—can and must enter into contradiction with one another, because the *division of*

* Here Marx wrote in the margin: "With this coincides the first form of ideologists (priests).—*Ed.*

** Here Marx wrote in the margin: "*Religion*. The Germans with *ideology* as such."—*Ed.*

labour implies the possibility, nay, the reality, that spiritual and material activity—enjoyment and work, production and consumption fall to different individuals; the only possibility that they will not enter into contradiction lies in the abolition of the division of labour. It is self-evident that the "ghosts," "bonds," "higher being," "concept," "doubtfulness" are but the idealistic spiritual expression, the idea of the apparently isolated individual, the idea of very empiric fetters and limitations within which the mode of production of life and the forms of intercourse corresponding to it move....

* * *

... The basis of this conception of history is, therefore, to disclose the real production process, with the material production of immediate life as the starting-point, to conceive the form of intercourse connected with and engendered by this mode of production—hence civil society in its various stages—as the foundation of all history, to represent this society in its state activity and to explain by society all the various theoretical products and forms of consciousness, religion, philosophy, morals, etc., and to trace its coming into being to them. Thereby the process in its totality (and hence the interreaction of these various sides) can be represented. This conception of history has not to seek a category in every epoch like the idealistic conception of history, but it remains constantly on the real *ground* of history; it does not explain practice by the idea but explains the formation of ideas by material practice. Accordingly it comes to the result that all forms and products of consciousness can be dissolved not by spiritual criticism, not by dissolution in "self-consciousness," or transformation into "phantoms," "ghosts," "freaks," etc., but by the practical overthrow of the real social relations which gave rise to these idealistic humbugs; that not criticism but revolution is the motive force of history as well as of religion, philosophy and all other forms of theory. It shows that history does not end by dissolving itself in "self-consciousness" as "the spirit of the spirit" but that there is present in it at every stage a material result, a sum of production forces, a historically created relation to nature and of individuals to one another handed down to each generation by its predecessor, a mass of production forces, capitals and circumstances which, on the one hand, are modified by the new generation but which, on the other hand, prescribe to that generation their own conditions of life and give it a definite development, a special character—that circumstances, therefore, make man just as much as man makes circumstances. This sum of productive forces, capitals and forms of social intercourse which every individual and every generation finds already in existence is the real basis of what the philosophers imagined to be the "substance" and "essence of man," what they apotheosized and fought against, a real basis which is not in the least disturbed in its action and influence on the development of man by those philosophers, as "self-consciousness" and "ego," rebelling against it. These already existing conditions of life of the various generations also decide whether the revolutionary upheavals that periodically recur in history are strong enough to overthrow the basis of all that is in existence; if these material elements of a complete overthrow, to wit, on one side the existing production forces and on the other the formation of a revolutionary mass which revolts not only against individual conditions of hitherto existing society but against the very "life-production" hitherto existing, the "whole of the activity" on which it is based—if these material elements are not to hand it is absolutely indifferent for practical development, as the history of communism proves, whether the *idea* of that revolution has already been formulated a hundred times.

All preceding conception of history has either completely ignored this real basis of history or has considered it only as incidental and in no way connected with the course of history. That is why history had always to be written according to a standard lying outside it; real life-production appeared as pre-historic while what was historical appeared as separated from common life and extra-supra-mundane. Man's relation to nature was thus excluded from history, as a result of which the antithesis of nature and history was produced. Hence this conception of history saw in history only the main official actions of the state and the religious and generally theoretical struggles; in particular it had to *share* with each historic epoch the *illusion of that epoch.* For instance, if an epoch imagines that it is determined by purely "political" or "religious" motives, although "religion" and "politics" are only forms of its real motive, its historian accepts that opinion. The "fancy," the "imagination" of these definite men concerning their real practice is transformed into the only determining and active force that dominates and determines the practice of those men. When the crude form in which division of labour appears among the Indians and the Egyptians leads to the caste system in the state and religion of those peoples, the historian believes that the caste system is the force that produced those crude social forms. While the French and the English keep at least to the political illusion which as yet is nearest to reality, the Germans move in the domain of the "pure spirit" and make the religious illusion the motive force of history. The Hegelian philosophy of history is the last product of this general German historiography carried to its "purest expression." It deals not with real, not even with political interests, but with pure thoughts which then must appear to the holy Bruno as a series of "thoughts" one of which devours the other and finally sinks in "self-consciousness."* With still greater consistency this course of history must appear to the holy Max Stirner, who knows nothing at all about real history, as a mere story of "knights," robbers and ghosts from the visions of which he naturally sees no salvation except in godlessness. This conception is really religious. It supposes religious man as primitive man from whom all history proceeds, and in its imagination it sets religious fantasy production in the place of the real production of the means of subsistence and of life itself. This whole conception of history together with its dissolution and the scruples and doubts arising from it is a mere *national* affair of the Germans and has only a *local* interest for Germany. An example is the important and of late repeatedly treated question of how, properly speaking, one "comes out of the kingdom of god into the kingdom of man." As if that "kingdom of god" ever existed anywhere except in the imagination, and erudite gentlemen had not always lived, without knowing it, in the "kingdom of man" the way into which they are now seeking. Or as if the scientific amusement—for it is no more than that—of explaining the curiosity of this theoretical nebular kingdom did not, on the contrary, consist in proving its origin to lie in real earthly relations. In general the question with these Germans is always to dissolve the existing nonsense in some other folly, i.e., to presuppose that all this nonsense has some *sense* of its own that must be discovered, whereas it is a case of explaining these theoretical phrases from the existing real relations. The real, practical dissolution of these phrases, the elimination of these notions from the consciousness of man, will, as we have already said, be accomplished by

* Here Marx wrote in the margin: "So-called *objective* historiography consisted precisely in conceiving historical relations separate from activity. Reactionary."—*Ed.*

altered circumstances, not by theoretic deductions. For the mass of human beings, i.e., for the proletariat, these theoretic notions do not exist and therefore do not need to be dissolved and if ever this mass had any such notions, e.g. religion, they have been dissolved long ago by circumstances. . . .

KARL MARX

THE COMMUNISM OF THE PAPER *RHEINISCHER BEOBACHTER*[29]

(Extract)

...Besides income tax, the Consistorial Councillor has another means of introducing communism as he conceives it:

"What is the alpha and omega of Christian faith? The dogma of original sin and the redemption. And therein lies the solidary link between men at its highest potential; one for all and all for one."

Happy people! The *cardinal question* is solved for ever. Under the double wings of the Prussian eagle and the Holy Ghost the proletariat will find two inexhaustible sources of life: first the surplus of income tax over and above the ordinary and extraordinary needs of the state, a surplus which is equal to nought; second, the revenues from the heavenly domains of original sin and the redemption which are also equal to nought. These two noughts provide a splendid ground for one-third of the nation who have no ground for their subsistence and a wonderful support for another third which is on the decline. In any case, the imaginary surpluses, original sin and the redemption, will appease the hunger of the people in quite a different way than the long speeches of the liberal deputies!

Further we read:

"In the 'Our Father' we say: lead us not into temptation. And we must practise towards our neighbour what we ask for ourselves. But our social conditions tempt man and excessive need incites to crime."

And we, the honourable bureaucrats, judges and consistorial councillors of the Prussian state, take this into consideration by having people racked on the wheel, beheaded, imprisoned, and flogged and thereby "lead" the proletarians "into temptation" to have us later similarly racked on the wheel, beheaded, imprisoned and flogged. And that will not fail to happen.

"Such conditions," the Consistorial Councillor declares, "a Christian state *cannot* tolerate, it must find a remedy for them."

Yes, with absurd prattle on society's duties of solidarity, with imaginary surpluses and unprovided bills drawn on God the Father, Son and Co.

"We can also be spared the already boring talk about communism," our observant Consistorial Councillor asserts. "If only those whose calling it is to develop the social principles of Christianity do so, the Communists will soon be put to silence."

The social principles of Christianity have now had eighteen hundred years to develop and need no further development by Prussian consistorial councillors.

The social principles of Christianity justified the slavery of Antiquity, glorified the serfdom of the Middle Ages and equally know, when necessary, how to defend the oppression of the proletariat, although they make a pitiful face over it.

The social principles of Christianity preach the necessity of a ruling and an oppressed class, and all they have for the latter is the pious wish the former will be charitable.

The social principles of Christianity transfer the consistorial councillors' adjustment of all infamies to heaven and thus justify the further existence of those infamies on earth.

The social principles of Christianity declare all vile acts of the oppressors against the oppressed to be either the just punishment of original sin and other sins or trials that the Lord in his infinite wisdom imposes on those redeemed.

The social principles of Christianity preach cowardice, self-contempt, abasement, submission, dejection, in a word all the qualities of the *canaille*; and the proletariat, not wishing to be treated as *canaille*, needs its courage, its self-feeling, its pride and its sense of independence more than its bread.

The social principles of Christianity are sneakish and the proletariat is revolutionary.

So much for the social principles of Christianity.

To continue:

"We acknowledged social reform as the noblest calling of the monarchy."

Did we? There has been no question of that so far. But grant it. And in what does the social reform of the monarchy consist? In putting into force an income tax purloined from the organs of liberalism and which is supposed to provide a surplus that the finance minister knows nothing about; in the fiasco of the *Landrentenbanken*, in the Prussian East Railway, and in the first place in the profit of an enormous capital of original sin and redemption!

"The interest of the monarchy itself advises that"—how low monarchy must have sunk!

"That is demanded by the need of society"—which at present requires protective barriers far more than dogmas.

"That is recommended by the Gospel"—it is recommended by everything in general, except the frightfully desolate state of the Prussian treasury, that abyss which will have irretrievably swallowed up the fifteen Russian millions within three years. The Gospel, by the way, recommends much, including castration as the beginning of social reform for itself (Math. XXV).

"The monarchy," our Consistorial Councillor says, "is one with the people."

This expression is only another form of the old "*l'état c'est moi*" and indeed it is the very form which Louis XVI used on June 23, 1789, against his rebellious Estates: "if you do not listen to me, I shall send you home—*et seul je ferai le bonheur de mon peuple*."*

The monarchy must be very hard pressed when it decides to make use of that form, and our learned Consistorial Councillor must know how the French people at the time thanked Louis XVI for using it.

"The throne," the Consistorial Councillor further assures, "must rest on the broad basis of the people," there it will be firmest.

As long, of course, as those broad shoulders do not throw the heavy superstructure into the gutter with a mighty jerk.

"*The aristocracy*," the Consistorial Councillor concludes, "leaves monarchy its dignity and gives it poetic embellishment but deprives it of real power. *The bourgeoisie* robs it of power and dignity alike and gives it only a Civil List. *The people* leaves the monarchy its power, its dignity and its poetry."

At this point the Consistorial Councillor unfortunately takes Frederick William's bombastic appeal *to his people* in the speech from the throne too seriously. His last words are: overthrow of the aristocracy, overthrow of the bourgeoisie, establishment of a monarchy relying on the support of the people.

Were these demands not pure fantasies they would contain a complete revolution.

---

* I alone shall make the happiness of my people.—*Ed.*

We shall not dwell on the fact that the aristocracy can be overthrown only by the bourgeoisie and the people together, that the rule of the people in a country where the aristocracy and the bourgeoisie still exist side by side is pure nonsense. Such fables from one of Eichhorn's consistorial councillors are not worth answering with serious arguments.

We shall make but a few well-meaning remarks to those gentlemen who wish to save the imperilled Prussian monarchy by a *somersault* into the people.

Of all political elements the people is the most dangerous for a king. Not the people that Frederick William speaks of, which thanks with tears in its eyes for a kick and a silver *groschen*; that people is by no means dangerous, for it exists nowhere except in the king's imagination. But the real people, the proletariat, the small peasants and the populace, there you have, as Hobbes said, *puer robustus, sed malitiosus*, a sturdy but malicious boy, who will not let himself be made a fool of either by thin kings or by fat ones.

This people would first and foremost force His Majesty to grant a constitution with universal suffrage, freedom of association, freedom of the press and other unpleasant things.

And having obtained all that it would use it to show as quickly as possible how it understands the *power*, the *dignity* and the *poetry* of the monarchy.

The present worthy holder of the monarchy could consider himself lucky if the people gave him a job as public declaimer in the Berlin Artisan Association with a Civil List of 250 thalers and a cool pale ale every day.

If the consistorial councillors who now rule the destiny of the Prussian monarchy and of *Rheinischer Beobachter* have any doubt about it, let them have a good look at history. History makes out quite different horoscopes for kings who appeal to their people.

Charles I of England also appealed *to his people* against his Estates. He called his people to arms against Parliament. But the people declared against the king, threw out of Parliament all the members who did not represent the people and finally had the king beheaded by Parliament which had thus become really representative of the people. That was how Charles I's appeal to his people ended. This happened on January 30, 1649, and 1849 is the second centenary.

Louis XVI of France also appealed *to his people.* For three years he appealed to one part of the people against another; he was looking for *his* people, the true people, the people that was enthusiastic for him, and he did not find it anywhere. In the end he found it in Coblenz camp behind the lines of the Prussian and Austrian armies. But that was too much for his people in France. On August 10, 1792, it imprisoned the appealer in the Temple and convened the National Convention which represented it in every way.

This Convention declared itself competent to decide the ex-king's *appeal* and after a few debates it sent the appealer to Place de la Révolution where he was guillotined on January 21, 1793.

That is what happens when kings *appeal to their peoples.* But we must wait and see what happens when consistorial councillors want to establish a democratic monarchy.

KARL MARX AND FREDERICK ENGELS

MANIFESTO OF THE COMMUNIST PARTY

(Extracts from Chapters II and III)

. . . The charges against communism made from a religious, a philosophical, and, generally, from an ideological standpoint, are not deserving of serious examination.

Does it require deep intuition to comprehend that man's ideas, views and conceptions, in one word, man's consciousness, changes with every change in the conditions of his material existence, in his social relations and in his social life?

What else does the history of ideas prove, than that intellectual production changes its character in proportion as material production is changed? The ruling ideas of each age have ever been the ideas of its ruling class.

When people speak of ideas that revolutionize society, they do but express the fact that within the old society the elements of a new one have been created, and that the dissolution of the old ideas keeps even pace with the dissolution of the old conditions of existence.

When the ancient world was in its last throes, the ancient religions were overcome by Christianity. When Christian ideas succumbed in the eighteenth century to rationalist ideas, feudal society fought its death battle with the then revolutionary bourgeoisie. The ideas of religious liberty and freedom of conscience merely gave expression to the sway of free competition within the domain of knowledge.

"Undoubtedly," it will be said, "religious, moral, philosophical and juridical ideas have been modified in the course of historical development. But religion, morality, philosophy, political science, and law, constantly survived this change."

"There are, besides, eternal truths, such as Freedom, Justice, etc., that are common to all states of society. But communism abolishes eternal truths, it abolishes all religion, and all morality, instead of constituting them on a new basis; it therefore acts in contradiction to all past historical experience."

What does this accusation reduce itself to? The history of all past society has consisted in the development of class antagonisms, antagonisms that assumed different forms at different epochs.

But whatever form they may have taken, one fact is common to all past ages, viz., the exploitation of one part of society by the other. No wonder, then, that the social consciousness of past ages, despite all the multiplicity and variety it displays, moves within certain common forms, or general ideas, which cannot completely vanish except with the total disappearance of class antagonisms.

The communist revolution is the most radical rupture with traditional property relations; no wonder that its development involves the most radical rupture with traditional ideas.

* * *

...As the parson has ever gone hand in hand with the landlord, so has Clerical Socialism with Feudal Socialism.

Nothing is easier than to give Christian asceticism a Socialist tinge. Has not Christianity declaimed against private property, against marriage, against the State? Has it not preached in the place of these, charity and poverty, celibacy and mortification of the flesh, monastic life and Mother Church? Christian Socialism is but the holy water with which the priest consecrates the heart-burnings of the aristocrat....

KARL MARX AND FREDERICK ENGELS

REVIEW OF G. FR. DAUMER'S *THE RELIGION OF THE NEW AGE*

An Attempt at a Combinative and Aphoristic Foundation, 2 Vols., Hamburg, 1850*

"An otherwise free-thinking man in *Nuremberg* who was not insensitive to the new had a monstrous hatred of democratic activities. He was a devotee of Ronge, whose portrait he had in his room. But when he heard that Ronge had sided with the democrats he removed the portrait to the lavatory. He once said: 'Oh, if only we lived under the Russian knout, how happy I would feel!' He died during disturbances and I presume that although he was already old, it was despondency and grief at the course of events that led him to the grave." (Vol. 2, pp. 321, 322.)

If, instead of dying, this pitiable Nuremberger had gleaned his scraps of thought from *Correspondent on and for Germany*, from Schiller and Goethe, from old school-books and modern lending-library books he would have spared himself the trouble of dying and Mr. Daumer his acidly elaborated two volumes of combinative and aphoristic foundation. We, of course, should not then have had the edifying opportunity to become acquainted with the religion of the new age and at the same time with its first martyr.

Mr. Daumer's work is divided into two parts, the "preliminary" and the "main" one. In the preliminary part

---

* G. Fr. Daumer. „Die Religion des neuen Weltalters. Versuch einer combinatorisch-aphoristischen Grundlegung". 2 Bände, Hamburg, 1850.—*Ed.*

the faithful Eckart of German philosophy expresses his profound concern that even thinking and educated Germans have let themselves be led astray for the past two years and have given up the inestimable achievements of thought for mere "external" revolutionary activity. He considers the present moment appropriate to appeal once more to the better feelings of the nation and points out what it means so light-mindedly to let all German culture, through which alone the German burgher was still anything at all, to depart. He resumes the whole content of German culture in the pithiest sayings that the casket of his erudition contains and thus discredits German culture no less than German philosophy. His anthology of the loftiest products of the German mind surpasses in platitude and triviality even the most ordinary reading book for young ladies in the educated walks of life. From Schiller's and Goethe's philistine sallies against the first French revolution, from the classic "Dangerous it is to rouse the lion"[30] down to the most modern literature, the high priest of the new religion zealously digs up every passage in which German pettifoggery stiffens with sleepy ill-humour against the historical movement it loathes. Authorities of the weight of a Friedrich Raumer, Berthold Auerbach, Lochner, Moritz Carrière, Alfred Meissner, Krug, Dingelstedt, Ronge, *Nürnberger Bote*, Max Waldau, Sternberg, Herman Mäurer, Louise Aston, Eckermann, Noack, *Blätter für literarische Unterhaltung*, A. Kunze, Ghillany, Th. Mundt, Saphir, Gutzkow, a certain "*née* Gatterer" and the like are the pillars on which the temple of the new religion rests. The revolutionary movement, which is here declared anathema in so many voices, is confined for Mr. Daumer on the one hand to the tritest prattle about politics as carried on in Nuremberg under the auspices of *Correspondent on and for Germany*, and on the other hand to ruffianism of which he has a most fantastic idea. The sources on which he draws are worthy of being placed on a par with those already mentioned: side by side with the oft-named *Nürnberger Korrespondent* figure *Bamberger Zeitung, Münchner Landbötin, Augsburger Allgemeine Zeitung* and others. The same petty-bourgeois vulgarity that sees nothing in the proletarian but a disgusting, corrupt ragamuffin and which rubs its hands with satisfaction at the Paris massacres in June 1848, when 3,000 of those "ragamuffins" are butchered—that very vulgarity is indignant at the raillery of which sentimental societies for the prevention of cruelty to animals are the object.

"The frightful tortures," Mr. Daumer exclaims on page 293 of Volume I, "that unfortunate beasts suffer at the tyrannous and cruel hand of man are for these barbarians 'rubbish' that nobody should bother about!"

The entire class struggle of our times seems to Mr. Daumer only a struggle of "coarseness" against "culture." Instead of explaining it by the historical conditions of these classes, he finds its origin in the seditious doings of a few malevolent individuals who incite the base appetites of the populace against the educated estates.

"This democratic reformism . . . excites the envy, the rage, the rapacity of the lower classes of society against the upper classes—a clean way of making man better and nobler and founding a higher degree of culture!" (Vol. I, p. 289.)

Mr. Daumer does not know what struggles "of the lower classes against the upper classes" it took to bring forth even a Nuremberg "degree of culture" and to make possible a Moloch-fighter à la Daumer.[31]

The second, "main," section contains the positive aspect of the new religion. It voices all the annoyance of the German philosopher over the oblivion into which his struggles against Christianity have fallen, over the people's indifference towards religion, the only object worthy to be considered by the philosopher. To restore credit to his trade, which has been ousted by competition, all our world-wise man can do is to invent a new religion after long barking against the old. But this new religion is confined, in accordance with the first section, to a continuation of the anthology of maxims, verses from genealogical registers and *versus memoriales* of German petty-bourgeois culture. The chapters of the new Koran[32] are nothing but a series of phrases morally palliating and poetically embellishing existing German conditions—phrases which, though divested of their immediately religious form, are still part and parcel of the old religion.

"Completely new world conditions and world relations can arise only through new religions. Examples and proofs of what religions are capable of are Christianity and Islam; a most vivid and sensible evidence of the powerlessness and futility of abstract, exclusive politics is provided by the movements started in the year 1848." (Vol. I, p. 313.)

This proposition so full of content immediately brings out the flatness and ignorance of the German "thinker" who takes the small German and specifically Bavarian "March achievements" for the European movement of 1848 and 1849 and who demands that the first, in themselves very superficial, eruptions of a gradually developing and concentrating major revolution should bring forth "completely new world conditions and world relations."

The world-wise Daumer reduces all the complicated social struggle the first skirmishes of which ranged from Paris to Debrecen and from Berlin to Palermo in the last two years to the fact that in January 1849 "the hopes of the Constitutional Societies of Erlangen were postponed indefinitely" (Vol. I, p. 312) and to fear of a new struggle that could once more be unpleasantly shocking for Mr. Daumer in his occupations with Hafis, Mohammed and Berthold Auerbach.

The same shameless superficiality allows Mr. Daumer to ignore completely that Christianity was preceded by the complete collapse of ancient "world conditions" of which Christianity was the mere expression; that "completely new world conditions" arose not internally through Christianity but only when the Huns and the Germans "fell externally on the corpse of the Roman Empire"; that after the Germanic invasion the "new world conditions" did not adapt themselves to Christianity but that Christianity itself likewise changed with every new phase of these world conditions. We should like Mr. Daumer to give us an example of the old world conditions changing with a new religion without the mightiest "external and abstract political" convulsions setting in at the same time.

It is clear that with every great historical upheaval of social conditions the outlooks and ideas of men, and consequently their religious ideas, are revolutionized. The difference between the present upheaval and all earlier ones lies in the very fact that man has found out the secret of this historical upheaval and hence, instead of once again exalting this practical, "external," process to the rapturous form of a new religion, divests himself of all religion.

After the gentle moral doctrines of the new world wisdom, which are even superior to Knigge[33] inasmuch as they contain all that is necessary not on intercourse with men only, but on intercourse with animals—after the Proverbs of Solomon comes the Song of the new Solomon.

"*Nature* and *woman* are the really divine, as opposed to the *human* and to *man*. . . . The sacrifice of the human to the natural, of the male to the female, is the genuine, the only true subjection and self-alienation, the highest, nay, the only virtue and piety." (Vol. II, p. 257.)

We see here that the superficiality and ignorance of the speculating founder of a religion is transformed into very pronounced cowardice. Mr. Daumer flees before the historic tragedy that is threatening him too closely to alleged nature, i.e., to mere rustic idyll, and preaches the cult of the female to cloak his own effeminate resignation.

Mr. Daumer's cult of nature, by the way, is a peculiar one. He has managed to be reactionary even in comparison with Christianity. He tries to establish the old pre-Christian natural religion in a modernized form. Thus he achieves nothing but Christian-Germanic-patriarchal drivel on nature expressed, for example, as follows:

Nature holy, Mother sweet,
In Thy footsteps place my feet.
My baby hand to Thy hand clings,
Hold me as in leading strings!

"Such things have gone out of fashion, but not to the benefit of culture, progress or human felicity." (Vol. II, p. 157.)

We see that this cult of nature is limited to the Sunday walks of an inhabitant of a small provincial town who childishly wonders at the cuckoo laying its eggs in another bird's nest (Vol. II, p. 40), at tears being designed to keep the surface of the eyes moist (Vol. II, p. 73), and so on, and finally trembles with reverence as he recites Klopstock's *Ode to Spring* to his children. (Vol. II, p. 23 et seqq.) There is no question, of course, of modern sciences, which, with modern industry, have revolutionized the whole of nature and put an end to man's childish attitude towards nature as well as to other forms of childishness. But instead we get mysterious hints and astonished philistine notions about Nostradamus's prophecies, second sight in Scotsmen and animal magnetism. For the rest, it would be desirable that Bavaria's sluggish peasant economy, the ground on which priests and Daumers likewise grow, should at last be ploughed up by modern cultivation and modern machines.

The position as regards the worship of the female is the same as with nature worship. Mr. Daumer naturally does not say a word about the present social situation of women; on the contrary it is a question only of the female as such. He tries to console women for their social distress by making them the object of a cult in words which is as empty as it would fain be mysterious. Thus he puts them at ease over the fact that marriage puts an end to their talents through their having to take care of the children (Vol. II, p. 237) by telling them that they can suckle babes until the age of sixty (Vol. II, p. 244), and so on. Mr. Daumer calls this the "sacrificing of the male to the female." In order to find the necessary ideal women characters for his sacrificing of the male in his native country, he is forced to resort to various aristocratic ladies of the last century. Thus his woman cult is reduced to the depressed attitude of a man of letters to respected patronesses. (See Wilhelm Meister.)[34]

The "culture" whose decay Mr. Daumer laments is that of the time in which Nuremberg flourished as a free *Reichsstadt*, in which Nuremberg industry—that cross between art and craftsmanship—played a role of importance, the German petty-bourgeois culture which is falling with that petty bourgeoisie. If the downfall of former classes such as the knighthood could offer subjects for magnificent tragic works of art, the philistine bourgeoisie can achieve nothing but powerless expressions of fanatic spite and a collection of Sancho Panza maxims and rules of wisdom. Mr. Daumer is the dry, absolutely humourless continuation of Hans Sachs. German philosophy, wringing its hands and lamenting at the deathbed of its foster father, German philistine bourgeoisie—such is the touching picture opened up to us by the religion of the new age.

FREDERICK ENGELS

THE PEASANT WAR IN GERMANY

(Chapter II)

The grouping of the then numerous and variegated Estates into bigger entities was made virtually impossible by decentralization, local and provincial independence, the industrial and commercial isolation of the provinces from each other, and poor communications. It developed only with the general spread of revolutionary, politico-religious ideas during the Reformation. The various Estates that either embraced or opposed those ideas, concentrated the nation, painfully and only approximately, into three large camps—the reactionary or Catholic camp, the Lutheran bourgeois reformist camp, and the revolutionary camp. And should we discover little logic in this great division of the nation and find partly the same elements in the first two camps, this is explained by the dissolution of most of the official Estates that came down from the Middle Ages, and by the decentralization, which, for the moment, gave these Estates in different localities opposing orientations. In recent years we have so often encountered similar facts in Germany that this apparent jumble of Estates and classes under the much more complicated conditions of the sixteenth century can scarcely surprise us.

In spite of the latest experiences, the German ideology still sees nothing except violent theological bickering in the struggles that ended the Middle Ages. If only the people of that time, say our home-bred historians and sages, had come to an understanding concerning heavenly things, there would have been no ground whatever to quarrel over earthly affairs. These ideologists are gullible enough to accept unquestioningly all the illusions that an epoch makes about itself or that ideologists of some epoch make about that epoch. People of the kind, see, for instance, in the Revolution of 1789 nothing but a somewhat heated debate on the advantages of a constitutional monarchy over absolutism, in the July Revolution a practical controversy on the untenability of right "by the grace of God," and in the February Revolution an attempt to answer the question: republic or monarchy?, etc. They have hardly any idea to this day of the *class struggles* which were fought out in these upheavals and of which the political slogan on the banner is every time a bare expression, although notice of them is audible enough not only from abroad, but also in the roar and rumble of many thousands of home proletarians.

Even the so-called religious wars of the sixteenth century involved primarily positive material class interests; those were class wars, too, just as the later internal collisions in England and France were. Although the class struggles of that day were carried on under religious shibboleths, and though the interests, requirements, and demands of the various classes were concealed behind a religious screen, this changed nothing in the matter and is easily explained by the conditions of the time.

The Middle Ages had developed altogether from the raw. They wiped the old civilization, the old philosophy, politics and jurisprudence off the slate, to begin anew in everything. The only thing they kept from the old shattered world was Christianity and a number of half-ruined towns divested of all their civilization. As a consequence, just as in every primitive stage of development, the clergy obtained a monopoly on intellectual education, and education itself became essentially theological. In the hands of the clergy politics and jurisprudence, much like all other sciences, remained mere branches of theology, and were treated according to the principles prevailing in the latter. Church dogmas were at the same time political axioms, and Bible quotations had the force of law in any court. Even as a special estate of jurists was taking shape, jurisprudence long remained under the tutelage of theology. And this supremacy of theology in the entire realm of intellectual activity was at the same time an inevitable consequence of the place held by the Church as the most general synthesis and sanction of the existing feudal domination.

It is clear that under the circumstances, all the generally voiced attacks against feudalism were above all attacks against the Church, and all social and political, revolutionary doctrines were necessarily at the same time and mainly theological heresies. The existing social conditions had to be stripped of their halo of sanctity before they could be attacked.

Revolutionary opposition to feudalism lasted throughout the Middle Ages. It took the shape of mysticism, open heresy, or armed insurrection, all depending on the conditions of the time. As for mysticism, it is well known how much sixteenth-century reformers depended on it. Münzer himself was largely indebted to it. The heresies gave expression partly to the reaction of the patriarchal Alpine shepherds against the feudalism advancing upon them (Waldenses[35]), partly to the opposition to feudalism of the towns that had outgrown it (the Albigenses,[36] Arnold of Brescia, etc.), and partly to direct peasant insurrections (John Ball, the Hungarian teacher[37] in Picardy, etc.). We can here leave aside the patriarchal heresy of the Waldenses, as well as the Swiss insurrection, for it was in form and content a reactionary, purely local attempt at stemming the tide of history. In the other two forms of mediaeval heresy we see, as early as the twelfth century, the precursors of the great antithesis between the burgher and peasant-plebeian oppositions, which caused the failure of the Peasant War. This antithesis is evident all through the later Middle Ages.

The town heresy—and that was the actual official heresy of the Middle Ages—was directed primarily against the clergy, whose wealth and political importance it attacked. Just as the present-day bourgeoisie demands a "*gouvernement à bon marché*" (cheap government), the mediaeval burghers chiefly demanded an "*église à bon marché*" (cheap church). Reactionary in form, like any heresy that sees only degeneration in the further development of church and dogma, the burgher heresy demanded the revival of the simple Early Christian Church constitution and abolition of exclusive priesthood. This cheap arrangement would have eliminated monks, prelates, and the Roman court, in short, everything in the Church that was expensive. The towns, republics themselves, albeit under the protection of monarchs, first enunciated in general terms through their attacks upon the Papacy that a republic was the normal form of bourgeois rule. Their hostility to a number of dogmas and church laws is explained partly by what has already been said and partly by the conditions in which they lived. Their bitter opposition to celibacy, for instance, has never been better explained than by Boccaccio. Arnold of Brescia in Italy and Germany, the Albigenses in Southern France, John Wycliffe in England, Huss and the Calixtines[38] in Bohemia, were the principal representatives of this trend. The towns were already a recognized Estate everywhere, and were sufficiently capable of fighting secular feudalism using their privileges, either by force of arms or in the Estate assemblies, and that explains quite simply why the opposition to feudalism appeared only as an opposition to *clerical* feudalism.

We also find, in Southern France as well as in England and Bohemia, that most of the lesser nobility joined the towns in their struggle against the clergy, and in their heresies—a phenomenon explained by the dependence of the lesser nobility upon the towns, and by their community of interests as opposed to the princes and prelates. We shall see the same thing in the Peasant War.

The heresy that directly expressed the peasant and plebeian demands, and almost invariably accompanied an insurrection, was of a totally different nature. Though it shared all the demands of burgher heresy with regard to the clergy, the Papacy, and revival of the early Christian Church constitution, it also went infinitely further. It demanded the restoration of early Christian equality among members of the community and the recognition of this equality as a prescript for the burgher world as well. From "equality of the children of God" it inferred civil equality, and partly even equality of property. Equality of nobleman and peasant, of patrician, privileged burgher and plebeian, abolition of the *corvée*, ground-rents, taxes, privileges, and at least the most crying differences in property—those were demands advanced with more or less determination as natural implications of the early Christian doctrine. At the time when feudalism was at its zenith there was little to choose between this peasant-plebeian heresy, among the Albigenses, for example, and the burgher opposition, but in the fourteenth and fifteenth centuries it developed into a clearly defined party opinion and usually took an independent stand alongside the heresy of the burghers. That was the case with John Ball, preacher of Wat Tyler's Rebellion in England, alongside the Wycliffe movement, and with the Taborites alongside the Calixtines in Bohemia. The Taborites even showed a republican trend under a theocratic cloak, a view further developed by representatives of the plebeians in Germany in the fifteenth and early sixteenth centuries.

The fanaticism of mystically-minded sects, of the Flagellants and Lollards,[39] etc., which continued the revolutionary tradition in times of suppression, rallied round this form of heresy.

At that time the plebeians were the only class that stood outside the existing official society. They stood outside both the feudal and the burgher associations. They had neither privileges nor property; they did not even have the kind of property the peasant or petty burgher had, weighed down as it was with burdensome taxes. They were unpropertied and rightless in every respect; their living conditions never even brought them into direct contact with the existing institutions, which ignored them completely. They were a living symptom of the decay of the feudal and guild-burgher society and at the same time the first precursors of the modern bourgeois society.

This explains why the plebeian opposition even then could not confine itself to fighting only feudalism and the privileged burghers; why, in fantasy at least, it reached beyond the then scarcely dawning modern bourgeois society; why, an absolutely propertyless group, it questioned the institutions, views and conceptions common to all societies based on class antagonisms. In this respect, the chiliastic dream-visions[40] of early Christianity offered a very convenient starting-point. On the other hand, this sally beyond both the present and even the future could be nothing but violent and fantastic, and of necessity fell back into the narrow limits set by the contemporary situation. The attack on private property, the demand for common ownership was bound to resolve into a primitive organization of charity; vague Christian equality could at best resolve into civic "equality before the law"; elimination of all authorities finally culminates in the establishment of republican governments elected by the people. The anticipation of communism by fantasy became in reality an anticipation of modern bourgeois conditions.

This violent anticipation of coming historical developments, easily explained by the living conditions of the plebeians, is first observed in *Germany*, in *Thomas Münzer* and his party. The Taborites had a kind of chiliastic common ownership, but that was a purely military measure. Only in the teachings of Münzer did these communist strains express the aspirations of a real fraction of society. He was the first to formulate them with a certain definiteness, and since him they have been observed in every great popular upheaval, until they gradually merged with the modern proletarian movement just as the struggles of free peasants in the Middle Ages against feudal domination which was ensnaring them more and more merged with the struggles of serfs and bondsmen for complete abolition of the feudal system.

While the first of the three large camps, the *conservative Catholic* camp, embraced all the elements interested in maintaining the existing conditions, i.e., the imperial authorities, the ecclesiastical and a section of the lay princes, the richer nobility, the prelates and the city patricians, the camp of *burgher-like moderate Lutheran* reforms, attracted all the propertied elements of the opposition, the bulk of the lesser nobility, the burghers, and even a portion of the lay princes who hoped to enrich themselves through confiscation of church estates and wanted to seize the opportunity of gaining greater independence from the Empire. As to the peasants and plebeians, they united in a *revolutionary* party whose demands and doctrines were most clearly expressed by Münzer.

Luther and Münzer each fully represented his party by his doctrine as well as by his character and actions.

From 1517 to 1525 *Luther* underwent quite the same changes as the present-day German constitutionalists did between 1846 and 1849, and which are undergone by every bourgeois party which, placed for a while at the head of the movement, is outflanked by the plebeian-proletarian party standing behind it.

When in 1517 Luther first opposed the dogmas and statutes of the Catholic Church, his opposition by no means possessed a definite character. While it did not overstep the demands of the earlier burgher heresy, it did not, and could not, rule out any trend which went further. At that early stage all the oppositional elements had to be united, the most aggressive revolutionary energy displayed, and the sum of the existing heresies against the Catholic orthodoxy had to find a protagonist. In much the same way our liberal bourgeoisie of 1847 was still revolutionary, called itself socialist and communist, and clamoured for the emancipation of the working class. Luther's sturdy peasant nature asserted itself in the stormiest fashion in that first period of his activities.

"If the raging madness" (of the Roman churchmen) "were to continue, it seems to me no better counsel and remedy could be found against it than that kings and princes apply force, arm themselves, attack those evil people who have poisoned the entire world, and put an end to this game once for all, *with arms, not with words*. Since we punish thieves with the halter, murderers with the sword, and heretics with fire, why do we not turn on all those evil teachers of perdition, those popes, cardinals and bishops, and the entire swarm of the Roman Sodom *with arms in hand, and wash our hands in their blood*?"

But this revolutionary ardour was short-lived. Luther's lightning struck home. The entire German people was set in motion. On the one hand, peasants and plebeians saw the signal to revolt in his appeals against the clergy and in his preaching of Christian freedom; and on the other, he was joined by the moderate burghers and a large section of the lesser nobility, and even princes were drawn into the current. The former believed the day had come to wreak vengeance upon all their oppressors, the latter only wished to break the power of the clergy, the dependence upon Rome and the Catholic hierarchy, and to enrich themselves on the confiscation of church property. The parties defined their positions, and each found its spokesmen. Luther had to choose between them. He, the protégé of the Elector of Saxony, the revered professor of Wittenberg who had become powerful and famous overnight, the great man with his coterie of servile creatures and flatterers, did not hesitate a single moment. He dropped the popular elements of the movement, and took the side of the burghers, the nobility, and the princes. His appeals for a war of extermination against Rome were heard no more. Luther now preached *peaceful progress* and *passive resistance* (cf., for example, *The Address to the German Nobility*, 1520, etc.). Invited by Hutten to visit him and Sickingen at Ebernburg, the seat of the nobility's conspiracy against clergy and princes, Luther replied:

"I do not wish the Gospel *defended by force and bloodshed.* The world was conquered by the Word, the Church is maintained by the Word, by the Word also the Church will be revived, and Antichrist, who gained his own without violence, will fall without violence."

From this turn, or, to be more exact, from this more exact definition of Luther's policy, sprang that bartering and haggling over institutions and dogmas to be retained or reformed, that disgusting diplomatizing, conciliating, intriguing and compromising, which resulted in the Augsburg Confession,[41] the finally negotiated articles of a reformed burgher church. It was quite the same kind of petty bargaining that was recently repeated in political form *ad nauseam* at the German national assemblies, conciliatory gatherings, chambers of revision, and Erfurt parliaments.[42] The philistine nature of the official Reformation was most markedly evident at these negotiations.

There were good reasons for Luther, henceforth the recognized representative of the burgher reform, to preach progress within the pale of the law. The bulk of towns espoused the cause of moderate reform, the petty nobility became more and more devoted to it, and a section of the princes struck in, while another vacillated. Success was as good as won, at least in a large part of Germany. The remaining regions could not in the long run withstand the pressure of moderate opposition in the event of continued peaceful development. Any violent upheaval, meanwhile, was bound to bring the moderate party into conflict with the extremist plebeian and peasant party, to alienate the princes, the nobility, and certain towns from the movement, leaving the alternative of either the burgher party being outflanked by the peasants and plebeians, or the entire movement being crushed by a Catholic restoration. And there have been examples enough lately of how bourgeois parties seek to steer their way by means of progress within the pale of the law between the Scylla of revolution and the Charybdis of restoration, as soon as they have gained the slightest victory.

Under the general social and political conditions prevailing in that day the results of every change were necessarily advantageous to the princes, and inevitably increased their power. Thus the more sharply the burgher reform broke away from the plebeian and peasant elements the more completely it was bound to fall under the control of the reformed princes. Luther himself became more and more their vassal, and the people well knew what they were doing when they accused him of having become, like the others, a flunkey of the princes, and when they stoned him at Orlamünde.

When the Peasant War broke out Luther strove to adopt a mediatory attitude in regions where the nobility and the princes were mostly Catholic. He resolutely attacked the governments. He said they were to blame for the rebellion because of their oppression; it was not the peasants, but God himself, who rose against them. Yet, on the other hand, he said, the revolt was ungodly, and contrary to the Gospel. In conclusion he called upon both parties to yield and reach a friendly settlement.

But in spite of these well-meaning mediatory offers, the revolt spread swiftly and even involved Protestant regions dominated by Lutheran princes, lords and towns, rapidly outgrowing the "circumspect" burgher reform. The most determined group of the insurgents under Münzer made its headquarters in Luther's immediate proximity in Thuringia. A few more successes, and the whole of Germany would be in flames, Luther surrounded and perhaps piked as a traitor, and the burgher reform swept away by the tide of a peasant-plebeian revolution. There was no more time for circumspection. All the old animosities were forgotten in the face of the revolution. Compared with the hordes of peasants, the servants of the Roman Sodom were innocent lambs, sweet-tempered children of God. Burgher and prince, noble and clergyman, Luther and the Pope, all joined hands "against the murderous and plundering peasant hordes."[43]

"They must be knocked to pieces, strangled and stabbed, covertly and overtly, by everyone who can, just as one must kill a *mad dog*!" Luther cried. "Therefore, dear sirs, help here, save there, stab, knock, strangle them everyone who can, and should you lose your life, bless you, no better death can you ever attain."

Only there should be no false mercy for the peasant. Whoever hath pity on those whom God pities not, whom He wishes punished and destroyed, belongs among the rebels himself. Later the peasants would themselves learn to thank God when they had to give up one cow in order to enjoy the other in peace, and the princes would learn through the revolution the spirit of the mob that must be ruled by force only. "The wise man says: *cibum, onus et virgam asino.** The peasants must have nothing but chaff. They do not hearken to the Word, and are foolish, so they must hearken to the rod and the gun, and that serves them right. We must pray for them that they obey. Where they do not there should not be much mercy. *Let the guns roar among them*, or else they will make things a thousand times worse."

That was exactly what our late socialist and philanthropic bourgeoisie said when the proletariat claimed its share in the fruits of victory after the March events.

Luther had put a powerful weapon into the hands of the plebeian movement by translating the Bible. Through the Bible he contrasted the feudalized Christianity of his day with the unassuming Christianity of the first century, and the decaying feudal society with a picture of a society that knew nothing of the complex and artificial feudal hierarchy. The peasants had made extensive use of this instrument against the princes, the nobility, and the clergy. Now Luther turned it against them, extracting from the Bible a real hymn to the God-ordained authorities such as no bootlicker of absolute monarchy had ever been able to achieve. Princedom by the grace of God, resigned obedience, even serfdom, were sanctioned with the aid of the Bible. Not the peasant revolt alone, but Luther's own mutiny against ecclesiastical and secular authority was

* Latin for "food, pack, and lash for the ass."—*Ed.*

thereby disavowed; and not only the popular movement, but the burgher movement as well, were betrayed to the princes.

Need we name the bourgeois who recently also gave us examples of such a disavowal of their own past?

Let us now compare the plebeian revolutionary *Münzer*, with Luther, the burgher reformist.

Thomas Münzer was born at *Stolberg*, in the Harz, in 1498. His father is said to have died on the scaffold, a victim of the tyranny of the Count of Stolberg. At the age of fifteen Münzer organized a secret union at a Halle school against the Archbishop of Magdeburg and the Roman Church in general. His learning in the theology of his time brought him an early doctor's degree and the position of chaplain in a Halle nunnery. Here he treated the church dogmas and rites with the greatest contempt. At mass he omitted the words of the transubstantiation, and ate, as Luther said, the almighty gods unconsecrated. Mediaeval mystics, and particularly the chiliastic works of Joachim the Calabrese, were the main subject of his studies. What with the Reformation and the general unrest of his time, the millennium and the day of judgment over the degenerated church and corrupted world propounded and described by that mystic, seemed to Münzer imminently close. He preached in the neighbourhood with great success. In 1520 he went to Zwickau as the first evangelical preacher. There he found one of those fanatical chiliastic sects that continued their existence on the quiet in many localities, and whose momentary dejection and retirement concealed the incessantly growing opposition of the lowest strata of society to the prevailing conditions, and who, with the growing unrest, now came into the open ever more boldly and persistently. It was the sect of the Anabaptists headed by Niklas *Storch*. They preached the approach of the day of judgment and of the millennium; they had "visions, transports, and the spirit of prophecy." They soon came into conflict with the Council of Zwickau. Münzer defended them, though he never joined them unconditionally and would have rather brought them under his own influence. The Council took drastic measures against them; they had to leave the town, and Münzer with them. This was at the close of 1521.

He went to Prague and sought to gain a foothold by joining the remnants of the Hussite movement. But his proclamation only had the effect of compelling him to flee from Bohemia as well. In 1522 he became preacher at Allstedt in Thuringia. Here he started with reforming the cult. Even before Luther dared to go so far, he entirely discarded the Latin language and ordered the entire Bible, and not only the prescribed Sunday Gospels and epistles, to be read to the people. At the same time, he organized propaganda in his locality. People flocked to him from all directions, and Allstedt soon became the centre of the popular anti-priest movement for the whole of Thuringia.

Münzer was as yet a theologian before everything else. He still directed his attacks almost exclusively against the priests. He did not, however, preach quiet debate and peaceful progress, as Luther was already then doing, but continued Luther's earlier violent sermons, calling upon the princes of Saxony and the people to rise in arms against the Roman priests.

"Does not Christ say, 'I came not to bring peace, but the sword'? What must you (the princes of Saxony) do with that sword? Only one thing if you wish to be the servants of God, and that is to drive out and destroy the evil ones who stand in the way of the Gospel. Christ ordered very earnestly (Luke, 19, 27): 'Bring hither mine enemies and slay them before me.' Do not give us any empty phrases that the power of God will do without the aid of your sword, since then it would rust in its sheath. . . . Those who stand in the way of God's revelation must be destroyed mercilessly, as Hezekiah, Cyrus, Josiah, Daniel and Elias destroyed the priests of Baal, else the Christian Church will never come back to its source. We must uproot the weeds in God's vineyard at harvest time. . . . God said in the Fifth Book of Moses, 7: 'Ye shall not show mercy unto the idolators, but ye shall destroy their altars, and break down their images and burn them with fire that I shall not be wroth at you.'"

But these appeals to the princes were of no avail, whereas revolutionary sentiments among the people grew day by day. Münzer, whose ideas became ever more sharply defined and bolder, now broke resolutely away from the burgher Reformation, and henceforth became an outright political agitator.

His philosophico-theological doctrine attacked all the main points not only of Catholicism, but of Christianity generally. Under the cloak of Christian forms he preached a kind of pantheism, which curiously resembles modern speculative contemplation[44] and at times even approaches atheism. He repudiated the Bible both as the only and the infallible revelation. The real and living revelation, he said, was reason, a revelation which has always existed among all peoples at all times. To hold up the Bible against reason, he maintained, was to kill the spirit by the letter, for the Holy Spirit of which the Bible speaks is not something that exists outside; the Holy Spirit is our reason. Faith is nothing else but reason come to life in man, and pagans could therefore also have faith. Through this faith, through reason come to life, man became goldlike and blessed. Heaven is, therefore, not a thing of another world, and is to be sought in this life and it is the task of believers to establish this Heaven, the kingdom of God, here on earth. Just as there is no Heaven in the beyond, there is also no Hell and no damnation. Similarly, there is no devil but man's evil lusts and greed. Christ was a man as we are, a prophet and a teacher, and his Eucharist is a mere commemoration meal wherein bread and wine are consumed without any mystic garnishing.

Münzer preached these doctrines mostly cloaked in the same Christian phraseology under which the new philosophy had to hide for some time. But the arch heretical fundamental idea is easily discerned in all his writings, and he obviously took the biblical cloak much less in earnest than many a disciple of Hegel in modern times. And yet three hundred years separate Münzer from modern philosophy.

Münzer's political doctrine followed his revolutionary religious conceptions very closely, and just as his theology overstepped the current conceptions of his time, so his political doctrine went beyond the directly prevailing social and political conditions. Just as Münzer's religious philosophy approached atheism, so his political programme approached communism, and even on the eve of the February Revolution, there was more than one modern communist sect that had not such a well-stocked theoretical arsenal as was "Münzer's" in the sixteenth century. This programme, less a compilation of the demands of the plebeians of that day than a visionary anticipation of the conditions for the emancipation of the proletarian element that had scarcely begun to develop among the plebeians—this programme demanded the immediate establishment of the kingdom of God, of the prophesied millennium, by restoring the Church to its original condition and abolishing all the institutions that conflicted with this allegedly early-Christian, but, in fact, very novel church. By the kingdom of God Münzer understood a society in which there would be no class differences or private property and no state authority independent of or foreign to the members of society. All the existing authorities, insofar as they refused to submit and join the revolution, were to be overthrown, all work and all property shared in common, and complete equality introduced. A union was to be established to implement all this, not only throughout Germany, but throughout Christendom. Princes and lords were to be invited to join, and should they refuse, the union was to take up arms and overthrow or kill them at the first opportunity.

Münzer set to work at once to organize the union. His sermons became still more militant and revolutionary. He thundered forth against the princes, the nobility and the patricians with a passion that equalled the fervour of his attacks upon the clergy. He depicted the prevailing oppression in fiery colours, and countered it with his dream-vision of the millennium of social republican equality. He published one revolutionary pamphlet after another and sent emissaries in all directions, while personally organizing the union in Allstedt and its vicinity.

The first fruit of this propaganda was the destruction of the Marienkapelle at Mellerbach near Allstedt, according to the command of the Bible (Deut. 7, 6): "Ye shall destroy their altars, and break down their images and burn their graven images with fire." The princes of Saxony came in person to Allstedt to quell the unrest, and summoned Münzer to the castle. There he delivered a sermon the like of which they had not heard from Luther, "that easy-living flesh of Wittenberg," as Münzer called him. Münzer maintained that ungodly rulers, especially priests and monks, who treated the Gospel as heresy, should be killed, and referred to the New Testament for confirmation. The ungodly had no right to live save by the mercy of God's elect. If the princes would not exterminate the ungodly, God would take their sword from them, *because the entire community had the power of the sword.* The princes and lords are the prime movers of usury, thieving and robbery;

they take all creatures into their private possession—the fish in the water, the birds in the air, and the plants in the soil—and still preach to the poor the commandment, "Thou shalt not steal," while they themselves take everything they find, rob and oppress the peasant and the artisan; but when one of the latter commits the slightest transgression, he has to hang, and Dr. Lügner says to all this: Amen.

"The masters themselves are to blame that the poor man becomes their enemy. If they do not remove the causes of the upheaval, how can things go well in the long run? Oh, dear sirs, how the Lord will smite these old pots with an iron rod! If I say so, I shall stir up the people. So be it!" (Cf. Zimmermann's *Bauernkrieg*, II, p. 75.[45])

Münzer had the sermon printed. His Allstedt printer was punished by Duke Johann of Saxony with banishment, while Münzer's writings were to be henceforth censored by the ducal government in Weimar. But he paid no heed to this order. He lost no time in publishing a highly seditious paper[46] in the imperial city of Mühlhausen, in which he called on the people "to widen the hole so that all the world may see and understand who our great personages are that have blasphemously turned our Lord into a painted manikin," and which ended with the following words:

"All the world must suffer a big jolt. There will be such a game that the ungodly will be thrown off their seats, and the downtrodden will rise."

Thomas Münzer, "the man with the hammer," wrote the following motto on the title page:

"Behold, I have put my words in thy mouth. I have this day set thee over the nations and over the kingdoms to root out, and to pull down, and to destroy, and to throw down, to build, and to plant. A wall of iron against the kings, princes, priests, and against the people of the land hath been erected. Let them fight, for victory will wondrously lead to the perdition of the strong and godless tyrants."*

Münzer's breach with Luther and his party had long been an accomplished fact. Luther had to accept some of the church reforms introduced by Münzer without consulting him. He watched Münzer's activities with a moderate reformer's nettled mistrust of a more energetic farther-aiming party. As early as the spring of 1524, in a letter to Melanchthon, that model of a hectic stay-at-home philistine, Münzer wrote that he and Luther did not understand the movement at all. He said they sought to choke it by the letter of the Bible, and that their doctrine was worm-eaten.

"Dear brethren," he wrote, "cease your procrastinations and vacillations. It is time, summer is knocking at the door. Do not keep friendship with the ungodly who hinder the Word from working its full force. Do not flatter your princes, or you may perish with them. Ye tender bookish scholars, be not wroth, for I cannot do otherwise."

Luther challenged Münzer more than once to an open debate. The latter, however, always ready to take up the battle before the people, had not the least desire to let himself in for a theological squabble before the partial public of Wittenberg University. He did not wish "to bring the testimony of the Spirit exclusively before the high school of learning." If Luther were sincere he should use his influence to stop the chicaneries against his, Münzer's printer, and lift the censorship so that their controversy might be freely fought out in the press.

But now, when Münzer's above-mentioned revolutionary brochure appeared, Luther openly denounced him. In his *Letter to the Princes of Saxony against the Rebellious*

* In the epigraph to his essay Münzer paraphrases a passage from the book of the Prophet Jeremiah, infusing it with a revolutionary meaning.—*Ed.*

Spirit, he declared Münzer to be an instrument of Satan, and demanded of the princes to intervene and drive the instigators of the upheaval out of the country, since they did not confine themselves to preaching their evil doctrine, but incited to insurrection, to violent action against the authorities.

On August 1, Münzer was compelled to appear before the princes in the castle of Weimar on the charge of incitement to mutiny. Highly compromising facts were brought against him; they were on the scent of his secret union; his hand was detected in the societies of the miners and the peasants. He was threatened with banishment. No sooner had he returned to Allstedt than he learned that Duke Georg of Saxony demanded his extradition. Union letters in his handwriting had been intercepted, in which he called Georg's subjects to armed resistance against the enemies of the Gospel. The Council would have extradited him had he not left the town.

In the meantime, the growing unrest among the peasants and plebeians had made Münzer's propaganda work incomparably easier. In the Anabaptists he found invaluable agents for that purpose. This sect, which had no definite dogmas, held together only by its common opposition to all ruling classes and by the common symbol of the second baptism, ascetic in their mode of living, untiring, fanatical and intrepid in carrying on propaganda, had grouped itself more and more closely around Münzer. Made homeless by persecutions, its members wandered all over Germany and carried everywhere word of the new teaching, in which Münzer had made their own demands and wishes clear to them. Countless Anabaptists were put on the rack, burned or otherwise executed, but the courage and endurance of these emissaries were unshakeable, and the success of their activities amidst the rapidly growing unrest of the people was enormous. Thus, on his flight from Thuringia, Münzer found the ground prepared wherever he turned.

Near Nuremberg, where Münzer first went,[47] a peasant revolt had been nipped in the bud a month before. Münzer conducted his propaganda clandestinely; people soon appeared who defended his most audacious theological propositions on the non-obligatory nature of the Bible and the meaninglessness of the sacraments, who declared Christ a mere man, and the power of the secular authorities ungodly. "There is Satan stalking, the Spirit of Allstedt!" Luther exclaimed. In Nuremberg Münzer printed his reply to Luther.[48] He accused him of flattering the princes and supporting the reactionary party through his insipid moderation. But the people would free themselves nonetheless, he wrote, and it would go with Dr. Luther as with a captive fox. The Council ordered the confiscation of the paper, and Münzer had to leave Nuremberg.

Now he went via Swabia to Alsace, then to Switzerland, and then back to the Upper Black Forest, where an insurrection had broken out several months before, largely precipitated by his Anabaptist emissaries. This propaganda tour of Münzer's unquestionably and substantially contributed to the establishment of the people's party, to a clear formulation of its demands and to the final general outbreak of the insurrection in April 1525. This trip particularly brought out the dual effect of Münzer's activities—on the one hand, on the people, whom he addressed in the only language they could then understand, that of religious prophecy; and, on the other hand, on the initiated, to whom he could disclose his ultimate aims. Even before his journey he had assembled in Thuringia a group of resolute men from among the people and the lower clergy, whom he had put at the head of his secret society. Now he became the soul of the entire revolutionary movement in South-Western Germany, organized ties between Saxony and Thuringia through Franconia and Swabia as far as Alsace and the Swiss border, and counted among his disciples and the heads of the union South-German agitators such as Hubmaier of Waldshut, Conrad Grebel of Zürich, Franz Rabmann of Griessen, Schappeler of Memmingen, Jakob Wehe of Leipheim, and Dr. Mantel in Stuttgart, who were mostly revolutionary priests. He himself stayed mostly in Griessen on the Schaffhausen border, journeying from there through Hegau, Klettgau, etc. The bloody persecutions undertaken everywhere by the alarmed princes and lords against this new plebeian heresy, contributed not a little to fan the spirit of rebellion and consolidate the ranks of the society. In this way Münzer conducted his agitation for about five months in Upper Germany, and returned to Thuringia when the outbreak of the conspiracy was near at hand, because he wished to lead the movement personally. There we shall find him later.

We shall see how truly the character and behaviour of the two party leaders reflected the attitude of their respective parties, how Luther's indecision and fear of the movement, which was assuming serious proportions, and his cowardly servility to the princes, fully corresponded to the hesitant and ambiguous policy of the burghers, and how Münzer's revolutionary energy and resolution was reproduced among the most advanced section of the plebeians and peasants. The only difference was that while Luther confined himself to expressing the conceptions and wishes of the majority of his class and thereby won an extremely cheap popularity among it, Münzer, on the contrary, went far beyond the immediate ideas and demands of the plebeians and peasants, and first organized a party of the élite of the then existing revolutionary elements, which, inasmuch as it shared his ideas and energy, was never more than a small minority of the insurgent masses.

ENGELS TO MARX

[Manchester, approx. May 24, 1853]

... Yesterday I read the book about the Arabian inscriptions of which I told you. The thing is not devoid of interest although priest and bible apologist are written disgustingly all over it. Its greatest triumph consists in being able to prove that *Gibbon* committed some blunders in ancient geography, from which it may be deduced that Gibbon's theology is also unsound. The thing is called *The Historical Geography of Arabia* by the Reverend Charles Forster. The best one can get out of it is the following:

1. The genealogy given in Genesis, purporting to be that of Noah, Abraham, etc., is a fairly exact enumeration of the Bedouin tribes of that time, according to their major or minor dialectal kinship, etc. As we know, the Bedouin tribes have to the present day always called themselves Beni Saled, Beni Jussuff, and so on, i.e., the sons of so and so. This appellation, which springs from the ancient patriarchal mode of existence, leads in the end to this kind of genealogy. The enumeration in Genesis is corroborated more or less by the ancient geographers, and the more recent travellers prove that the old names, with dialectal changes, still exist in their majority. However, it follows from this that the Jews themselves were nothing more than a small Bedouin tribe, just like the rest, which local conditions, agriculture, and so forth placed in opposition to the other Bedouins.

2. With regard to the great Arabian invasion of which we spoke previously: the Bedouins made periodic invasions, just like the Mongols, the Assyrian Empire as

well as the Babylonian was founded by Bedouin tribes, on the same spot where later the caliphate of Baghdad arose. The founders of the Babylonian Empire, the Chaldeans, still exist under the same name, Beni Chaled, in the same locality. The rapid rise of big cities like Niniveh and Babylon occurred in exactly the same way as only three hundred years ago similar giant cities, such as Agra, Delhi, Lahore and Muttan, in East India, were created by an Afghan or Tatar invasion. Thus the Mohammedan invasion loses much of its distinctive character.

3. It seems that the Arabians, where they had settled down in the South-West, were just as civilized a people as the Egyptians, Assyrians, etc., as is proved by the buildings they erected. This too explains much in the Mohammedan invasion. As far as that fake, religion, is concerned, it seems to follow from the ancient inscriptions in the South, in which the old national-Arabian tradition of monotheism still predominates (as it does among the American Indians) and of which tradition the Hebrew constitutes only a *small part*, that Mohammed's religious revolution, like *every* religious movement, was *formally a reaction*, an alleged return to the old, the simple.

That Jewish so-called Holy Scripture is nothing more than a record of the old-Arabian religious and tribal tradition, modified by the early separation of the Jews from their consanguineous but nomadic neighbours—that is now perfectly clear to me. The circumstance that Palestine is surrounded on the Arabian side by nothing but deserts, Bedouin land, explains the separate exposition. But the old-Arabian inscriptions, traditions, and the Koran, and the ease with which all genealogies, etc., can now be unravelled testify that the main content was Arabic or rather Semitic in general, like our Edda and German heroic saga.

Yours,

F. E.

MARX TO ENGELS

London, June 2, 1853

. . . With regard to the Hebrews and Arabians your letter interested me very much. By the way: 1) a *general* relationship can be proved, since history began, among all Oriental tribes, between the settlement of one part of the tribes and the continued nomadic life of the others. 2) In Mohammed's time the trade route from Europe to Asia had been considerably modified and the cities of Arabia, which had taken a great part in the trade with India, etc., were in a state of commercial decay; this in any case also lent impetus. 3) As to religion, the question resolves itself into the general and therefore easily answered one: Why does the history of the East *appear* as a history of religions?

On the formation of Oriental cities one can read nothing more brilliant, graphic and striking than old François Bernier (nine years physician to Aurang-zeb): *Travels Containing a Description of the Dominions of the Great Mogul, etc.* He also describes the military system, the way these great armies were fed, etc., very well. On these two points he remarks, among other things:

"The cavalry forms the principal section, the infantry is not so big as is generally rumoured, unless all the servants and people from the bazaars or markets who follow the army are thrown in with the real fighting force; for in that case I could well believe that they would be right in putting the number of men in the army alone accompanying the king at 200,000 or 300,000 and sometimes even more, when for example it is certain that he will be absent from the capital for a long time. And this will not appear so very astonishing to one who knows the strange encumbrance of tents, kitchens, clothes, furniture and quite frequently even of women, and consequently also the elephants, camels, oxen, horses, porters, foragers, provisioners, merchants of all kinds and servitors whom these armies carry in their wake; or to one who understands the particular condition and government of the country, namely that the *king is the one and only proprietor of all the land* in the kingdom, from which it follows as a necessary consequence that a whole *capital city* like Delhi or Agra lives almost entirely on the army and is therefore obliged to follow the king if he takes the field for any length of time. For these towns neither are nor can be anything like Paris, *being virtually nothing but military camps*, only a little better and more conveniently situated than in the open country."

On the occasion of the march of the Great Mogul into Kashmir with an army of 400,000 men, etc., he says:

"The difficulty is to know whence and how such a great army, such a great number of men and animals, can subsist in the field. For this it is only necessary to suppose, what is perfectly true, that the Indians are very sober and very simple in their food, and that of all that great number of horsemen not the tenth nor even the twentieth part eats meat during the march. So long as they have their *kicheri*, or mixture of rice and other vegetables, over which when it is cooked they pour melted butter, they are satisfied. Further it is necessary to know that camels are possessed of extreme endurance at work, and can long resist hunger and thirst, live on little and eat anything, and that as soon as the army has arrived the camel drivers lead them to graze in the open country where they eat whatever they can find. Moreover, the same merchants who keep the bazaars in Delhi are forced to maintain them during campaigns too, and so are the small merchants, etc.... And finally with regard to forage, all these poor folks go roaming all over the countryside to buy it and thus earn something. Their great and usual resort is to rasp whole fields with a sort of small trowel, thrash or cleanse the small herb rasped, and bring it along to sell to the army...."

Bernier rightly considered the basis of all phenomena in the East—he refers to Turkey, Persia, Hindustan—to be the *absence of private property in land.* This is the real key, even to the Oriental heaven....

ENGELS TO MARX

Manchester, June 6, 1853

...The absence of property in land is indeed the key to the whole of the East. Herein lies its political and religious history. But how does it come about that the Orientals did not arrive at landed property, even in its feudal form? I think it is mainly due to the climate, taken in connection with the nature of the soil, especially with the great stretches of desert which extend from the Sahara straight across Arabia, Persia, India and Tatary up to the highest Asiatic plateau. Artificial irrigation is here the first prerequisite for agriculture and this is a matter either for the communes, the provinces or the central government. An Oriental government never had more than three departments: finance (plunder at home), war (plunder at home and abroad), and public works (provision for reproduction). The British Government in India has administered Nos. 1 and 2 in a rather narrow-minded spirit and dropped No. 3 entirely, so that Indian agriculture is being ruined. Free competition discredits itself there completely. This artificial fertilization of the land which immediately ceased when the irrigation system fell into decay, explains the otherwise curious fact that whole stretches which were once brilliantly cultivated are now waste and bare (Palmyra, Petra, the ruins in the Yemen, districts in Egypt, Persia and Hindustan); it explains the fact that one single devastating war could depopulate a country for centuries and strip it of its whole civilization. Here too, I think, comes in the destruction of the South-Arabian trade before Mohammed, which you very rightly regard as one of the chief factors in the Mohammedan revolution. I do not know the commercial history of the first six centuries after Christ thoroughly enough to be able to judge how far general material world conditions caused the trade route through Persia to the Black Sea and through the Persian Gulf to Syria and Asia Minor to be preferred to the route over the Red Sea. But in any case the relative security of the caravans in the orderly Persian Empire of the Sassanids was not without considerable effect, while between the years 200 and 600 the Yemen was almost continuously subjugated, invaded and plundered by the Abyssinians. The cities of Southern Arabia, which were still flourishing in the time of the Romans, were sheer wastes and ruins in the seventh century; within five hundred years the neighbouring Bedouins had adopted purely mythical, fabulous traditions of their origin (see the Koran and the Arabian historian Novaïri), and the alphabet in which the inscriptions in those parts are written was almost totally unknown, *although there was no other*, so that even *writing* had actually fallen into oblivion. Things of this sort imply, besides a "superseding" caused by general trade conditions, some absolutely direct and violent destruction which can only be explained by the Abyssinian invasion. The expulsion of the Abyssinians took place about forty years before Mohammed and was obviously the first act of the awakening Arabian national consciousness, which was also spurred by Persian invasions from the North, pushing forward almost to Mecca. I shall take up the history of Mohammed himself in the next few days; so far, however, it seems to me to bear the character of a Bedouin reaction against the settled but degenerating fellaheen of the towns, who at that time had also become very decadent in their religion, mingling a corrupt nature-cult with corrupt Judaism and Christianity.

Old Bernier's things are really very fine. It is a real delight once more to read something by a sober, clear-headed old Frenchman who keeps hitting the nail on the head without appearing to notice it. . . .

KARL MARX

ANTI-CHURCH MOVEMENT—DEMONSTRATION IN HYDE PARK

London, June 25, 1855

It is an old and historically established maxim that obsolete social forces, nominally still in possession of all the attributes of power and continuing to vegetate long after the basis of their existence has rotted away, inasmuch as the heirs are quarrelling among themselves over the inheritance even before the obituary notice has been printed and the testament read—that these forces once more summon all their strength before their agony of death, pass from the defensive to the offensive, challenge instead of giving way, and seek to draw the most extreme conclusions from premises which have not only been put in question but already condemned. Such is today the English oligarchy. Such is the *Church*, its twin sister. Countless attempts at reorganization have been made within the Established Church, both the High and the Low, attempts to come to an understanding with the Dissenters and thus to set up a compact force to oppose the profane mass of the nation. There has been a rapid succession of measures of religious coercion. The pious Earl of Shaftesbury, formerly known as Lord Ashley, bewailed the fact in the House of Lords that in England alone five millions had become wholly alienated not only from the Church but from Christianity altogether. "*Compelle intrare*," replies the Established Church. It leaves it to Lord Ashley and similar dissenting, sectarian and hysterical pietists to pull the chestnuts out of the fire for it.

The first measure of religious coercion was the Beer Bill, which shut down all places of public entertainment on Sundays, except between 6 and 10 p. m. This bill was smuggled through the House at the end of a sparsely attended sitting, after the pietists had bought the support of the big public-house owners of London by guaranteeing them that the license system would continue, that is, that big capital would retain its monopoly. Then came the Sunday Trading Bill, which has now passed its third reading in the Commons and separate clauses of which have just been discussed by commissions in both Houses. This new coercive measure too was ensured the vote of big capital, because only small shopkeepers keep open on Sunday and the proprietors of the big shops are quite willing to do away with the Sunday competition of the small fry by parliamentary means. In both cases there is a conspiracy of the Church with monopoly capital, but in both cases there are religious penal laws against the lower classes to set the consciences of the privileged classes at rest. The *Beer Bill* was as far from hitting the aristocratic clubs as the *Sunday Trading Bill* is from hitting the Sunday occupations of genteel society. The workers get their wages late on Saturday; they are the only ones for whom shops open on Sundays. They are the only ones compelled to make their purchases, small as they are, on Sundays. The new bill is therefore directed against them alone. In the eighteenth century the French aristocracy said: For us, Voltaire; for the people, the mass and the tithes. In the nineteenth century the English aristocracy says: For us, pious phrases; for the people, Christian practice. The classical saint of Christianity mortified *his* body for the salvation of the souls of the masses; the modern, educated saint mortifies *the bodies of the masses* for the salvation of his own soul.

This alliance of a dissipated, degenerating and pleasure-seeking aristocracy with a church propped up by the filthy profits calculated upon by the big brewers and monopolizing wholesalers was the occasion yesterday of a *mass demonstration* in Hyde Park, the like of which London has not seen since the death of George IV, "the first gentleman of Europe." We were spectators from beginning to end and do not think we are exaggerating in saying that *the English Revolution began yesterday in Hyde Park.* The latest news from the Crimea acted as an effective ferment upon this "*unparliamentary*," "*extra-parliamentary*" and "*anti-parliamentary*" demonstration.

Lord *Robert Grosvenor*, who fathered the Sunday Trading Bill, when reproached on the score of this measure being directed solely against the poor and not against the rich classes, retorted that "the aristocracy was largely refraining from employing its servants and horses on Sundays." The last few days of the past week the following poster, put out *by the Chartists* and affixed to all the walls of London, announced in huge letters:

"*New Sunday Bill* prohibiting newspapers, shaving, smoking, eating and drinking and all kinds of recreation and nourishment, both corporal and spiritual, which the *poor people* still enjoy at the present time. *An open-air meeting* of artisans, workers and '*the lower orders*' generally of the capital will take place in Hyde Park on Sunday afternoon to see how religiously the aristocracy is observing the Sabbath and how anxious it is not to employ its servants and horses on that day, as Lord Robert Grosvenor said in his speech. The meeting is called for three o'clock on the right bank of the Serpentine" (a small river in Hyde Park), "on the side towards Kensington Gardens. Come and bring your wives and children in order that they may profit by the example their '*betters*' set them!"

It should be borne in mind, of course, that what *Longchamps** means to the Parisians, the road along the Serpentine in Hyde Park means to English high society—the place where of an afternoon, particularly on Sunday, they parade their magnificent horses and carriages with all their trappings, followed by swarms of lackeys. It will be realized from the above placard that the struggle against clericalism assumes the same character in England as every other serious struggle there—the character of a *class struggle* waged by the poor against the rich, the people against the aristocracy, the "lower orders" against their "betters."

At three o'clock approximately 50,000 people had gathered at the spot announced on the right bank of the Serpentine in Hyde Park's immense meadows. Gradually the assembled multitude swelled to a total of at least 200,000 due to additions from the other bank. Milling groups of people could be seen shoved about from place to place. The police, who were present in force, were obviously endeavouring to deprive the organizers of the meeting of what Archimedes had asked for to move the earth, namely, a place to stand upon. Finally a rather large crowd made a firm stand and *Bligh* the Chartist constituted himself chairman on a small eminence in the midst of the throng. No sooner had he begun his harangue than Police Inspector Banks at the head of 40 truncheon-swinging constables explained to him that the Park was the private property of the *Crown* and that no meeting might be held in it. After some *pourparlers* in which Bligh sought to demonstrate to him that parks were public property and in which Banks rejoined he had strict orders to arrest him if he

* *Longchamps*: a hippodrome in the outskirts of Paris.—*Ed.*

should insist on carrying out his intention, Bligh shouted amidst the bellowing of the masses surrounding him:

"Her Majesty's police declare that Hyde Park is private property of the Crown and that Her Majesty is unwilling to let her land be used by the people for their meetings. So let's move to Oxford Market."

With the ironical cry: "God save the Queen!" the throng broke up to journey to Oxford Market. But meanwhile, Finlen, a member of the Chartist executive, rushed to a tree some distance away followed by a crowd who in a twinkle formed so close and compact a circle around him that the police abandoned their attempt to get at him.

"Six days a week," he said, "we are treated like slaves and now Parliament wants to rob us of the bit of freedom we still have on the seventh. These oligarchs and capitalists allied with sanctimonious parsons wish to do *penance* by mortifying us instead of themselves for the unconscionable murder in the Crimea of the sons of the people."

We left this group to approach another where a speaker stretched out on the ground addressed his audience from this horizontal position. Suddenly shouts could be heard on all sides: "Let's go to the road, to the carriages!" The heaping of insults upon horse riders and occupants of carriages had meanwhile already begun. The constables, who constantly received reinforcements from the city, drove the promenading pedestrians off the carriage road. They thus helped to bring it about that either side of it was lined deep with people, from Apsley House up Rotten-Row along the Serpentine as far as Kensington Gardens—a distance of more than a quarter of an hour. The spectators consisted of about two-thirds workers and one-third members of the middle class, all with women and children. The procession of elegant ladies and gentlemen, "commoners and Lords," in their high coaches-and-four with liveried lackeys in front and behind, joined, to be sure, by a few mounted venerables slightly under the weather from the effects of wine, did not this time pass by in review but played the role of involuntary actors who were made to run the gauntlet. A babel of jeering, taunting, discordant ejaculations, in which no language is as rich as English, soon bore down upon them from both sides. As it was an improvised concert, instruments were lacking. The chorus therefore had only its own organs at its disposal and was compelled to confine itself to vocal music. And what a devil's concert it was: a cacophony of grunting, hissing, whistling, squeaking, snarling, growling, croaking, shrieking, groaning, rattling, howling, gnashing sounds! A music that could drive one mad and move a stone. To this must be added outbursts of genuine old-English humour peculiarly mixed with long-contained seething wrath. "Go to church!" were the only articulate sounds that could be distinguished. One lady soothingly offered a prayer-book in orthodox binding from her carriage in her outstretched hand. "Give it to your horses to read!" came the thundering reply, echoing a thousand voices. When the horses started to shy, rear, buck and finally run away, jeopardizing the lives of their genteel burdens, the contemptuous din grew louder, more menacing, more ruthless. Noble lords and ladies, among them Lady Granville, the wife of a minister and President of the Privy Council, were forced to alight and use their own legs. When elderly gentlemen rode past wearing broad-brimmed hats and otherwise so apparelled as to betray their special claim to perfectitude in matters of belief, the strident outbursts of fury were extinguished, as if in obedience to a command, by inextinguishable laughter. One of these gentlemen lost his patience. Like Mephistopheles he made an impolite gesture, sticking out his tongue at the enemy. "He is a windbag, a parliamentary man! He fights with his own weapons!" someone shouted on one side of the road. "He is a psalm-singing saint!" was the antistrophe from the opposite side. Meanwhile the metropolitan electric telegraph had informed all police stations that a riot was about to break out in Hyde Park and the police were ordered to the theatre of military operations. Soon one detachment of them after another marched at short intervals through the double file of people, from Apsley House to Kensington Gardens, each received with the popular ditty:

Where are the geese?
Ask the police!

This was a hint at a notorious theft of geese recently committed by a constable in Clerkenwell.

The spectacle lasted three hours. Only English lungs could perform such a feat. During the performance opinions such as, "This is only the beginning!" "That is the first step!" "We hate them!" and the like were voiced by the various groups. While rage was inscribed on the faces of the workers, such smiles of blissful self-satisfaction covered the physiognomies of the middle classes as we had never seen there before. Shortly before the end the demonstration increased in violence. Canes were raised in menace of the carriages and through the welter of discordant noises could be heard the cry of "you rascals!" During the three hours zealous Chartists, men and women, ploughed their way through the throng distributing leaflets which stated in big type:

"Reorganization of Chartism!

"A big public meeting will take place next Tuesday, June 26th, in the Literary and Scientific Institute in Friar Street, Doctors' Commons, to elect delegates to a conference for the reorganization of Chartism in the capital. Admission free."

Most of the London papers carry today only a brief account of the events in Hyde Park. No leading articles as yet, except in Lord Palmerston's *Morning Post*.

It claims that "a spectacle both disgraceful and dangerous in the extreme has taken place in Hyde Park, an open violation of law and decency—an illegal interference by physical force in the free action of the Legislature." It urges that "this scene must not be allowed to be repeated the following Sunday, as was threatened."

At the same time, however, it declares that the "fanatical" Lord Grosvenor is solely "responsible" for this mischief, being the man who provoked the "just indignation of the people." As if Parliament had not adopted Lord Grosvenor's bill in three readings! Or perhaps he too brought his influence to bear "by physical force on the free action of the Legislature"?

KARL MARX

CAPITAL, Book I

(Extracts)[49]

. . . The religious world is but the reflex of the real world. And for a society based upon the production of commodities, in which the producers in general enter into social relations with one another by treating their products as commodities and values, whereby they reduce their individual private labour to the standard of homogeneous human labour—for such a society, Christianity with its *cultus* of abstract man, more especially in its bourgeois developments, Protestantism, Deism, &c., is the most fitting form of religion. In the ancient Asiatic and other ancient modes of production, we find that the conversion of products into commodities, and therefore the conversion of men into producers of commodities, holds a subordinate place, which, however, increases in importance as the primitive communities approach nearer and nearer to their dissolution. Trading nations, properly so called, exist in the ancient world only in its interstices, like the gods of Epicurus in the Intermundia, or like Jews in the pores of Polish society. Those ancient social organisms of production are, as compared with bourgeois society, extremely simple and transparent. But they are founded either on the immature development of man individually, who has not yet severed the umbilical cord that unites him with his fellowmen in a primitive tribal community, or upon direct relations of subjection. They can arise and exist only when the development of the productive power of labour has not risen beyond a low stage, and when, therefore, the social relations within the sphere of material life, between man and man, and between man and nature, are correspondingly narrow. This narrowness is reflected in the ancient worship of nature, and in the other elements of the popular religions. The religious reflex of the real world can, in any case, only then finally vanish, when the practical relations of every-day life offer to man none but perfectly intelligible and reasonable relations with regard to his fellowmen and to nature.

The life-process of society, which is based on the process of material production, does not strip off its mystical veil until it is treated as production by freely associated men, and is consciously regulated by them in accordance with a settled plan. This, however, demands for society a certain material groundwork or set of conditions of existence which in their turn are the spontaneous product of a long and painful process of development.

Political Economy has indeed analyzed, however incompletely, value and its magnitude, and has discovered what lies beneath these forms. But it has never once asked the question why labour is represented by the value of its product and labour-time by the magnitude of that value. These formulae, which bear stamped upon them in unmistakable letters, that they belong to a state of society, in which the process of production has the mastery over man, instead of being controlled by him, such formulae appear to the bourgeois intellect to be as much a self-evident necessity imposed by nature as productive labour itself. Hence forms of social production that preceded the bourgeois form, are treated by the bourgeoisie in much the same way as the Fathers of the Church treated pre-Christian religions. . . .

* * *

. . . A critical history of technology would show how little any of the inventions of the 18th century are the work of a single individual. Hitherto there is no such book. Darwin has interested us in the history of Nature's Technology, *i.e.*, in the formation of the organs of plants and animals, which organs serve as instruments of production for sustaining life. Does not the history of the productive organs of man, of organs that are the material basis of all social organization, deserve equal attention? And would not such a history be easier to compile, since, as Vico says, human history differs from natural history in this, that we have made the former, but not the latter? Technology discloses man's mode of dealing with nature, the process of production by which he sustains his life, and thereby also lays bare the mode of formation of his social relations, and of the mental conceptions that flow from them. Every history of religion even, that fails to take account of this material basis, is uncritical. It is, in reality, much easier to discover by analysis the earthly core of the misty creations of religion, than, conversely, it is, to develop from the actual relations of life the corresponding celestialized forms of those relations. The latter method is the only materialistic, and therefore the only scientific one. The weak points in the abstract materialism of natural science, a materialism that excludes history and its process, are at once evident from the abstract and ideological conceptions of its spokesmen, whenever they venture beyond the bounds of their own speciality.

* * *

. . . If the reader reminds me of Malthus, whose *Essay on Population* appeared in 1798, I remind him that this work in its first form is nothing more than a schoolboyish, superficial plagiary of De Foe, Sir James Steuart, Townsend, Franklin, Wallace, &c., and does not contain a single sentence thought out by himself. The great sensation this pamphlet caused was due solely to party interest. The French Revolution had found passionate defenders in the United Kingdom; the "principle of population," slowly worked out in the eighteenth century, and then, in the midst of a great social crisis, proclaimed with drums and trumpets as the infallible antidote to the teachings of Condorcet, &c., was greeted with jubilance by the English oligarchy as the great destroyer of all hankerings after human development. Malthus, hugely astonished at his success, gave himself to stuffing into his book materials superficially compiled, and adding to it new matter, not discovered but annexed by him. Note further: Although Malthus was a parson of the English State Church, he had taken the monastic vow of celibacy—one of the conditions of holding a Fellowship in Protestant Cambridge University: "*Socios collegiorum maritos esse non permittimus, sed statim postquam quis uxorem duxerit, socius collegii desinat esse.*" ("Reports of Cambridge University Commission," p. 172.) This circumstance favourably distinguishes Malthus from the other Protestant parsons, who have shuffled off the command enjoining celibacy of the priesthood and have taken, "Be fruitful and multiply," as their special Biblical mission in such a degree that they generally contribute to the increase of population to a really unbecoming extent, whilst they preach at the same time to the labourers the "principle of population." It is characteristic that the economic fall of man, the Adam's apple, the urgent appetite, "the checks which tend to blunt the shafts of Cupid," as Parson Townsend waggishly puts it, that this delicate question was and is monopolized by the Reverends of Protestant Theology, or rather of the Protestant Church. With the exception of the Venetian monk, Ortes, an original and clever writer, most of the population-theory teachers are Protestant parsons. For instance, Bruckner, *Théorie du Système animal*, Leyde, 1767, in which the whole subject of the modern population theory is exhausted, and to which the passing quarrel between Quesnay and his pupil, the elder Mirabeau, furnished ideas on the same topic; then Parson Wallace, Parson Townsend, Parson Malthus and his pupil, the arch-Parson Thomas Chalmers, to say nothing of lesser reverend scribblers in this line. Originally, Political Economy was studied by philosophers like Hobbes, Locke, Hume; by businessmen and statesmen, like Thomas More, Temple, Sully, De Witt, North, Law, Wanderlint, Cantillon, Franklin; and especially, and with the greatest success, by medical men like Petty, Barbon, Mandeville, Quesnay. Even in the middle of the eighteenth century, the Rev. Mr. Tucker, a notable economist of his time, excused himself for meddling with the things of Mammon. Later on, and in truth with this very "principle of population," struck the hour of the Protestant parsons. Petty, who regarded the population as the basis of wealth, and was, like Adam Smith, an outspoken foe to parsons, says, as if he had a presentiment of their bungling interference, "that Religion best flourishes when the priests are most mortified, as was before said of the Law, which best flourisheth when lawyers have least to do." He advises the Protestant priests, therefore, if they, once for all, will not follow the Apostle Paul and "mortify" themselves by celibacy, "not to breed more Churchmen than the Benefices, as they now stand shared out, will receive, that is to say, if there be places for about twelve thousand in England and Wales, it will not be safe to breed up 24,000 ministers, for then the twelve thousand which are unprovided for, will seek ways how to get themselves a livelihood, which they cannot do more easily than by persuading the people that the twelve thousand incumbents do poison or starve their souls, and misguide them in their way to Heaven." (Petty,

A Treatise of Taxes and Contributions, London, 1667, p.57.) Adam Smith's position with the Protestant priesthood of his time is shown by the following. In *A Letter to A. Smith, L. L. D. On the Life, Death, and Philosophy of His Friend, David Hume. By one of the People called Christians*, 4th edition, Oxford, 1784, Dr. Horne, Bishop of Norwich, reproves Adam Smith, because in a published letter to Mr. Strahan, he "embalmed his friend David" (sc. Hume); because he told the world how "Hume amused himself on his death-bed with Lucian and Whist," and because he even had the impudence to write of Hume: "I have always considered him, both in his life-time and since his death, as approaching as nearly to the idea of a perfectly wise and virtuous man, as, perhaps, the nature of human frailty will permit." The bishop cries out, in a passion: "Is it right in you, Sir, to hold up to our view as 'perfectly wise and virtuous,' the *character* and *conduct* of one, who seems to have been possessed with an incurable antipathy to all that is called *Religion*; and who strained every nerve to explode, suppress and extirpate the spirit of it among men, that its very name, if he could effect it, might no more be had in remembrance?" (1. c., p.8.) "But let not the lovers of truth be discouraged. Atheism cannot be of long continuance" (p. 17). Adam Smith, "had the atrocious wickedness to propagate atheism through the land (viz., by his "Theory of Moral Sentiments"). Upon the whole, Doctor, your meaning is good; but I think you will not succeed this time. You would persuade us, by the example of *David Hume, Esq.*, that atheism is the only cordial for low spirits, and the proper antidote against the fear of death. . . . You may smile over *Babylon* in ruins and congratulate the hardened *Pharaoh* on his overthrow in the Red Sea" (1. c., pp. 21, 22). One orthodox individual, amongst Adam Smith's college friends, writes after his death: "Smith's well-placed affection for Hume . . . hindered him from being a Christian.... When he met with honest men whom he liked ... he would believe almost anything they said. Had he been a friend of the worthy ingenious Horrox he would have believed that the moon sometimes disappeared in a clear sky without the interposition of a cloud.... He approached to republicanism in his political principles." (*The Bee.* By James Anderson, 18 Vols., Vol. 3, pp. 166, 165, Edinburgh, 1791-93.) Parson Thomas Chalmers has his suspicions as to Adam Smith having invented the category of "unproductive labourers," solely for the Protestant parsons, in spite of their blessed work in the vineyard of the Lord....

FREDERICK ENGELS

EMIGRANT LITERATURE

(Extract from the Second Article)

... Our Blanquists share the Bakuninists' desire to represent the most far-reaching, most extreme trend. That, by the way, is why they often adopt the same means as the Bakuninists, though with opposite ends in view. The point is, therefore, to be more radical than everybody else as far as atheism is concerned. Fortunately it is easy enough to be an atheist today. Atheism is so near to being self-obvious with European working-class parties nowadays—although in certain countries it is often enough like that of the Spanish Bakuninist who maintained that it was against all socialism to believe in God but that the Virgin Mary was a different matter, every decent socialist ought naturally to believe in her. It can even be said of the German Social-Democratic workers that atheism has already outlived itself with them: this purely negative word no longer has any application as far as they are concerned inasmuch as their opposition to faith in God is no longer one of theory but one of practice; they have *purely and simply finished with God*, they live and think in the world of reality and are therefore materialists. This seems to be the case in France too. If not, nothing would be simpler than to have the splendid French materialistic literature of the past century spread on a large scale among the workers. For in that literature French thought made its greatest achievement both in form and in content and, considering the level of science at that time, it is still infinitely high today as far as content is concerned and has not been equalled as to form. But that cannot be to the liking of our Blanquists. In order to prove that they are the most radical of all they abolish God by decree as was done in 1793:

"Let the Commune free mankind for ever from the ghost of past misery" (God), "from that cause" (non-existing God a cause!) "of their present misery. There is no room for priests in the Commune; every religious manifestation, every religious organization must be prohibited."

And this demand that men should be changed into atheists *par ordre du mufti* is signed by two members of the Commune who have really had opportunity enough to find out that first a vast amount of things can be ordered on paper without necessarily being carried out, and second, that persecution is the best means of promoting undesirable convictions! This much is sure: the only service that can be rendered to God today is to declare atheism a compulsory article of faith and to outdo Bismarck's *Kirchenkulturkampf*[50] laws by prohibiting religion generally. . . .

KARL MARX

CRITIQUE OF THE GOTHA PROGRAMME

(Extract)

...*"Freedom of conscience!"* If one had desired at the time of the *Kulturkampf* to remind liberalism of its old catchwords, it surely could have been done only in the following form: Everyone should be able to attend to his religious as well as his bodily needs without the police sticking their noses in. But the workers' party ought at any rate in this connection to have expressed its awareness of the fact that bourgeois "freedom of conscience" is nothing but the toleration of all possible kinds of *religious freedom of conscience*, and that for its part it endeavours rather to liberate the conscience from the witchery of religion. But one chooses not to overstep the "bourgeois" level....

FREDERICK ENGELS

ANTI-DÜHRING

(Extracts[51])

. . . Christianity knew only *one* point in which all men were equal: that all were equally born in original sin—which corresponded perfectly to its character as the religion of the slaves and the oppressed. Apart from this it recognized, at most, the equality of the elect, which however was only stressed at the very beginning. The traces of common ownership which are also found in the early stages of the new religion can be ascribed to solidarity among the proscribed rather than to real equalitarian ideas. Within a very short time the establishment of the distinction between priests and laymen put an end even to this incipient Christian equality.

The overrunning of Western Europe by the Germans abolished for centuries all ideas of equality, through the gradual building up of such a complicated social and political hierarchy as had never existed before. But at the same time the invasion drew Western and Central Europe into the course of historical development, created for the first time a compact cultural area, and within this area also for the first time a system of predominantly national states exerting mutual influence on each other and mutually holding each other in check. Thereby it prepared the ground on which alone the question of the equal status of men, of the rights of man, could at a later period be raised. . . .

* * *

. . . Now the sovereignty of the individual consists essentially in that "the individual *is subject to absolute compulsion* by the state"; this compulsion, however, can only be justified in so far as it "really serves natural justice." With this end in view there will be "legislative and judicial authority," which, however, "must remain in the hands of the community"; and there will also be an alliance for defence, which will find expression in "joint action in the army or in an executive section for the maintenance of internal security"—that is to say, there will also be army, police, *gendarmerie.* Herr Dühring has many times already shown that he is a good Prussian; here he proves himself a peer of that model Prussian, who, as the late Minister von Rochow put it, "carries his gendarme in his breast." This *gendarmerie* of the future, however, will not be so dangerous as the police thugs of the present day. Whatever the sovereign individual may suffer at their hands, he will always, have *one consolation*: "the right or wrong which, according to the circumstances, may then be dealt to him by free society can never be *any worse* than that which the *state of nature* would have brought with it." And then, after Herr Dühring has once more tripped us up on those authors' rights of his which are always getting in the way, he assures us that in his world of the future there will be, "of course, an absolutely free Bar available to all." "The free society, as it is conceived today," gets steadily more and more mixed. Architects, porters, professional writers, gendarmes, and now also barristers! This "world of sober and critical thought" and the various heavenly kingdoms of the different religions, in which the believer always finds in transfigured form the things which have sweetened his earthly existence, are as like as two peas. And Herr Dühring is a citizen of the state where "everyone can be happy in his own way." What more do we want?

But it does not matter what we want. What matters is what Herr Dühring wants. And he differs from Frederick II in this, that in the Dühringian future state certainly not everyone will be able to be happy in his own way. The constitution of this future state provides: "In the free society there can be no religious worship; *for* every member of it has got beyond the primitive childish superstition that there are beings, behind nature or above it, who can be influenced by sacrifices or prayers." A "socialitarian system, rightly conceived, *has* therefore . . . to *abolish* all the paraphernalia of religious magic, and therewith all the essential elements of religious worship." Religion is prohibited.

All religion, however, is nothing but the fantastic reflection in men's minds of those external forces which control their daily life, a reflection in which the terrestrial forces assume the form of supernatural forces. In the beginnings of history it was the forces of nature which were first so reflected and which in the course of further evolution underwent the most manifold and varied personifications among the various peoples. This early process has been traced back by comparative mythology, at least in the case of the Indo-European peoples, to its origin in the Indian Vedas, and in its further evolution it has been demonstrated in detail among the Indians, Persians, Greeks, Romans, Germans and, so far as material is available, also among the Celts, Lithuanians and Slavs. But it is not long before, side by side with the forces of nature, social forces begin to be active—forces which confront man as equally alien and at first equally inexplicable, dominating him with the same apparent natural necessity as the forces of nature themselves. The fantastic figures, which at first only reflected the mysterious forces of nature, at this point acquire social attributes, become representatives of the forces of history.* At a still further stage of evolution, all the natural and social attributes of the numerous gods are transferred to *one* almighty god, who is but a reflection of the abstract man. Such was the origin of monotheism, which was historically the last product of the vulgarized philosophy of the later Greeks and found its incarnation in the exclusively national god of the Jews, Jehovah.** In this convenient, handy and universally adaptable form, religion can continue to exist as the immediate, that is, the sentimental form of men's relation to the alien natural and social forces which dominate them, so long as men remain under the control of these forces. However, we have seen repeatedly that in existing bourgeois society men are dominated by the economic conditions created by themselves, by the means of production which they themselves have produced, as if by an alien force. The actual basis of the reflective activity that gives rise to religion therefore continues to exist, and with it the religious reflection itself. And although bourgeois political economy has given a certain insight into the causal connection of this alien domination, this makes no essential difference. Bourgeois economics can neither prevent crises in general, nor protect the individual capitalists from losses, bad debts and bankruptcy, nor secure the individual workers against unemployment and destitution. It is still true that man proposes and God (that is, the alien domination of the capitalist mode of

* This two-fold character assumed later on by the divinities was one of the causes of the subsequently widespread confusion of mythologies—a cause which comparative mythology has overlooked, as it pays attention exclusively to their character as reflections of the forces of nature. Thus in some Germanic tribes the war-god is called Tyr (Old Nordic) or Zio (Old High German) and corresponds therefore to the Greek Zeus, Latin Jupiter for Diu-piter; in other Germanic tribes, Er, Eor, corresponds therefore to the Greek Ares, Latin Mars. [*Note by Engels.*]

** See p. 197 of the present collection.—*Ed.*

production) disposes. Mere knowledge, even if it went much further and deeper than that of bourgeois economic science, is not enough to bring social forces under the domination of society. What is above all necessary for this, is a social *act*. And when this act has been accomplished, when society, by taking possession of all means of production and using them on a planned basis, has freed itself and all its members from the bondage in which they are now held by these means of production which they themselves have produced but which confront them as an irresistible alien force; when therefore man no longer merely proposes, but also disposes—only then will the last alien force which is still reflected in religion vanish; and with it will also vanish the religious reflection itself, for the simple reason that then there will be nothing left to reflect.

Herr Dühring, however, cannot wait until religion dies this, its natural, death. He proceeds in more deep-rooted fashion. He out-Bismarcks Bismarck; he decrees sharper May laws[52] not merely against Catholicism, but against all religion whatsoever; he incites his gendarmes of the future against religion, and thereby helps it to martyrdom and a prolonged lease of life. Wherever we turn, we find specifically Prussian socialism. . . .

Equality—Justice.—The idea that equality is the expression of justice, the principle of consummated political and social regulation, arose quite historically. It did not exist in primitive communities, or only very limitedly so, for full members of individual communities, and was saddled with slavery. Ditto in the democracy of antiquity. Equality of all people—Greeks, Romans, and barbarians, freemen and slaves, subjects and aliens, citizens and peregrines, etc.—was not only insane but criminal to the mind of the ancients, and in Christendom its first beginnings were strictly persecuted.

In Catholicism there was first the *negative equality of*

all human beings before God as sinners, and, more narrowly construed, the equality of all children of God redeemed by the grace and the blood of Christ. Both versions are grounded on the role of Christianity as the religion of the slaves, the banished, the dispossessed, the persecuted, the oppressed. With the victory of Christianity this circumstance was relegated to the rear and prime importance attached next to the antithesis between believers and pagans, orthodox and heretics.

With the rise of the cities and thereby of the more or less developed elements of the bourgeoisie, as well as of the proletariat, the demand for equality as a condition of bourgeois existence was bound gradually to resurge, interlinked with the proletariat's drawing of the conclusion to proceed from political to social equality. This naturally assumed a religious form, sharply expressed for the first time in the Peasant War.

The bourgeois side was first formulated by Rousseau, in trenchant terms but still on behalf of all humanity. As was the case with all demands of the bourgeoisie, so here too the proletariat cast a fateful shadow beside it and drew its own conclusions (Babeuf). This connection between bourgeois equality and the proletariat's drawing of conclusions should be developed in greater detail....

* * *

...Even the correct reflection of *nature* is extremely difficult, the product of a long history of experience. To primitive man the forces of nature were something alien, mysterious, superior. At a certain stage, through which *all* civilized peoples passed, he assimilates them by means of personification. It was this urge to personify that created gods everywhere, and the *consensus gentium*,* as regards

* Consensus of the peoples.—*Ed.*

proof of the existence of God, proves after all only the universality of this urge to personify as a necessary transition stage, and consequently the universality of religion too. Only real knowledge of the forces of nature ejects the gods or God from one position after another (Secchi and his solar system). This process has now advanced so far that theoretically it may be considered concluded.

In the sphere of *society* reflection is still more difficult. Society is determined by economic relations, production and exchange, and besides by the historically prerequisite conditions. . . .

FREDERICK ENGELS

DIALECTICS OF NATURE

(Extracts)

INTRODUCTION

Modern research into nature, which alone has achieved a scientific, systematic, all-round development, in contrast to the brilliant natural-philosophical intuitions of antiquity and the extremely important but sporadic discoveries of the Arabs, which for the most part vanished without results—this modern research into nature dates, like all more recent history, from that mighty epoch which we Germans term the Reformation, from the national misfortune that overtook us at that time, and which the French term the Renaissance and the Italians the Cinquecento, although it is not fully expressed by any of these names. It is the epoch which had its rise in the latter half of the fifteenth century. Royalty, with the support of the burghers of the towns, broke the power of the feudal nobility and established the great monarchies, based essentially on nationality, within which the modern European nations and modern bourgeois society came to development. And while the burghers and nobles were still fighting one another, the German Peasant War pointed prophetically to future class struggles by bringing on to the stage not only the peasants in revolt—that was no longer anything new—but behind them the beginnings of the modern proletariat, with the red flag in their hands and the demand for common ownership of goods on their lips.

In the manuscripts saved from the fall of Byzantium, in the antique statues dug out of the ruins of Rome, a new world was revealed to the astonished West, that of ancient Greece: the ghosts of the Middle Ages vanished before its shining forms; Italy rose to an undreamt-of flowering of art, which seemed like a reflection of classical antiquity and was never attained again. In Italy, France, and Germany a new literature arose, the first modern literature; shortly afterwards came the classical epochs of English and Spanish literature. The bounds of the old *orbis terrarum* were pierced, only now for the first time was the world really discovered and the basis laid for subsequent world trade and the transition from handicraft to manufacture, which in its turn formed the starting-point for modern large-scale industry. The dictatorship of the Church over men's minds was shattered; it was directly cast off by the majority of the Germanic peoples, who adopted Protestantism, while among the Latins a cheerful spirit of free thought, taken over from the Arabs and nourished by the newly discovered Greek philosophy, took root more and more and prepared the way for the materialism of the eighteenth century.

It was the greatest progressive revolution that mankind had so far experienced, a time which called for giants and produced giants—giants in power of thought, passion and character, in universality and learning. The men who founded the modern rule of the bourgeoisie had anything but bourgeois limitations. On the contrary, the adventurous character of the time inspired them to a greater or lesser degree. There was hardly any man of importance then living who had not travelled extensively, who did not speak four or five languages, who did not shine in a number of fields. Leonardo da Vinci was not only a great painter but also a great mathematician, mechanician, and engineer, to whom the most diverse branches of physics are indebted for important discoveries. Albrecht Dürer was painter, engraver, sculptor, and architect, and in addition invented a system of fortification embodying many of the ideas that much later were again taken up by Montalembert and the modern German science of fortification. Machiavelli was statesman, historian, poet, and at the same time the first notable military author of modern times. Luther not only cleaned the Augean stable of the Church but also that of the German language; he created modern German prose and composed the text and melody of that triumphal hymn which became the Marseillaise of the sixteenth century. The heroes of that time were not yet in thrall to the division of labour, the restricting effects of which, with its production of one-sidedness, we so often notice in their successors. But what is especially characteristic of them is that they almost all live and pursue their activities in the midst of the contemporary movements, in the practical struggle; they take sides and join in the fight, one by speaking and writing, another with the sword, many with both. Hence the fulness and force of character that makes them complete men. Men of the study are the exception—either persons of second or third rank or cautious philistines who do not want to burn their fingers.

At that time natural science also developed in the midst of the general revolution and was itself thoroughly revolutionary; it had indeed to win in struggle its right of existence. Side by side with the great Italians from whom modern philosophy dates, it provided its martyrs for the stake and the dungeons of the Inquisition. And it is characteristic that Protestants outdid Catholics in persecuting the free investigation of nature. Calvin had Servetus burnt at the stake when the latter was on the point of discovering the circulation of the blood, and indeed he kept him roasting alive for two hours; for the Inquisition at least it sufficed to have Giordano Bruno simply burnt alive.

The revolutionary act by which natural science declared its independence and, as it were, repeated Luther's burning of the Papal Bull, was the publication of the immortal work[53] by which Copernicus, though timidly and, so to speak, only from his death-bed, threw down the gauntlet to ecclesiastical authority in the affairs of nature. The emancipation of natural science from theology dates from this, although the fighting out of particular mutual claims has dragged on down to our day and in many minds is still far from completion. Thenceforward, however, the development of the sciences proceeded with giant strides, and, it might be said, gained in force in proportion to the square of the distance (in time) from its point of departure. It was as if the world were to be shown that henceforth, for the highest product of organic matter, the human mind, the law of motion that holds good is the reverse of that for inorganic matter.

The main work in the first period of natural science that now opened lay in mastering the material immediately at hand. In most fields a start had to be made from the very beginning. Antiquity had bequeathed Euclid[54] and the Ptolemaic solar system[55]; the Arabs had left behind the decimal notation, the beginnings of algebra, the modern numerals, and alchemy, the Christian Middle Ages nothing at all. Of necessity, in this situation the most fundamental natural science, the mechanics of terrestrial and heavenly bodies, occupied first place, and alongside of it, as handmaiden to it, the discovery and perfecting of mathematical methods. Great things were achieved here. At the end of the period typified by Newton and Linnaeus we find these branches of science brought to a certain perfection. The basic features of the most essential mathematical methods were established: analytical geometry by Descartes especially, logarithms by Napier, and differential and integral calculus by Leibniz and perhaps Newton. The same holds good of the mechanics of rigid bodies, the main laws of which were made clear once for all. Finally in the astronomy of the solar system Kepler discovered the laws of planetary movement and Newton formulated them from the point of view of the general laws of motion of matter. The other branches of natural science were far removed even from this preliminary perfection. Only towards the end of the period did the mechanics of fluid and gaseous bodies receive further treatment.* Physics proper had still not gone beyond its first beginnings, with the exception of optics, the exceptional progress of which was due to the practical needs of astronomy. By the phlogistic theory,[56] chemistry for the first time emancipated itself from alchemy. Geology had not yet gone beyond the embryonic stage of mineralogy; hence palaeontology could not yet exist at all. Finally, in the field of biology the essential preoccupation was still the collection and first sifting of the immense material, not only botanical and zoological but also anatomical and properly physiological. There could as yet be hardly any talk of the comparison of the various forms of life, of the investigation of their geographical distribution and their climatic, etc., conditions of existence. Here only botany and zoology arrived at an approximate completion owing to Linnaeus.

But what is especially typical of this period is the elaboration of a peculiar general outlook, the central point of which is the view *of the absolute immutability of nature.* In whatever way nature itself might have come into being, once present it remained as it was as long as it continued to exist. The planets and their satellites, once set in

---

* In the margin of the manuscript Engels noted: "Torricelli in connection with the control of alpine rivers."—*Ed.*

motion by the mysterious "first impulse," circled on and on in their pre-appointed ellipses for all eternity, or at any rate until the end of all things. The stars remained for ever fixed and immovable in their places, keeping one another therein by "universal gravitation." The earth had remained the same without alteration from all eternity or, alternatively, from the first day of its creation. The "five continents" of the present day had always existed, and they had always had the same mountains, valleys, and rivers, the same climate, and the same flora and fauna, except in so far as change or transplantation had taken place at the hand of man. The species of plants and animals had been established once for all when they came into existence; like continually produced like, and it was already a good deal for Linnaeus to have conceded that possibly here and there new species could have arisen by crossing. In contrast to the history of mankind, which develops in time, there was ascribed to the history of nature only an unfolding in space. All change, all development in nature, was denied. Natural science, so revolutionary at the outset, suddenly found itself confronted by an out-and-out conservative nature, in which even today everything was as it had been from the beginning and in which—to the end of the world or for all eternity—everything would remain as it had been since the beginning.

High as the natural science of the first half of the eighteenth century stood above Greek antiquity in knowledge and even in the sifting of its material, it stood just as far below Greek antiquity in the theoretical mastery of this material, in the general outlook on nature. For the Greek philosophers the world was essentially something that had emerged from chaos, something that had developed, that had come into being. For the natural scientists of the period that we are dealing with it was something ossified, something immutable, and for most of them something that had been created at one stroke. Science was still deeply enmeshed in theology. Everywhere it sought and found the ultimate cause in an impulse from outside that was not to be explained from nature itself. Even if attraction, pompously christened "universal gravitation" by Newton, was conceived as an essential property of matter, whence comes the unexplained tangential force which first gives rise to the orbits of the planets? How did the innumerable varieties of animals and plants arise? And how, above all, did man arise, since after all it was certain that he was not present from all eternity? To such questions natural science only too frequently answered by making the creator of all things responsible. Copernicus, at the beginning of the period, shows theology the door; Newton closes the period with the postulate of a divine first impulse. The highest general idea to which this natural science attained was that of the purposiveness of the arrangements of nature, the shallow teleology of Wolff, according to which cats were created to eat mice, mice to be eaten by cats, and the whole of nature to testify to the wisdom of the creator. It is to the highest credit of the philosophy of the time that it did not let itself be led astray by the restricted state of contemporary natural knowledge, and that—from Spinoza down to the great French materialists—it insisted on explaining the world from the world itself and left the justification in detail to the natural science of the future.

I include the materialists of the eighteenth century in this period because no material of natural science was available to them other than that described above. Kant's epoch-making work remained a secret to them, and Laplace came long after them. We should not forget that this obsolete outlook on nature, although shattered by the progress of science, dominated the entire first half of the nineteenth century, and in substance is even now still taught in all schools.*

The first breach in this petrified outlook on nature was made not by a natural scientist but by a philosopher. In 1755 appeared Kant's *Allgemeine Naturgeschichte und Theorie des Himmels.* The question of the first impulse was done away with; the earth and the whole solar system appeared as something that had *come into being* in the course of time. If the great majority of the natural scientists had had a little less of the repugnance to thinking that Newton expressed in the warning: Physics, beware of metaphysics!, they would have been compelled to draw from this single brilliant discovery of Kant's conclusions that would have spared them endless deviations and immeasurable amounts of time and labour wasted in false directions. For Kant's discovery contained the point of departure for all further progress. If the earth was some-

---

* How tenaciously even in 1861 this view could be held by a man whose scientific achievements had provided highly important material for abolishing it is shown by the following classic words.

"All the arrangements of our solar system, so far as we are capable of comprehending them, aim at preservation of what exists and at unchanging continuance. Just as since the most ancient times no animal and no plant on the earth has become more perfect or in any way different, just as we find in all organisms only stages *alongside of* one another and not *following* one another, just as our own race has always remained the same in corporeal respects—so even the greatest diversity in the co-existing heavenly bodies does not justify our assuming that these forms are merely different stages of development; it is rather that everything created *is equally* perfect in itself." (Mädler, *Der Wunderbau des Weltalls oder populäre Astronomie,* 5th edition, Berlin 1861, p. 316.) [*Note by Engels.*]

In the margin of the manuscript is a note "The rigidity of the old outlook on nature provided the basis for the general comprehension of all natural science as a single whole. The French encyclopaedists, still purely mechanically—alongside of one another; and then simultaneously St.-Simon and German philosophy of nature, perfected by Hegel."—*Ed.*

thing that had come into being, then its present geological, geographical, and climatic state, and its plants and animals likewise, must be something that had come into being; it must have had a history not only of co-existence in space but also of succession in time. If at once further investigations had been resolutely pursued in this direction, natural science would now be considerably further advanced than it is. But what good could come of philosophy? Kant's work remained without immediate results until many years later Laplace and Herschel expounded its contents and gave them a deeper foundation, thereby gradually bringing the "nebular hypothesis"[57] into favour. Further discoveries finally brought it victory; the most important of these were: the proper motion of the fixed stars, the demonstration of a resistant medium in universal space, the proof furnished by spectral analysis of the chemical identity of the matter of the universe and of the existence of such glowing nebular masses as Kant had postulated.*

It is, however, permissible to doubt whether the majority of natural scientists would so soon have become conscious of the contradiction of a changing earth that bore immutable organisms, had not the dawning conception that nature does not just *exist*, but *comes into being* and *passes away*, derived support from another quarter. Geology arose and pointed out not only the terrestrial strata formed one after another and deposited one upon another, but also the shells and skeletons of extinct animals and the trunks, leaves, and fruits of no longer existing plants contained in these strata. The decision had to be taken to acknowledge that not only the earth as a whole but also its present surface and the plants and animals living on it possessed a

* In the margin of the manuscript Engels added: "Retardation of the earth's rotation by the tides, also from Kant, only now understood."—*Ed.*

history in time. At first the acknowledgement occurred reluctantly enough. Cuvier's theory of the revolutions of the earth was revolutionary in phrase and reactionary in substance. In place of a *single* divine creation, he put a whole series of repeated acts of creation, making the miracle an essential natural agent. Lyell first brought sense into geology by substituting for the sudden revolutions due to the moods of the creator the gradual effects of a slow transformation of the earth.*

Lyell's theory was even more incompatible than any of its predecessors with the assumption of constant organic species. Gradual transformation of the earth's surface and of all conditions of life led directly to gradual transformation of the organisms and their adaptation to the changing environment, to the mutability of species. But tradition is a power not only in the Catholic Church but also in natural science. For years, Lyell himself did not see the contradiction, and his pupils still less. This can only be explained by the division of labour that had meanwhile become dominant in natural science, which more or less restricted each person to his special sphere, there being only a few whom it did not rob of a comprehensive view.

Meanwhile physics had made mighty advances, the results of which were summed up almost simultaneously by three different persons in the year 1842, an epoch-making year for this branch of natural investigation. Mayer in Heilbronn and Joule in Manchester demonstrated the transformation of heat into mechanical force and of mechanical force into heat. The determination of the mechanical equivalent of heat put this result beyond question.

* The defect of Lyell's view—at least in its first form—lay in conceiving the forces at work on the earth as constant, both in quality and quantity. The cooling of the earth does not exist for him; the earth does not develop in a definite direction but merely changes in an inconsequent fortuitous manner. [*Note by Engels.*]

Simultaneously, by simply working up the separate results of physics already arrived at, Grove—not a natural scientist by profession, but an English lawyer—proved that all so-called physical forces, mechanical force, heat, light, electricity, magnetism, indeed even so-called chemical force, become transformed into one another under definite conditions without any loss of force occurring, and so proved additionally along physical lines Descartes' principle that the quantity of motion present in the world is constant. With that the special physical forces, the as it were immutable "species" of physics, were resolved into variously differentiated forms of the motion of matter, passing into one another according to definite laws. The fortuitousness of the existence of such and such a number of physical forces was abolished from science by the proof of their interconnections and transitions. Physics, like astronomy before it, had arrived at a result that necessarily pointed to the eternal cycle of matter in motion as the ultimate conclusion.

The wonderfully rapid development of chemistry since Lavoisier, and especially since Dalton, attacked the old ideas about nature from another aspect. The preparation by inorganic means of compounds that hitherto had been produced only in the living organism proved that the laws of chemistry have the same validity for organic as for inorganic bodies, and to a large extent bridged the gulf between inorganic and organic nature, a gulf that even Kant regarded as for ever impassable.

Finally, in the sphere of biological research also the scientific journeys and expeditions that had been systematically organized since the middle of the previous [i.e., eighteenth] century, the more thorough exploration of the European colonies in all parts of the world by specialists living there, and further the progress of palaeontology, anatomy, and physiology in general, particularly since the systematic use of the microscope and the discovery of the cell, had accumulated so much material that the application of the comparative method became possible and at the same time indispensable.* On the one hand the conditions of life of the various floras and faunas were established by means of comparative physical geography; on the other hand the various organisms were compared with one another according to their homologous organs, and this not only in the adult condition but at all stages of their development. The more deeply and exactly this research was carried on, the more did the rigid system of an immutably fixed organic nature crumble away at its touch. Not only did the separate species of plants and animals become more and more inextricably intermingled, but animals turned up, such as *Amphioxus* and *Lepidosiren*,[58] that made a mockery of all previous classification,** and finally organisms were encountered of which it was not possible to say whether they belonged to the plant or animal kingdom. More and more the gaps in the palaeontological record were filled up, compelling even the most reluctant to acknowledge the striking parallelism between the history of the development of the organic world as a whole and that of the individual organism, the Ariadne's thread that was to lead the way out of the labyrinth in which botany and zoology appeared to have become more and more deeply lost. It was characteristic that, almost simultaneously with Kant's attack on the eternity of the solar system, K. F. Wolff in 1759 launched the first attack on the fixity of species and proclaimed the theory of descent. But what in his case was still only a brilliant anticipation took firm shape in the hands of Oken, Lamarck, Baer, and was

* In the margin of the manuscript Engels added: "Embryology." —*Ed.*

** In the margin of the manuscript Engels added: "*Ceratodus*. Ditto *Archaeopteryx, etc.*"[59]—*Ed.*

victoriously carried through by Darwin in 1859, exactly a hundred years later. Almost simultaneously it was established that protoplasm and the cell, which had already been shown to be the ultimate morphological constituents of all organisms, occurred independently existing as the lowest forms of organic life. This not only reduced the gulf between inorganic and organic nature to a minimum but removed one of the most essential difficulties that had previously stood in the way of the theory of descent of organisms. The new outlook on nature was complete in its main features; all rigidity was dissolved, all fixity dissipated, all particularity that had been regarded as eternal became transient, the whole of nature was shown as moving in eternal flux and cyclical course.

Thus we have once again returned to the mode of outlook of the great founders of Greek philosophy, the view that the whole of nature, from the smallest element to the greatest, from grains of sand to suns, from Protista to man, has its existence in eternal coming into being and passing away, in ceaseless flux, in unresting motion and change. Only with the essential difference that what in the case of the Greeks was a brilliant intuition, is in our case the result of strictly scientific research in accordance with experience, and hence also it emerges in a much more definite and clear form. It is true that the empirical proof of this cyclical course is not wholly free from gaps, but these are insignificant in comparison with what has already been firmly established and with each year they become more and more filled up. And how could the proof in detail be other than one containing gaps when one bears in mind that the most important branches of science—trans-planetary astronomy, chemistry, geology—have a scientific existence of barely a century, and the comparative method in physiology one of barely fifty years, and that the basic form of almost all organic development, the cell, is a discovery not yet forty years old?

The innumerable suns and solar systems of our island universe, bounded by the outermost stellar rings of the Milky Way, developed by contraction and cooling from swirling, glowing masses of vapour, the laws of motion of which will perhaps be disclosed after the observations of some centuries have given us an insight into the proper motion of the stars. Obviously, this development did not proceed everywhere at the same rate. Astronomy is more and more being forced to recognize the existence of dark bodies, not merely planetary in nature, hence extinct suns in our stellar system (Mädler); on the other hand (according to Secchi) a part of the vaporous nebular patches belong to our stellar system as suns not yet fully formed, which does not exclude the possibility that other nebulae are, as Mädler maintains, distant independent island universes, the relative stage of development of which must be determined by the spectroscope.

How a solar system develops from an individual nebular mass has been shown in detail by Laplace in a manner still unsurpassed; subsequent science has more and more confirmed him.

On the separate bodies so formed—suns as well as planets and satellites—the form of motion of matter at first prevailing is that which we call heat. There can be no question of chemical compounds of the elements even at a temperature like that still possessed by the sun; the extent to which heat is transformed into electricity or magnetism under such conditions, continued solar observations will show; it is already as good as proved that the mechanical motion taking place in the sun arises solely from the conflict of heat with gravity.

The smaller the individual bodies, the quicker they cool down, the satellites, asteroids, and meteors first of all, just as our moon has long been extinct. The planets cool more slowly, the central body slowest of all.

With progressive cooling the interplay of the physical forms of motion which become transformed into one another comes more and more to the forefront until finally a point is reached from when on chemical affinity begins to make itself felt, the previously chemically indifferent elements become differentiated chemically one after another, acquire chemical properties, and enter into combination with one another. These compounds change continually with the decreasing temperature, which affects differently not only each element but also each separate compound of the elements, changing also with the consequent passage of part of the gaseous matter first to the liquid and then the solid state, and with the new conditions thus created.

The time when the planet acquires a firm shell and accumulations of water on its surface coincides with that from when on its intrinsic heat diminishes more and more compared with the heat emitted to it from the central body. Its atmosphere becomes the arena of meteorological phenomena in the sense in which we now understand the term; its surface becomes the arena of geological changes in which the deposits resulting from atmospheric precipitation become of ever greater importance compared with the slowly decreasing external effects of the hot fluid interior.

If, finally, the temperature becomes so far equalized that over a considerable portion of the surface at least it no longer exceeds the limits within which protein is capable of life, then, if other chemical preconditions are favourable, living protoplasm is formed. What these preconditions are, we do not yet know, which is not to be wondered at since so far not even the chemical formula of protein has been established—we do not even know how many chemically different protein bodies there are—and since it is only about ten years ago that the fact became known that completely structureless protein exercises all the essential functions of life: digestion, excretion, movement, contraction, reaction to stimuli, and reproduction.[60]

Thousands of years may have passed before the conditions arose in which the next advance could take place and this shapeless protein produce the first cell by formation of nucleus and cell membrane. But this first cell also provided the foundation for the morphological development of the whole organic world; the first to develop, as it is permissible to assume from the whole analogy of the palaeontological record, were innumerable species of non-cellular and cellular Protista, of which *Eozoon canadense*[61] alone has come down to us, and of which some were gradually differentiated into the first plants and others into the first animals. And from the first animals were developed, essentially by further differentiation, the numerous classes, orders, families, genera, and species of animals; and finally mammals, the form in which the nervous system attains its fullest development; and among these again finally that mammal in which nature attains consciousness of itself—man.

Man, too, arises by differentiation. Not only individually—by development from a single egg-cell to the most complicated organism that nature produces—but also historically. When after thousands of years of struggle the differentiation of hand from foot, and erect gait, were finally established, man became distinct from the ape and the basis was laid for the development of articulate speech and the mighty development of the brain that has since made the gulf between man and the ape an unbridgeable one. The specialization of the hand—this implies the *tool*, and the tool implies specific human activity, the transforming reaction of man on nature, production. Animals in the narrower sense also have tools, but only as limbs of their bodies: the ant, the bee, the beaver; animals also produce, but their productive effect on surrounding nature in relation to the latter amounts to nothing at all. Man alone has succeeded in impressing his stamp on nature, not only by shifting plant and animal species from one place to another, but also by so altering the aspect and climate of his dwelling-place, and even the plants and animals themselves, that the consequences of his activity can disappear only with the general extinction of the terrestrial globe. And he has accomplished this primarily and essentially by means of *the hand.* Even the steam-engine, so far his most powerful tool for the transformation of nature, depends, because it is a tool, in the last resort on the hand. But step by step with the development of the hand went that of the brain; first of all came consciousness of the conditions for separate practically useful actions, and later among the more favoured peoples and arising from that consciousness, insight into the natural laws governing them. And with the rapidly growing knowledge of the laws of nature the means for reacting on nature also grew; the hand alone would never have achieved the steam-engine if, along with and parallel to the hand, and partly owing to it, the brain of man had not correspondingly developed.

With man we enter *history.* Animals also have a history, that of their descent and gradual evolution to their present position. This history, however, is made for them, and in so far as they themselves take part in it, this occurs without their knowledge and desire. On the other hand, the more human beings become removed from animals in the narrower sense of the word, the more they make their history themselves, consciously, the less becomes the influence of unforeseen effects and uncontrolled forces on this history, and the more accurately does the historical result correspond to the aim laid down in advance. If, however, we apply this measure to human history, to that of even the most developed peoples of the present day, we find that there still exists here a colossal disproportion between the proposed aims and the results arrived at, that unforeseen effects predominate, and that the uncontrolled forces are far more powerful than those set into motion according to plan. And this cannot be otherwise as long as the most essential historical activity of men, the one which has raised them from the animal to the human state and which forms the material foundation of all their other activities, namely the production of their requirements of life, i. e., in our day social production, is above all subject to the interplay of unintended effects from uncontrolled forces and achieves its desired end only by way of exception, but much more frequently the exact opposite. In the most advanced industrial countries we have subdued the forces of nature and pressed them into the service of mankind; we have thereby infinitely multiplied production, so that a child now produces more than a hundred adults previously did. And what is the result? Increasing overwork and increasing misery of the masses, and every ten years a great collapse. Darwin did not know what a bitter satire he wrote on mankind, and especially on his countrymen, when he showed that free competition, the struggle for existence, which the economists celebrate as the highest historical achievement, is the normal state of the *animal kingdom.* Only conscious organization of social production, in which production and distribution are carried on in a planned way, can lift mankind above the rest of the animal world as regards the social aspect, in the same way that production in general has done this for mankind in the specifically biological aspect. Historical evolution makes such an organization daily more indispensable, but also with every day more possible. From it will date a new epoch of history, in which mankind itself, and with mankind all branches of its activity, and particularly natural science, will experience an advance that will put everything preceding it in the deepest shade.

Nevertheless, "all that comes into being deserves to perish."[62] Millions of years may elapse, hundreds of thousands of generations be born and die, but inexorably the time will come when the declining warmth of the sun will no longer suffice to melt the ice thrusting forward from the poles; when the human race, crowding more and more about the equator, will finally no longer find even there enough heat for life; when gradually even the last trace of organic life will vanish; and the earth, an extinct frozen globe like the moon, will circle in deepest darkness and in an ever narrower orbit about the equally extinct sun, and at last fall into it. Other planets will have preceded it, others will follow it; instead of the bright, warm solar system with its harmonious arrangement of members, only a cold, dead sphere will still pursue its lonely path through universal space. And what will happen to our solar system will happen sooner or later to all the other systems of our island universe; it will happen to all the other innumerable island universes, even to those the light of which will never reach the earth while there is a living human eye to receive it.

And when such a solar system has completed its life history and succumbs to the fate of all that is finite, death, what then? Will the sun's corpse roll on for all eternity through infinite space, and all the once infinitely diversely differentiated natural forces pass for ever into one single form of motion, attraction? "Or"—as Secchi asks (p. 810) —"are there forces in nature which can reconvert the dead system into its original state of glowing nebula and re-awaken it to new life? We do not know."[63]

Of course, we do not know it in the sense that we know that 2×2=4, or that the attraction of matter increases and decreases according to the square of the distance. In theoretical natural science, however, which as far as possible builds up its outlook on nature into a harmonious whole, and without which nowadays even the most unthinking empiricist cannot get anywhere, we have very often to calculate with incompletely known magnitudes, and consistency of thought must at all times help to get over defective knowledge. Modern natural science has had to take over from philosophy the principle of the indestructibility of motion; it cannot any longer exist without this principle. But the motion of matter is not merely crude mechanical motion, mere change of place, it is heat and light, electric and magnetic tension, chemical combination and dissociation, life and, finally, consciousness. To say that matter during the whole unlimited time of its existence has only once, and for what is an infinitesimal period in comparison to its eternity, found itself able to differentiate its motion and thereby to unfold the whole wealth of this motion, and that before and after this it remains restricted for eternity to mere change of place—this is equivalent to maintaining that matter is mortal and motion transient. The indestructibility of motion cannot be conceived merely quantitatively, it must also be conceived qualitatively; matter whose purely mechanical change of place includes indeed the possibility under favourable conditions of being transformed into heat, electricity, chemical action, life, but which is not capable of producing these conditions from out of itself, such matter *has forfeited motion*; motion which has lost the capacity of being transformed into the various forms appropriate to it may indeed still have *dynamis** but no longer *energeia***, and so has become partially destroyed. Both, however, are unthinkable.

This much is certain: there was a time when the matter of our island universe had transformed into heat such an

---

* Power.—*Ed.*

** Activity.—*Ed.*

amount of motion—of what kind we do not yet know—that there could be developed from it the solar systems appertaining (according to Mädler) to at least twenty million stars, the gradual extinction of which is likewise certain. How did this transformation take place? We know that just as little as Father Secchi knows whether the future *caput mortuum* of our solar system will once again be converted into the raw material of new solar systems. But here either we must have recourse to a creator, or we are forced to the conclusion that the incandescent raw material for the solar systems of our universe was produced in a natural way by transformations of motion which are *by nature inherent* in moving matter and the conditions for which, therefore, must also be reproduced by matter, even if only after millions and millions of years and more or less by chance, but with the necessity that is also inherent in chance.

The possibility of such a transformation is more and more being conceded. The view is being arrived at that the heavenly bodies are ultimately destined to fall into one another and calculations are even made of the amount of heat which must be developed on such collisions. The sudden flaring up of new stars, and the equally sudden increase in brightness of familiar ones, of which we are informed by astronomy, is most easily explained by such collisions. Moreover, not only does our group of planets move around the sun, and our sun within our island universe, but our whole island universe also moves in space in temporary relative equilibrium with the other island universes, for even the relative equilibrium of freely floating bodies can only exist where the motion is reciprocally determined; and it is assumed by many that the temperature in space is not everywhere the same. Finally, we know that, with the exception of an infinitesimal portion, the heat of the innumerable suns of our island universe vanishes into space and fails to raise the temperature of space even by a millionth of a degree Centigrade. What becomes of all this enormous quantity of heat? Is it for ever dissipated in the attempt to heat universal space, has it ceased to exist practically, and does it only continue to exist theoretically, in the fact that universal space has become warmer by a decimal fraction of a degree beginning with ten or more noughts? Such an assumption denies the indestructibility of motion; it concedes the possibility that by the successive falling into one another of the heavenly bodies all existing mechanical motion will be converted into heat and the latter radiated into space, so that in spite of all "indestructibility of force" all motion in general would have ceased. (Incidentally, it is seen here how inaccurate is the term "indestructibility of force" instead of "indestructibility of motion.") Hence we arrive at the conclusion that in some way, which it will later be the task of scientific research to demonstrate, it must be possible for the heat radiated into space to be transformed into another form of motion, in which it can once more be stored up and become active. Thereby the chief difficulty in the way of the reconversion of extinct suns into incandescent vapour disappears.

For the rest, the eternally repeated succession of worlds in infinite time is only the logical complement to the co-existence of innumerable worlds in infinite space—a principle the necessity of which has forced itself even on the antitheoretical Yankee brain of Draper.*

It is an eternal cycle that matter moves in, a cycle that certainly only completes its orbit in periods of time for which our terrestrial year is no adequate measure, a cycle in which the time of highest development, the time of or-

* "The multiplicity of worlds in infinite space leads to the conception of a succession of worlds in infinite time." (J. W. Draper, *History of the Intellectual Development of Europe*, Vol. 2, London, 1864, p. 325.) [*Note by Engels.*]

ganic life and still more that of the life of beings conscious of nature and of themselves, is just as narrowly restricted as the space in which life and self-consciousness come into operation; a cycle in which every finite mode of existence of matter, whether it be sun or nebular vapour, single animal or genus of animals, chemical combination or dissociation, is equally transient, and wherein nothing is eternal but eternally changing, eternally moving matter and the laws according to which it moves and changes. But however often, and however relentlessly, this cycle is completed in time and space; however many millions of suns and earths may arise and pass away, however long it may last before, in one solar system and only on *one* planet, the conditions for organic life develop; however innumerable the organic beings, too, that have to arise and to pass away before animals with a brain capable of thought are developed from their midst, and for a short span of time find conditions suitable for life, only to be exterminated later without mercy—we have the certainty that matter remains eternally the same in all its transformations, that none of its attributes can ever be lost, and therefore, also, that with the same iron necessity that it will exterminate on the earth its highest creation, the thinking mind, it must somewhere else and at another time again produce it.

NATURAL SCIENCE IN THE SPIRIT WORLD

The dialectics that has found its way into popular consciousness is expressed in the old saying that extremes meet. In accordance with this we should hardly err in looking for the extreme degree of fantasy, credulity, and superstition, not in that trend of natural science which, like the German philosophy of nature, tries to force the objective world into the framework of its subjective thought but rather in the opposite trend, which, exalting mere experience, treats thought with sovereign disdain and really has gone to the furthest extreme in emptiness of thought. This school prevails in England. Its father, the much lauded Francis Bacon, already advanced the demand that his new empirical, inductive method should be pursued to attain, above all, by its means: longer life, rejuvenation—to a certain extent, alteration of stature and features, transformation of one body into another, the production of new species, power over the air and the production of storms. He complains that such investigations have been abandoned, and in his natural history he gives definite recipes for making gold and performing various miracles. Similarly Isaac Newton in his old age greatly busied himself with expounding the Revelation of St. John. So it is not to be wondered at if in recent years English empiricism in the person of some of its representatives—and not the worst of them—should seem to have fallen a hopeless victim to the spirit-rapping and spirit-seeing imported from America.

The first natural scientist belonging here is the very eminent zoologist and botanist, Alfred Russel Wallace, the man who simultaneously with Darwin put forward the theory of the alteration of species by natural selection. In his little work, *On Miracles and Modern Spiritualism*, London, Burns, 1875, he relates that his first experiences in this branch of natural knowledge date from 1844, when he attended the lectures of Mr. Spencer Hall on mesmerism and as a result carried out similar experiments on his pupils. "I was intensely interested in the subject and pursued it with ardour." (P. 119.) He not only produced magnetic sleep together with the phenomena of articular rigidity and local loss of sensation, he also confirmed the correctness of Gall's map of the skull, because on touching any one of Gall's organs the corresponding activity was aroused in the magnetized patient and exhibited by appropriate and lively gestures. Further, he established that his patient, merely by being touched, partook of all the sensations of the operator; he made him drunk with a glass of water as soon as he told him that it was brandy. He could make one of the young men so stupid, even in the waking condition, that he no longer knew his own name, a feat, however, that other schoolmasters are capable of accomplishing without any mesmerism. And so on.

Now it happens that I also saw this Mr. Spencer Hall in the winter of 1843-44 in Manchester. He was a very mediocre charlatan, who travelled the country under the patronage of some parsons and undertook magnetico-phrenological performances with a young woman in order to prove thereby the existence of God, the immortality of the soul, and the incorrectness of the materialism that was being preached at that time by the Owenites in all big towns. The lady was sent into a magnetic sleep and then, as soon as the operator touched any part of the skull corresponding to one of Gall's organs, she gave a bountiful display of theatrical, demonstrative gestures and poses representing the activity of the organ concerned; for instance, for the organ of philoprogenitiveness she fondled and kissed an imaginary baby, etc. Moreover, the good Mr. Hall had enriched Gall's geography of the skull with a new island of Barataria[64]: right at the top of the skull he had discovered an organ of veneration, on touching which his hypnotic miss sank on to her knees, folded her hands in prayer, and depicted to the astonished philistine audience an angel wrapt in veneration. That was the climax and conclusion of the exhibition. The existence of God had been proved.

The effect on me and one of my acquaintances was similar to that on Mr. Wallace; the phenomena interested us and we tried to find out how far we could reproduce them. A wide-awake young boy of 12 years offered himself as subject. Gently gazing into his eyes, or stroking, sent him without difficulty into the hypnotic condition. But since we were rather less credulous than Mr. Wallace and set to work with rather less fervour, we arrived at quite different results. Apart from muscular rigidity and loss of sensation, which were easy to produce, we found also a state of complete passivity of the will bound up with a peculiar hypersensitivity of sensation. The patient, when aroused from his lethargy by any external stimulus, exhibited very much greater liveliness than in the waking condition. There was no trace of any mysterious relation to the operator: anyone else could just as easily set the sleeper into activity. To put Gall's cranial organs into operation was a mere trifle for us; we went much further, we could not only exchange them for one another, or make their seat anywhere in the whole body, but we also fabricated any amount of other organs, organs of singing, whistling, piping, dancing, boxing, sewing, cobbling, tobacco-smoking, etc., and we could make their seat wherever we wanted. Wallace made his patients drunk on water, but we discovered in the great toe an organ of drunkenness which only had to be touched in order to cause the finest drunken comedy to be enacted. But it must be well understood, no organ showed a trace of action until the patient was given to understand what was expected of him; the boy soon perfected himself by practice to such an extent that the merest indication sufficed. The organs produced in this way then retained their validity for later occasions of putting to sleep, as long as they were not altered in the same way. The patient had indeed a double memory, one for the waking state and a second quite separate one for the hypnotic condition. As regards the passivity of the will and its absolute subjection to the will of a third person, this loses all its miraculous appearance when we bear in mind that the whole condition began with the subjection of the will of the patient to that of the operator, and cannot be produced without it. The most powerful magician of a magnetizer in the world will come to the end of his resources as soon as his patient laughs him in the face.

While we with our frivolous scepticism thus found that the basis of magnetico-phrenological charlatanry lay in a series of phenomena which for the most part differ only in degree from those of the waking state and require no mystical interpretation, Mr. Wallace's "ardour" led him into a series of self-deceptions, in virtue of which he confirmed Gall's map of the skull in all its details and noted a mysterious relation between operator and patient.* Everywhere in Mr. Wallace's account, the sincerity of which reaches the degree of *naïveté*, it becomes apparent that he was much less concerned in investigating the factual background of charlatanry than in reproducing all the phenomena at any cost. Only this frame of mind is needed for one who was originally a scientist to be quickly converted

* As already said, the patients perfect themselves by practice. It is therefore quite possible that when the subjection of the will has become habitual the relation between the participants becomes more intimate, individual phenomena are intensified and are reflected weakly even in the waking state. [*Note by Engels.*]

into an adept by means of simple and facile self-deception. Mr. Wallace ended up with faith in magnetico-phrenological miracles and so already stood with one foot in the world of spirits.

He drew the other foot after him in 1865. On returning from his twelve years of travel in the tropics, experiments in table-turning introduced him to the society of various "mediums." How rapid his progress was, and how complete his mastery of the subject, is testified to by the above-mentioned booklet. He expects us to take for good coin not only all the alleged miracles of Home, the brothers Davenport, and other "mediums" who all more or less exhibit themselves for money and have for the most part been frequently exposed as impostors, but also a whole series of allegedly authentic spirit histories from early times. The pythonesses of the Greek oracle, the witches of the Middle Ages, were all "mediums," and Iamblichus in his *De divinatione* already described quite accurately "the most startling phenomena of modern spiritualism." (P. 229.)

Just one example to show how lightly Mr. Wallace deals with the scientific establishment and authentication of these miracles. It is certainly a strong assumption that we should believe that the above-mentioned spirits would allow themselves to be photographed, and we have surely the right to demand that such spirit photographs should be authenticated in the most indubitable manner before we accept them as genuine. Now Mr. Wallace recounts on p. 187 that in March, 1872, a leading medium, Mrs. Guppy, *née* Nicholls, had herself photographed together with her husband and small boy at Mr. Hudson's in Notting Hill, and on two different photographs a tall female figure, finely draped in white gauzy robes, with somewhat Eastern features, was to be seen behind her in a pose as if giving a benediction.

"Here, then, one of two things *are* absolutely certain.* Either there was a living, intelligent, but invisible being present, or Mr. and Mrs. Guppy, the photographer, and some fourth person planned a wicked imposture, and have maintained it ever since. Knowing Mr. and Mrs. Guppy as well as I do, I feel an *absolute conviction* that they are as incapable of an imposture of this kind as any earnest inquirer after truth in the department of natural science." (P. 188.)

Consequently, either deception or spirit photography. Quite so. And, if deception, either the spirit was already on the photographic plates, or four persons must have been concerned, or three if we leave out as weak-minded or duped old Mr. Guppy, who died in January, 1875, at the age of 84 (it only needed that he should be sent behind the Spanish screen of the background). That a photographer could obtain a "model" for the spirit without difficulty does not need to be argued. But shortly afterwards the photographer Hudson was publicly prosecuted for habitual falsification of spirit photographs, so Mr. Wallace remarks in mitigation: "One thing is clear; that if there has been imposture, it was at once detected by spiritualists themselves." (P. 189).

Hence there is not much reliance to be placed on the photographer. Remains Mrs. Guppy, and for her there is only the "absolute conviction" of our friend Wallace and nothing more.—Nothing more? Not at all. The absolute trustworthiness of Mrs. Guppy is evidenced by her assertion that one evening, early in June, 1871, she was carried through the air in a state of unconsciousness from her house in Highbury Hill Park to 69, Lamb's Conduit Street—three English miles as the crow flies—and deposited in the

* The spirit world is superior to grammar. A joker once caused the spirit of the grammarian Lindley Murray to testify. To the question whether he was there, he answered: "I are." The medium was from America. [*Note by Engels.*]

said house of No. 69 on the table in the midst of a spiritualistic *séance*. The doors of the room were closed, and although Mrs. Guppy was one of the stoutest women in London, which is certainly saying a good deal, nevertheless her sudden incursion did not leave behind the slightest hole either in the doors or in the ceiling. (Reported in the London *Echo*, June 8, 1871.) And if anyone still does not believe in the genuineness of spirit photography, there's no helping him.

The second eminent adept among English natural scientists is Mr. William Crookes, the discoverer of the chemical element thalium and of the radiometer[65] (in Germany also called *Lichtmühle*). Mr. Crookes began to investigate spiritualistic manifestations about 1871, and employed for this purpose a number of physical and mechanical appliances, spring balances, electric batteries, etc. Whether he brought to his task the main apparatus required, a sceptically critical mind, or whether he kept it to the end in a fit state for working, we shall see. At any rate, within a not very long period, Mr. Crookes was just as completely captivated as Mr. Wallace.

"For some years," he relates, "a young lady, Miss Florence Cook, has exhibited remarkable mediumship, which latterly culminated in the production of an entire female form purporting to be of spiritual origin, and which appeared barefooted and in white flowing robes while she lay entranced, in dark clothing and securely bound in a cabinet or adjoining room."

This spirit, which called itself Katie, and which looked remarkably like Miss Cook, was one evening suddenly seized round the waist by Mr. Volckman—the present husband of Mrs. Guppy—and held fast in order to see whether it was not indeed Miss Cook in another edition. The spirit proved to be a quite sturdy damsel, it defended itself vigorously, the onlookers intervened, the gas was turned out, and when, after some scuffling, peace was re-established and the room re-lit, the spirit had vanished and Miss Cook lay bound and unconscious in her corner. Nevertheless, Mr. Volckman is said to maintain up to the present day that he had seized hold of Miss Cook and nobody else. In order to establish this scientifically, Mr. Varley, a well-known electrician, on the occasion of a new experiment, arranged for the current from a battery to flow through the medium, Miss Cook, in such a way that she could not play the part of the spirit without interrupting the current. Nevertheless, the spirit made its appearance. It was, therefore, indeed a being different from Miss Cook. To establish this further was the task of Mr. Crookes. His first step was to win the *confidence* of the spiritualistic lady. This confidence, so he says himself in the *Spiritualist*, June 5, 1874, "increased gradually to such an extent that she refused to give a *séance* unless *I made the arrangements*. She said that she always wanted *me* to be near her and in the neighbourhood of the cabinet; I found that—when this confidence had been established and she was sure that *I would not break any promise made to her*—the phenomena increased considerably in strength and there was freely forthcoming evidence that would have been unobtainable in any other way. She frequently *consulted me* in regard to the persons present at the *séances* and the places to be given them, for she had recently become very nervous as a result of certain ill-advised suggestions that, besides other more scientific methods of investigation, *force* also should be applied."

The spirit lady rewarded this confidence, which was as kind as it was scientific, in the highest measure. She even made her appearance—which can no longer surprise us—in Mr. Crookes' house, played with his children and told them "anecdotes from her adventures in India," treated Mr. Crookes to an account of "some of the bitter experiences of her past life," allowed him to take her by the arm so that he could convince himself of her evident materiality, allowed him to take her pulse and count the number of her respirations per minute, and finally allowed herself to be photographed next to Mr. Crookes. "This figure," says Mr. Wallace, "after being seen, felt, conversed with, and photographed, *absolutely disappeared* from a small room from which there was no other exit than an adjoining room filled with spectators" (p. 183)—which was not such a great feat, provided that the spectators were polite enough to show as much faith in Mr. Crookes, in whose house this happened, as Mr. Crookes did in the spirit.

Unfortunately these "fully authenticated phenomena" are not immediately credible even for spiritualists. We saw above how the very spiritualistic Mr. Volckman permitted himself to make a very material grab. And now a clergyman, a member of the committee of the "British National Association of Spiritualists," has also been present at a *séance* with Miss Cook, and he established without difficulty that the room through the door of which the spirit came and disappeared communicated with the outer world by a *second door*. The behaviour of Mr. Crookes, who was also present, gave "the final death-blow to my belief that there might be 'something' in the face manifestations." (*Mystic London*, by the Rev. C. Maurice Davies, London, Tinsley Brothers [319].) And, over and above that, it came to light in America how "Katies" were "materialized." In Philadelphia a married couple named Holmes held *séances* in which likewise a "Katie" appeared and received bountiful presents from the believers. However, one sceptic refused to rest until he got on the track of the said Katie, who, anyway, had already gone on strike once because of lack of pay; he discovered her in a boarding-house as a young lady of unquestionable flesh and bone, and in possession of all the presents that had been given to the spirit.

Meanwhile the Continent also had its scientific spirit-seers. A scientific association in St. Petersburg—I do not know exactly whether the University or even the Academy itself—charged the Councillor of State, Aksakov, and the chemist, Butlerov, to examine the basis of the spiritualistic phenomena, but it does not seem that very much came of this.[66] On the other hand—if the noisy announcements of the spiritualists are to be believed—Germany has now also put forward its man in the person of Professor Zöllner in Leipzig.

For years, as is well known, Herr Zöllner has been hard at work on the "fourth dimension" of space, and has discovered that many things that are impossible in a space of three dimensions are a simple matter in a space of four dimensions. Thus, in the latter kind of space, a closed metal sphere can be turned inside out like a glove without making a hole in it; similarly a knot can be tied in an endless string or one which has both ends fastened, and two separate closed rings can be interlinked without opening either of them, and many more such feats. Now, according to recent triumphant reports from the spirit world, Professor Zöllner has addressed himself to one or more mediums in order with their aid to determine more details of the locality of the fourth dimension. The success is said to have been surprising. After the session the arm of the chair on which he rested his arm while his hand never left the table was found to have become interlocked with his arm, a string that had both ends sealed to the table was found tied into four knots, and so on. In short, all the miracles of the fourth dimension are said to have been performed by the spirits with the utmost ease. It must be borne in mind: *relata refero*, I do not vouch for the correctness of the spirit bulletin, and if it should contain any inaccuracy, Herr Zöllner ought to be thankful that I am giving him the opportunity to make a correction. If, however, it reproduces the experiences of Herr Zöllner without falsification, then it obviously signifies a new era both in the science of spiritualism and that of mathematics. The spirits prove the existence of the fourth dimension, just as the fourth dimension vouches for the existence of spirits. And this once established, an entirely new, immeasurable field is opened to science. All previous mathematics and natural science will be only a preparatory school for the mathematics of the fourth and still higher dimensions, and for the mechanics, physics, chemistry, and physiology of the spirits dwelling in these higher dimensions. Has not Mr. Crookes scientifically determined how much weight is lost by tables and other articles of furniture on their passage into the fourth dimension—as we may now well be permitted to call it—and does not Mr. Wallace declare it proven that fire there does no harm to the human body? And now we have even the physiology of the spirit bodies! They breathe, they have a pulse, therefore lungs, heart and a circulatory apparatus, and in consequence are at least as admirably equipped as our own in regard to the other bodily organs. For breathing requires carbohydrates which undergo combustion in the lungs, and these carbohydrates can only be supplied from without; hence, stomach, intestines, and their accessories—and if we have once established so much, the rest follows without difficulty. The existence of such organs, however, implies the possibility of their falling a prey to disease, hence it may still come to pass that Herr Virchow will have to compile a cellular pathology of the spirit world. And since most of these spirits are very handsome young ladies, who are not to be distinguished in any respect whatsoever from terrestrial damsels, other than by their supramundane beauty, it could not be very long before they come into contact with "men who feel the passion of love"[67]; and since, as established by Mr. Crookes from the beat of the pulse, "the female heart is not absent," natural selection also has opened before it the prospect of a fourth dimension, one in which it has no longer any need to fear being confused with wicked Social-Democracy.[68]

* * *

Enough. Here it becomes palpably evident which is the surest path from natural science to mysticism. It is not the extravagant theorizing of the philosophy of nature, but the shallowest empiricism that spurns all theory and distrusts all thought. It is not *a priori* necessity that proves the existence of spirits, but the empirical observations of Messrs. Wallace, Crookes, and Co. If we trust the spectrum-analysis observations of Crookes, which led to the discovery of the metal thallium, or the rich zoological discoveries of Wallace in the Malay Archipelago, we are asked to place the same trust in the spiritualistic experiences and discoveries of these two scientists. And if we express the opinion that, after all, there is a little difference between the two, namely, that we can verify the one but not the other, then the spirit-seers retort that this is not the case, and that they are ready to give us the opportunity of verifying also the spirit phenomena.

Indeed, dialectics cannot be despised with impunity. However great one's contempt for all theoretical thought, nevertheless one cannot bring two natural facts into relation with each other, or understand the connection existing between them, without theoretical thought. The only question is whether one's thinking is correct or not, and contempt of theory is evidently the surest way to think naturalistically, and therefore incorrectly. But, according to an old and well-known dialectical law, incorrect thinking, carried to its logical conclusion, inevitably arrives at the opposite of its point of departure. Hence, the empirical contempt for dialectics is punished by some of the most sober empiricists being led into the most barren of all superstitions, into modern spiritualism.

It is the same with mathematics. The ordinary, metaphysical mathematicians boast with enormous pride of the absolute irrefutability of the results of their science. But these results include also imaginary magnitudes, which thereby acquire a certain reality. When one has once become accustomed to ascribe some kind of reality outside of our minds to $\sqrt{-1}$, or to the fourth dimension, then it is not a matter of much importance if one goes a step further and also accepts the spirit world of the mediums. It is as Ketteler said about Döllinger:

"The man has defended so much nonsense in his life, he really could have accepted infallibility into the bargain!"[69]

In fact, mere empiricism is incapable of refuting the spiritualists. In the first place, the "higher" phenomena always show themselves only when the "investigator" concerned is already so far in the toils that he now only sees what he is meant to see or wants to see—as Crookes himself describes with such inimitable *naïveté*. In the second place, the spiritualists care nothing that hundreds of alleged facts are exposed as imposture and dozens of alleged mediums as ordinary tricksters. As long as *every* single alleged miracle has not been explained away, they have still room enough to carry on, as indeed Wallace says clearly enough in connection with the falsified spirit photographs. The existence of falsifications proves the genuineness of the genuine ones.

And so empiricism finds itself compelled to refute the importunate spirit-seers not by means of empirical experiments, but by theoretical considerations, and to say, with Huxley:

"The only good that I can see in the demonstration of the truth of 'spiritualism' is to furnish an additional argument against suicide. Better live a crossing-sweeper than die and be made to talk twaddle by a 'medium' hired at a guinea a *séance*!"[70]

THE PART PLAYED BY LABOUR IN THE TRANSITION FROM APE TO MAN

(Extract)

. . .And, in fact, with every day that passes we are learning to understand these laws more correctly, and getting to know both the more immediate and the more remote consequences of our interference with the traditional course of nature. In particular, after the mighty advances of natural science in the present century, we are more and more placed in a position where we can get to know, and hence to control, even the more remote natural consequences at least of our most ordinary productive activities. But the more this happens, the more will men once more not only feel, but also know, themselves to be one with nature, and thus the more impossible will be the senseless and antinatural idea of a contradiction between mind and matter, man and nature, soul and body, such as arose in Europe after the decline of classic antiquity and which obtained its highest elaboration in Christianity. . . .

NOTES AND FRAGMENTS[71]

HISTORICAL

Modern natural science—the only one which can come into consideration *qua* science as against the brilliant intuitions of the Greeks and the sporadic unconnected investigations of the Arabs—begins with that mighty epoch when feudalism was smashed by the burghers. In the background of the struggle between the burghers of the towns and the feudal nobility this epoch showed the peasant in revolt, and behind the peasant the revolutionary beginnings of the modern proletariat, already red flag in hand and with communism on its lips. It was the epoch which brought into being the great monarchies in Europe, broke the spiritual dictatorship of the Pope, evoked the revival of Greek antiquity and with it the highest artistic development of the new age, broke through the boundaries of the old world, and for the first time really discovered the world.

It was the greatest revolution that the world had so far experienced. Natural science also flourished in this revolution, was revolutionary through and through, advanced hand in hand with the awakening modern philosophy of the great Italians, and provided its martyrs for the stake and the prisons. It is characteristic that Protestants and Catholics vied with one another in persecuting it. The former burned Servetus, the latter Giordano Bruno. It was a time that called for giants and produced giants, giants in learning, intellect, and character, a time that the French correctly called the Renaissance and Protestant Europe with one-sided prejudice called the Reformation.

At that time natural science also had its declaration of independence, though it is true it did not come right at the beginning, any more than that Luther was the first Protestant. What Luther's burning of the Papal Bull was in the religious field, in the field of natural science was the great work of Copernicus,[72] in which he, although timidly, after thirty-six years' hesitation and so to say on his death-bed, threw down a challenge to ecclesiastical superstition. From then on natural science was in essence emancipated from religion, although the complete settlement of accounts in all details has gone on to the present day and in many minds is still far from being complete. But from then on the development of science went forward with giant strides, increasing, so to speak, proportionately to the square of the distance in time from its point of departure, as if it wanted to show the world that for the motion of the highest product of organic matter, the human mind, the law that holds good is the reverse of that for the motion of inorganic matter.

The first period of modern natural science ends—in the inorganic sphere—with Newton. It is the period in which the available subject-matter was mastered; it performed a great work in the fields of mathematics, mechanics and astronomy, statics and dynamics, especially owing to Kepler and Galileo, from whose work Newton drew the conclusions. In the organic sphere, however, there was no progress beyond the first beginnings. The investigation of the forms of life historically succeeding one another and replacing one another, as well as the changing conditions of life corresponding to them—palaeontology and geology—did not yet exist. Nature was not at all regarded as something that developed historically, that had a history in time; only extension in space was taken into account; the various forms were grouped not one after the other, but only one beside the other; natural history was valid for all periods, like the elliptical orbits of the planets. For any closer analysis of organic structure both the immediate bases were lacking, viz., chemistry and knowledge of the essential organic structure, the cell. Natural science, at the outset revolutionary, was confronted by an out-and-out conservative nature, in which everything remained today as it was at the beginning of the world, and in which right to the end of the world everything would remain as it had been in the beginning.

It is characteristic that this conservative outlook on nature both in the inorganic and in the organic sphere [. . .]*

Astronomy	Physics	Geology
Mechanics	Chemistry	Palaeontology
Mathematics		Mineralogy
Plant physiology		Therapeutics
Animal physiology		Diagnostics
Anatomy		

The first breach: Kant and Laplace. The second: geology and palaeontology (Lyell, slow development). The third: organic chemistry, which prepares organic bodies and shows the validity of chemical laws for living bodies. The fourth: 1842, mechanical [theory of] heat, Grove. The fifth: Darwin, Lamarck, the cell, etc. (struggle, Cuvier and Agassiz). The sixth: the *comparative element* in anatomy, climatology (isotherms), animal and plant geography (scientific travel expeditions since the middle of the eighteenth century), physical geography in general (Humboldt), the assembling of the material in its interconnection. Morphology (embryology, Baer).

The old teleology has gone to the devil, but it is now firmly established that matter in its eternal cycle moves according to laws which at a definite stage—now here, now there—necessarily give rise to the thinking mind in organic beings.

---

* The sentence was not completed.—*Ed.*

The normal existence of animals is given by the contemporary conditions in which they live and to which they adapt themselves—those of man, as soon as he differentiates himself from the animal in the narrower sense, have as yet never been present, and are only to be elaborated by the ensuing historical development. Man is the sole animal capable of working his way out of the merely animal state—his normal state is one appropriate to his consciousness, *one that has to be created by himself.*

* * *

. . . God is nowhere treated worse than by the natural scientists who believe in him. Materialists simply explain the *facts,* without making use of such phrases, they do this first when importunate pious believers try to force God upon them, and then they answer curtly, either like Laplace: *Sire, je n'avais pas, etc.,*[73] or more rudely in the manner of the Dutch merchants who, when German commercial travellers press their shoddy goods on them, are accustomed to turn them away with the words: *Ik kan die zaken niet gebruiken,** and that is the end of the matter. But what God has had to suffer at the hands of his defenders! In the history of modern natural science, God is treated by his defenders as Frederick-William III was treated by his generals and officials in the Jena campaign. One division of the army after another lays down its arms, one fortress after another capitulates before the march of science, until at last the whole infinite realm of nature is conquered by science, and there is no place left in it for the Creator. Newton still allowed Him the "first impulse" but forbade Him any further interference in his solar system. Father Secchi bows Him out of the solar system altogether, with all canonical honours it is true, but none

* I have no use for the things.—*Ed.*

the less categorically for all that, and he only allows Him a creative act as regards the primordial nebula. And so in all spheres. In biology, his last great Don Quixote, Agassiz, even ascribes positive nonsense to Him; He is supposed to have created not only the actual animals but also abstract animals, the fish as such! And finally Tyndall[74] totally forbids Him any entry into nature and relegates Him to the world of emotional processes, only admitting Him because, after all, there must be somebody who knows more about all these things (nature) than John Tyndall! What a distance from the old God—the Creator of heaven and earth, the maintainer of all things—without whom not a hair can fall from the head!

Tyndall's emotional need proves nothing. The Chevalier des Grieux also had an emotional need to love and possess Manon Lescaut, who sold herself and him over and over again; for her sake he became a cardsharper and pimp, and if Tyndall wants to reproach him, he would reply with his "emotional need!"

God=*nescio*; but *ignorantia non est argumentum*[75] (Spinoza).

FREDERICK ENGELS

BRUNO BAUER AND EARLY CHRISTIANITY

In Berlin on April 13 a man died who once played a role as a philosopher and a theologian but was hardly heard of for years, only attracting the attention of the public from time to time as a "literary eccentric." Official theologians, including *Renan*, wrote him off and therefore maintained a silence of death about him. And yet he was worth more than them all and did more than all of them in a question which interests us Socialists too: the question of the historical origin of Christianity.

On the occasion of his death let us give a brief account of the present position on this question and Bauer's contribution to its solution.

The view that dominated from the free-thinkers of the Middle Ages to the Enlighteners of the eighteenth century, the latter included, that all religions, and therefore Christianity too, were the work of deceivers was no longer sufficient after Hegel had set philosophy the task of showing a rational evolution in world history.

It is clear that if spontaneously arising religions, like the fetish worship of the Negroes or the common primitive religion of the Aryans, come to being without deception playing any part, deception by the priests soon becomes inevitable in their further development. But in spite of all sincere fanaticism, artificial religions cannot even at their foundation do without deception and falsification of history. Christianity, too, has pretty achievements to boast of in this respect from the very beginning, as Bauer shows in his criticism of the New Testament. But that only confirms a general phenomenon and does not explain the particular case in question.

A religion that brought the Roman world empire into subjection and dominated by far the larger part of civilized humanity for 1,800 years cannot be disposed of merely by declaring it to be nonsense gleaned together by frauds. One cannot dispose of it before one succeeds in explaining its origin and its development from the historical conditions under which it arose and reached its dominating position. This applies to Christianity. The question to be solved, then, is how it came about that the popular masses in the Roman Empire so far preferred this nonsense—which was preached, into the bargain by slaves and oppressed—to all other religions that the ambitious *Constantine* finally saw in the adoption of this religion of nonsense the best means of exalting himself to the position of autocrat of the Roman world.

Bruno Bauer has contributed far more to the solution of this question than anybody else. No matter how much the half-believing theologians of the period of reaction have struggled against him since 1849, he irrefutably proved the chronological order of the Gospels and their mutual interdependence, shown by Wilke from the purely linguistic standpoint, by the very contents of the Gospels themselves. He exposed the utter lack of scientific spirit of Strauss's vague myth theory according to which anybody can hold for historical as much as he likes in the Gospel narrations. And if almost nothing from the whole content of the Gospels turns out to be historically provable—so that even the historical existence of a Jesus Christ can be questioned—Bauer has thereby only cleared the ground for the solution of the question: what is the origin of the ideas and thoughts that have been woven together into a sort of system in Christianity, and how came they to dominate the world?

Bauer studied this question until his death. His research reached its culminating point in the conclusion that the Alexandrian Jew *Philo*, who was still living about 40 A.D. but was already very old, was the real father of Christianity, and that the Roman stoic *Seneca* was, so to speak, its uncle. The numerous writings attributed to Philo which have reached us originate indeed in a fusion of allegorically and rationalistically conceived Jewish traditions with Greek, particularly stoic, philosophy. This conciliation of western and eastern outlooks already contains all the essentially Christian ideas: the inborn sinfulness of man, the *Logos*, the Word, which is with God and is God and which becomes the mediator between God and man; atonement, not by sacrifices of animals, but by bringing one's own heart to God, and finally the essential feature that the new religious philosophy reverses the previous world order, seeks its disciples among the poor, the miserable, the slaves and the rejected and despises the rich, the powerful and the privileged, whence the precept to despise all worldly pleasures and to mortify the flesh.

On the other hand, Augustus himself saw to it that not only the God-man, but also the so-called immaculate conception became formulae imposed by the state. He not only had Caesar and himself worshipped as gods, he also spread the notion that he, Augustus Caesar Divus, the Divine, was not the son of a human father but that his mother had conceived him of the god Apollo. But was not that Apollo perhaps a relation of the one sung by Heinrich Heine?[76]

As we see, we need only the keystone and we have the whole of Christianity in its basic features: the incarnation of the Word become man in a definite person and his sacrifice on the cross for the redemption of sinful mankind.

Truly reliable sources leave us uncertain as to when this keystone was introduced into the stoic-philonic doctrines. But this much is sure: it was not introduced by philosophers, either Philo's disciples or stoics. Religions are founded by people who feel a need for religion themselves and have a feeling for the religious needs of the masses. As a rule this is not the case with classical philosophers. On the other hand we find that in times of general decay, now, for instance, philosophy and religious dogmatism are generally current in a vulgarized and shallow form. While classic Greek philosophy in its last forms—particularly in the Epicurean school—led to atheistic materialism, Greek vulgar philosophy led to the doctrine of a one and only God and of the immortality of the human soul. Likewise rationally vulgarized Judaism in mixture and intercourse with aliens and half-Jews ended by neglecting the ritual and transforming the formerly exclusively Jewish national god, Jahveh,* into the one true God, the creator of heaven and earth and by adopting the idea of the immortality of the soul which was alien to early Judaism. Thus monotheistic vulgar philosophy came into contact with vulgar religion, which presented it with the ready-made one and only God. Thus the ground was prepared on which the elaboration among the Jews of the likewise vulgarized philonic notions could produce Christianity, which once produced would be acceptable to both Greeks and Romans.

---

* As Ewald proved, the Jews used dotted script (containing vowels and reading signs) to write under the consonants in the name of Jahveh, which it was forbidden to pronounce, the vowels of the word *Adonai*, which they read in its place. This was subsequently read as Jehovah. This word is therefore not the name of a god but only a vulgar mistake in grammar: in Hebrew it is simply impossible.

The fact that it was vulgarized philonic notions and not Philo's own works that Christianity proceeded from is proved by the New Testament's almost complete disregard of most of these works, particularly the allegorical and philosophical interpretation of the narrations of the Old Testament. This is an aspect to which Bauer did not devote enough attention.

One can get an idea of what Christianity looked like in its early form by reading the so-called Book of Revelation of John. Wild, confused fanaticism, only the beginnings of dogmas, only the mortification of the flesh of the so-called Christian morals, but on the other hand a multitude of visions and prophecies. The development of the dogmas and moral doctrine belongs to a later period, in which the Gospels and the so-called Epistles of the Apostles were written. In this—at least as regards morals—the philosophy of the stoics, of Seneca in particular, was unceremoniously made use of. Bauer proved that the Epistles often copy the latter word for word; in fact, even the faithful noticed this, but they maintained that Seneca had copied from the New Testament, though it had not yet been written in his time. Dogma developed on the one hand in connection with the legend of Jesus which was then taking shape and on the other hand in the struggle between Christians of Jewish and of pagan origin.

Bauer also gives very valuable data on the causes which helped Christianity to triumph and attain world domination. But here the German philosopher is prevented by his idealism from seeing clearly and formulating precisely. Phrases often replace substance in decisive points. Instead, therefore, of going into details of Bauer's views we shall give our own conception of this point, based on Bauer's works and also on our personal study.

The Roman conquest dissolved in all subjugated countries first directly the former political conditions and then indirectly also the social conditions of life. Firstly by substituting for the former organization according to estates (slavery apart) the simple distinction between Roman citizens and peregrines or subjects. Secondly, and mainly, by exacting tribute in the name of the Roman state. If under the empire a limit was set as far as possible in the interest of the state to the governors' thirst for wealth, that thirst was replaced by ever more effective and oppressive taxation for the benefit of the state treasury, the effect of which was terribly destructive. Thirdly, Roman law was finally administered everywhere by Roman judges while the native social system was declared invalid in so far as it was incompatible with the provisions of Roman law. These three levers necessarily developed a tremendous levelling power, particularly when they were applied for several hundred years to populations the most vigorous sections of which had been either suppressed or taken away into slavery in the battles preceding, accompanying and also often following the conquest. Social relations in the provinces came nearer and nearer to those obtaining in the capital and in Italy. The population became more and more sharply divided into three classes, thrown together out of the most varying elements and nationalities: rich people, including not a few emancipated slaves (cf. Petronius), big landowners or usurers or both at once, like Seneca, the uncle of Christianity; propertyless free people, who in Rome were fed and amused by the state—in the provinces they got on as they could by themselves—and finally the great mass, the slaves. In face of the state, i.e., the emperor, the first two classes had as few rights as the slaves in face of their masters. From the time of Tiberius to that of Nero, in particular, it was a practice to sentence rich Roman citizens to death in order to confiscate their property. The support of the government was—*materially*, the army, which was more like an army of hired foreign soldiers than the old Roman peasant army, and *morally*, the general view that there was no way out of that condition; that not, indeed, this or that Caesar, but the empire based on military domination was an immutable necessity. This is not the place to examine what very material facts this view was based on.

The general rightlessness and despair of the possibility of a better condition gave rise to a corresponding general slackening and demoralization. The few surviving old Romans of the patrician type and views either were removed or died out; Tacitus was the last of them. The others were glad when they were able to keep away from public life; all they existed for was to collect and enjoy riches, and to indulge in private gossip and private intrigue. The propertyless free citizens were state pensioners in Rome, but in the provinces their condition was an unhappy one. They had to work, and to compete with slave-labour into the bargain. But they were confined to the towns. Besides them there were also in the provinces peasants, free landowners (here and there probably still common ownership) or, as in Gaul, bondsmen for debts to the big landowners. This class was the least affected by the social upheaval; it was also the one to resist longest the religious upheaval.* Finally, there were the slaves, deprived of rights and of their own will and the possibility to free themselves, as the defeat of Spartacus had already proved; most of them, however, were former free citizens or sons of free-born citizens. It must therefore have been among them that hatred of their condition of life was still generally vigorous, though externally powerless.

We shall find that the type of ideologists at the time corresponded to this state of affairs. The philosophers were

---

* According to Fallmereyer the peasants in Main, Peloponnesus, still offered sacrifices to Zeus in the ninth century.

either mere money-earning schoolmasters or buffoons in the pay of wealthy revellers. Some were even slaves. An example of what became of them under good conditions is supplied by Seneca. This stoic and preacher of virtue and abstinence was Nero's first court intriguer, which he could not have been without servility; he secured from him presents in money, properties, gardens and palaces and while he preached the poor man Lazarus of the Gospel he was in reality the rich man in the same parable. Not until Nero wanted to get at him did he request the emperor to take back all his presents, his philosophy being enough for him. Only completely isolated philosophers like Persius had the courage to brandish the lash of satire over their degenerated contemporaries. But as for the second type of ideologists, the jurists, they were enthusiastic over the new conditions because the abolition of all differences between Estates allowed them broad scope in the elaboration of their favourite private right, in return for which they prepared for the emperor the vilest state system of right that ever existed.

With the political and social peculiarities of the various peoples the Roman Empire also doomed to ruin their particular religions. All religions of antiquity were spontaneous tribal and later national religions which arose from and merged with the social and political conditions of the respective peoples. Once these, their bases, were disrupted and their traditional forms of society, their inherited political institutions and their national independence shattered, the religion corresponding to these also naturally collapsed. The national gods could suffer other gods beside them, as was the general rule in antiquity, but not above them. The transplanting of Oriental divinities to Rome was harmful only to the Roman religion, it could not check the decay of the Oriental religions. As soon as the national gods were unable to protect the independence of their nation they met their own destruction. This was the case everywhere (except with peasants, especially in the mountains). What vulgar philosophical enlightenment —I almost said Voltairianism—did in Rome and Greece, was done in the provinces by Roman oppression and the replacing of men proud of their freedom by desperate subjects and self-seeking ragamuffins.

Such was the material and moral situation. The present was unbearable, the future still more menacing, if possible. There was no way out. Only despair or refuge in the commonest sensuous pleasure, for *those* who could afford it at least, and they were a tiny minority. Otherwise, nothing but surrender to the inevitable.

But in all classes there was necessarily a number of people who, despairing of material salvation, sought in its stead a spiritual salvation, a consolation in their consciousness to save them from utter despair. This consolation could not be provided by the stoics any more than by the Epicurean school, for the very reason that these philosophies were not intended for common consciousness and, secondly, because the conduct of the disciples of the schools cast discredit on their doctrines. The consolation was to be a substitute, not for the lost philosophy, but for the lost religion; it had to take on a religious form, the same as anything which had to grip the masses both then and as late as the seventeenth century.

We hardly need to note that the majority of those who were pining for such consolation of their consciousness, for this flight from the external world into the internal, were necessarily among the *slaves*.

It was in the midst of this general economic, political, intellectual and moral decadence that Christianity appeared. It entered into a resolute antithesis to all previous religions.

In all previous religions ritual had been the main thing. Only by taking part in the sacrifices and processions, and in the Orient by observing the most detailed diet and cleanliness precepts, could one show to what religion one belonged. While Rome and Greece were tolerant in the last respect, there was in the Orient a rage for religious prohibitions that contributed no little to the final downfall. People of two different religions (Egyptians, Persians, Jews, Chaldeans) could not eat or drink together, perform any every-day act together, or hardly speak to each other. It was largely due to this segregation of man from man that the Orient collapsed. Christianity knew no distinctive ceremonies, not even the sacrifices and processions of the classic world. By thus rejecting all national religions and their common ceremonies and addressing itself to all peoples without distinction it becomes the *first possible world religion*. Judaism too, with its new universal god, had made a start on the way to becoming a universal religion; but the children of Israel always remained an aristocracy among the believers and the circumcised, and Christianity itself had to get rid of the notion of the superiority of the Jewish Christians (still dominant in the so-called Book of Revelation of John) before it could really become a universal religion. Islam itself, on the other hand, by preserving its specifically Oriental ritual, limited the area of its propagation to the Orient and North Africa, conquered and populated anew by Arab Bedouins; here it could become the dominating religion, but not in the West.

Secondly, Christianity struck a chord that was bound to echo in countless hearts. To all complaints about the wickedness of the times and the general material and moral distress, Christian consciousness of sin answered: It is so and it cannot be otherwise; thou art to blame, ye are all to blame for the corruption of the world, thine and your own internal corruption! And where was the man who could deny it? *Mea culpa!* The admission of each one's share in the responsibility for the general unhappiness was irrefutable and was made the precondition for the spiritual salvation which Christianity at the same time announced. And this spiritual salvation was so instituted that it could be easily understood by members of every old religious community. The idea of atonement to placate the offended deity was current in all the old religions; how could the idea of the self-sacrifice of the mediator atoning once for all for the sins of humanity not easily find ground there? Christianity, therefore, clearly expressed the universal feeling that men themselves are guilty of the general corruption as the consciousness of sin of each one; at the same time it provided, in the death-sacrifice of his judge, a form of the universally longed-for internal salvation from the corrupt world, the consolation of consciousness; it thus again proved its capacity to become a world religion and, indeed, a religion which suited the world as it then was.

So it happened that among the thousands of prophets and preachers in the desert that filled that period of countless religious novations the founders of Christianity alone met with success. Not only Palestine, but the entire Orient swarmed with such founders of religions, and between them there raged what can be called a Darwinistic struggle for ideological existence. Thanks mainly to the elements mentioned above Christianity won the day. How it gradually developed its character of world religion by natural selection in the struggle of sects against one another and against the pagan world is taught in detail by the history of the Church in the first three centuries.

FREDERICK ENGELS

THE BOOK OF REVELATION

A science almost unknown in this country, except to a few liberalizing theologians who contrive to keep it as secret as they can, is the historical and linguistic criticism of the Bible, the inquiry into the age, origin, and historical value of the various writings comprising the Old and New Testament.

This science is almost exclusively German. And, moreover, what little of it has penetrated beyond the limits of Germany is not exactly the best part of it: it is that latitudinarian criticism which prides itself upon being unprejudiced and thoroughgoing, and, at the same time, Christian. The books are not exactly revealed by the holy ghost, but they are revelations of divinity through the sacred spirit of humanity, etc. Thus, the Tübingen school[77] (Baur, Gfrörer, etc.) are the great favourites in Holland and Switzerland, as well as in England, and, if people will go a little further, they follow Strauss. The same mild, but utterly unhistorical, spirit dominates the renowned Ernest Renan, who is but a poor plagiarist of the German critics. Of all his works nothing belongs to him but the aesthetic sentimentalism of the pervading thought, and the milk-and-water language which wraps it up.

One good thing, however, Ernest Renan has said:

"When you want to get a distinct idea of what the first

Christian communities were, do not compare them to the parish congregations of our day; they were rather like local sections of the International Working Men's Association."

And this is correct. Christianity got hold of the masses, exactly as modern socialism does, under the shape of a variety of sects, and still more of conflicting individual views—some clearer, some more confused, these latter the great majority—but all opposed to the ruling system, to "the powers that be."

Take, for instance, our Book of Revelation, of which we shall see that, instead of being the darkest and most mysterious, it is the simplest and clearest book of the whole New Testament. For the present we must ask the reader to believe what we are going to prove by-and-by. That it was written in the year of our era 68 or January, 69, and that it is therefore not only the only book of the New Testament, the date of which is really fixed, but also the oldest book. How Christianity looked in 68 we can here see as in a mirror.

First of all, sects over and over again. In the messages to the seven churches of Asia there are at least three sects mentioned, of which, otherwise, we know nothing at all: the Nicolaitans, the Balaamites, and the followers of a woman typified here by the name of Jezebel. Of all the three it is said that they permitted their adherents to eat of things sacrificed to idols, and that they were fond of fornication. It is a curious fact that with every great revolutionary movement the question of "free love" comes in to the foreground. With one set of people as a revolutionary progress, as a shaking off of old traditional fetters, no longer necessary; with others as a welcome doctrine, comfortably covering all sorts of free and easy practices between man and woman. The latter, the philistine sort, appear here soon to have got the upper hand; for the "fornication" is always associated with the eating of "things sacrificed to idols," which Jews and Christians were strictly forbidden to do, but which it might be dangerous, or at least unpleasant, at times to refuse. This shows evidently that the free lovers mentioned here were generally inclined to be everybody's friend, and anything but stuff for martyrs.

Christianity, like every great revolutionary movement, was made by the masses. It arose in Palestine, in a manner utterly unknown to us, at a time when new sects, new religions, new prophets arose by the hundred. It is, in fact, a mere average, formed spontaneously out of the mutual friction of the more progressive of such sects, and afterwards formed into a doctrine by the addition of theorems of the Alexandrian Jew, Philo, and later on of strong stoic infiltrations. In fact, if we may call Philo the doctrinal father of Christianity, Seneca was her uncle. Whole passages in the New Testament seem almost literally copied from his works; and you will find, on the other hand, passages in Persius' satires which seem copied from the then unwritten New Testament. Of all these doctrinal elements there is not a trace to be found in our Book of Revelation. Here we have Christianity in the crudest form in which it has been preserved to us. There is only one dominant dogmatic point: that the faithful have been saved by the sacrifice of Christ. But how, and why is completely indefinable. There is nothing but the old Jewish and heathen notion, that God, or the gods, must be propitiated by sacrifices, transformed into the specific Christian notion (which, indeed, made Christianity the universal religion) that the death of Christ is the great sacrifice which suffices once for all.

Of original sin, not a trace. Nothing of the trinity. Jesus is "the lamb," but subordinate to God. In fact, in one passage (XV, 3) he is placed upon an equal footing with Moses. Instead of one holy ghost there are "the seven spirits of god" (III, 1, and IV, 5). The murdered saints (the martyrs) cry to God for revenge: "How long, O Lord, dost thou not judge and avenge our blood on them that dwell on the earth?" (VI, 10)—a sentiment which has, later on, been carefully struck out from the theoretical code of morals of Christianity, but carried out practically with a vengeance as soon as the Christians got the upper hand over the heathens.

As a matter of course, Christianity presents itself as a mere sect of Judaism. Thus, in the messages to the seven churches: "I know the blasphemy of them which say that they are Jews (not Christians), and are not, but are the synagogue of Satan" (II, 9); and again, III, 9: "Them of the synagogue of Satan, which say they are Jews, but are not." Thus, our author, in the 69th year of our era, had not the remotest idea that he represented a new phase of religious development, destined to become one of the greatest elements of revolution. Thus also, when the saints appear before the throne of God, there are at first 144,000 Jews, 12,000 of each of the twelve tribes, and only after them are admitted the heathens who have joined this new phase of Judaism.

Such was Christianity in the year 68, as depicted in the oldest, and the only, book of the New Testament, the authenticity of which cannot be disputed. Who the author was we do not know. He calls himself John. He does not even pretend to be the "apostle" John, for in the foundations of the "new Jerusalem" are "the names of the twelve apostles of the lamb" (XXI, 14). They therefore must have been dead when he wrote. That he was a Jew is clear from the Hebraisms abounding in his Greek, which exceeds in bad grammar, by far, even the other books of the New Testament. That the so-called Gospel of John, the epistles of John, and this book have at least three different authors, their language clearly proves, if the doctrines they contain, completely clashing one with another, did not prove it.

The apocalyptic visions which make up almost the whole of the Revelation, are taken in most cases literally, from the classic prophets of the Old Testament and their later imitators, beginning with the Book of Daniel (about 190 before our era, and prophesying things which had occurred centuries before) and ending with the "Book of Henoch," an apocryphal concoction in Greek written not long before the beginning of our era. The original invention, even the grouping of the purloined visions, is extremely poor. Professor Ferdinand Benary, to whose course of lectures in Berlin University, in 1841, I am indebted for what follows, has proved, chapter and verse, whence our author borrowed every one of his pretended visions. It is therefore no use to follow our "John" through all his vagaries. We had better come at once to the point which discovers the mystery of this at all events curious book.

In complete opposition with all his orthodox commentators, who all expect that his prophecies are still to come off, after more than 1,800 years, "John" never ceases to say, "The time is at hand, all this will happen shortly." And this is especially the case with the crisis which he predicts, and which he evidently expects to see.

This crisis is the great final fight between God and the "antichrist," as others have named him. The decisive chapters are XIII and XVII. To leave out all unnecessary ornamentations, "John" sees a beast arising from the sea which has seven heads and ten horns (the horns do not concern us at all) "and I saw one of his heads, as it were, wounded as to death; and his deadly wound was healed." This beast was to have power over the earth, against God and the lamb for forty-two months (one half of the sacred seven years), and all men were compelled during that time to have the mark of the beast or the number of his name in their right hand, or in their forehead. "Here is wisdom. Let him that hath understanding *count the number of the beast; for it is the number of a man, and his number is six hundred threescore and six."*

Irenaeus, in the second century, knew still that by the head which was wounded and healed, the Emperor Nero was meant. He had been the first great persecutor of the Christians. At his death a rumour spread, especially through Achaia and Asia, that he was not dead, but only wounded, and that he would one day reappear and spread terror throughout the world (Tacitus, Ann. VI, 22). At the same time Irenaeus knew another very old reading, which made the number of the name 616, instead of 666.

In chapter XII, the beast with the seven heads appears again, this time mounted by the well-known scarlet lady, the elegant description of whom the reader may look out in the book itself. Here an angel explains to John:

"The beast that thou sawest was, and is not. . . . The seven heads are seven mountains on which the woman sitteth; and there are seven kings;*five are fallen, and one is, and the other is not yet come,* and when he cometh, he must continue a short space. And the beast that was, and is not, *even he is the eighth, and is of the seven.* . . . And the woman which thou sawest is the great city which reigneth over the kings of the earth."

Here, then, we have two clear statements: (1) The scarlet lady is Rome, the great city which reigneth over the kings of the earth; (2) at the time the book is written the sixth Roman emperor reigns; after him another will come to reign for a short time; and then comes the return of one who "is of the seven," who was wounded but healed, and whose name is contained in that mysterious number, and whom Irenaeus still knew to be Nero.

Counting from Augustus, we have Augustus, Tiberius, Caligula, Claudius, Nero the fifth. The sixth, who is, is Galba, whose ascension to the throne was the signal for an insurrection of the legions, especially in Gaul, led by

Otho, Galba's successor. Thus our book must have been written under Galba, who reigned from June 9th, 68, to January 15th, 69. And it predicts the return of Nero as imminent.

But now for the final proof—the number. This also has been discovered by Ferdinand Benary, and since then it has never been disputed in the scientific world.

About 300 years before our era the Jews began to use their letters as symbols for numbers. The speculative Rabbis saw in this a new method for mystic interpretation or cabbala. Secret words were expressed by the figure produced by the addition of the numerical values of the letters contained in them. This new science they called *gematriah,* geometry. Now this science is applied here by our "John." We have to prove (1) that the number contains the name of a man, and that man is Nero; and (2) that the solution given holds good for the reading 666 as well as for the equally old reading 616. We take Hebrew letters and their values—

נ (nun)	n = 50	ק (keph)	k = 100
ר (resh)	r = 200	ס (samech)	s = 60
ו (vau) for	o = 6	ר (resh)	r = 200
נ (nun)	n = 50		

Neron Kesar, the Emperor Neron, Greek Nêron Kaisar. Now, if instead of the Greek spelling, we transfer the Latin Nero Caesar into Hebrew characters, the *nun* at the end of *Neron* disappears, and with it the value of fifty. That brings us to the other old reading of 616, and thus the proof is as perfect as can be desired.*

The mysterious book, then, is now perfectly clear.

* The above spelling of the name, both with and without the second *nun,* is the one which occurs in the Talmud, and is therefore authentic.

"John" predicts the return of Nero for about the year 70, and a reign of terror under him which is to last forty-two months, or 1,260 days. After that term God arises, vanquishes Nero, the antichrist, destroys the great city by fire, and binds the devil for a thousand years. The millennium begins, and so forth. All this now has lost all interest, except for ignorant persons who may still try to calculate the day of the last judgment. But as an authentic picture of almost primitive Christianity, drawn by one of themselves, the book is worth more than all the rest of the New Testament put together.

FREDERICK ENGELS

LUDWIG FEUERBACH AND THE END OF CLASSICAL GERMAN PHILOSOPHY

FOREWORD

In the preface to *A Contribution to the Critique of Political Economy*, published in Berlin, 1859, Karl Marx relates how the two of us in Brussels in the year 1845 set about "jointly to expound the opposition between our view"—the materialist conception of history which was elaborated mainly by Marx—"and the ideological view of German philosophy, in fact, to settle accounts with our erstwhile philosophical conscience. The resolve was carried out in the form of a criticism of post-Hegelian philosophy. The manuscript, two large octavo volumes, had long reached its place of publication in Westphalia when we received the news that altered circumstances did not allow of its being printed. We abandoned the manuscript to the gnawing criticism of the mice all the more willingly as we had achieved our main purpose—self-clarification."[78]

Since then more than forty years have elapsed and Marx died without either of us having had an opportunity of returning to the subject. We have expressed ourselves in various places regarding our relation to Hegel, but nowhere in a comprehensive, connected account. To Feuerbach, who after all in many respects forms an intermediate link between Hegelian philosophy and our conception, we never returned.

In the meantime the Marxist world outlook has found representatives far beyond the boundaries of Germany and Europe and in all the literary languages of the world. On the other hand, classical German philosophy is experiencing a kind of rebirth abroad, especially in England and Scandinavia, and even in Germany itself people appear to be getting tired of the pauper's broth of eclecticism which is ladled out in the universities there under the name of philosophy.

In these circumstances a short, connected account of our relation to the Hegelian philosophy, of how we proceeded from as well as of how we separated from it, appeared to me to be required more and more. Equally, a full acknowledgement of the influence which Feuerbach, more than any other post-Hegelian philosopher, had upon us during our period of storm and stress, appeared to me to be an undischarged debt of honour. I therefore willingly seized the opportunity when the editors of *Neue Zeit* asked me for a critical review of Starcke's book on Feuerbach. My contribution was published in that journal in the fourth and fifth numbers of 1886 and appears here in revised form as a separate publication.

Before sending these lines to press I have once again ferreted out and looked over the old manuscript of 1845-46. The section dealing with Feuerbach is not completed. The finished portion consists of an exposition of the materialist conception of history which proves only how incomplete our knowledge of economic history still was at that time. It contains no criticism of Feuerbach's doctrine itself; for the present purpose, therefore, it was unusable. On the other hand, in an old notebook of Marx's I have found the eleven theses on Feuerbach printed here as an appendix. These are notes hurriedly scribbled down for later elaboration, absolutely not intended for publication, but invaluable as the first document in which is deposited the brilliant germ of the new world outlook.

Frederick Engels

London, February 21, 1888

LUDWIG FEUERBACH AND THE END OF CLASSICAL GERMAN PHILOSOPHY

I

The volume* before us carries us back to a period which, although in time no more than a generation behind us, has become as foreign to the present generation in Germany as if it were already a hundred years old. Yet it was the period of Germany's preparation for the Revolution of 1848; and all that has happened since then in our country has been merely a continuation of 1848, merely the execution of the last will and testament of the revolution.

Just as in France in the eighteenth century, so in Germany in the nineteenth, a philosophical revolution ushered in the political collapse. But how different the two looked! The French were in open combat against all official science, against the Church and often also against the State; their writings were printed abroad, in Holland or England, while they themselves were often in jeopardy of imprisonment in the Bastille. On the other hand, the Germans were professors, state-appointed instructors of youth; their writings were recognized textbooks, and the terminating system of the whole development—the Hegelian system—was even raised, as it were, to the rank of a royal Prussian philosophy of state! Was it possible that a revolution could hide behind these professors, behind their obscure, pedantic phrases, their ponderous, wearisome sentences? Were not precisely those people who were then regarded as the representatives of the revolution, the liberals, the bitterest opponents of this brain-confusing philosophy? But what neither the government nor the liberals saw was seen

* *Ludwig Feuerbach*, by C. N. Starcke, Ph. D., Stuttgart Ferd. Encke. 1885. [*Note by Engels.*]

at least by one man as early as 1833, and this man was indeed none other than Heinrich Heine.[79]

Let us take an example. No philosophical proposition has earned more gratitude from narrow-minded governments and wrath from equally narrow-minded liberals than Hegel's famous statement. "All that is real is rational; and all that is rational is real." That was tangibly a sanctification of things that be, a philosophical benediction bestowed upon despotism, police government, Star Chamber proceedings and censorship. That is how Frederick-William III and how his subjects understood it. But according to Hegel certainly not everything that exists is also real, without further qualification. For Hegel the attribute of reality belongs only to that which at the same time is necessary: "In the course of its development reality proves to be necessity." A particular governmental measure—Hegel himself cites the example of "a certain tax regulation"—is therefore for him by no means real without qualification. That which is necessary, however, proves itself in the last resort to be also rational; and, applied to the Prussian state of that time, the Hegelian proposition therefore, merely means: this state is rational, corresponds to reason, in so far as it is necessary; and if it nevertheless appears to us to be evil, but still, in spite of its evil character, continues to exist, then the evil character of the government is justified and explained by the corresponding evil character of its subjects. The Prussians of that day had the government that they deserved.

Now, according to Hegel, reality is, however, in no way an attribute predicable of any given state of affairs, social or political, in all circumstances and at all times. On the contrary. The Roman Republic was real, but so was the Roman Empire, which superseded it. In 1789 the French monarchy had become so unreal, that is to say, so robbed of all necessity, so irrational, that it had to be destroyed by the Great Revolution, of which Hegel always speaks with the greatest enthusiasm. In this case, therefore, the monarchy was the unreal and the revolution the real. And so, in the course of development, all that was previously real becomes unreal, loses its necessity, its right of existence, its rationality. And in the place of moribund reality comes a new, viable reality—peacefully if the old has enough intelligence to go to its death without a struggle; forcibly if it resists this necessity. Thus the Hegelian proposition turns into its opposite through Hegelian dialectics itself: All that is real in the sphere of human history becomes irrational in the process of time, is therefore irrational by its very destination, is tainted beforehand with irrationality; and everything which is rational in the minds of men is destined to become real, no matter how much it contradicts existing apparent reality. In accordance with all the rules of the Hegelian method of thought, the proposition of the rationality of everything which is real resolves itself into the other proposition: All that exists deserves to perish.

But precisely therein lay the true significance and the revolutionary character of the Hegelian philosophy (to which, as the close of the whole movement since Kant, we must here confine ourselves), that it once for all dealt the death-blow to the finality of all products of human thought and action. Truth, the cognition of which is the business of philosophy, was in the hands of Hegel no longer an aggregate of finished dogmatic statements, which, once discovered, had merely to be learned by heart. Truth lay now in the process of cognition itself, in the long historical development of science, which mounts from lower to ever higher levels of knowledge without ever reaching, by discovering so-called absolute truth, a point at which it can proceed no further, where it would have nothing more to do than to fold its arms and gaze with wonder at the absolute truth to which it had attained. And what holds good for the realm of philosophical knowledge holds good also for that of every other kind of knowledge and also for practical action. Just as knowledge is unable to reach a complete conclusion in a perfect, ideal condition of humanity, so is history unable to do so; a perfect society, a perfect "state," are things which can exist only in imagination. On the contrary, all successive historical systems are only transitory stages in the endless course of development of human society from the lower to the higher. Each stage is necessary, and therefore justified for the time and conditions to which it owes its origin. But in the face of new, higher conditions which gradually develop in its own womb, it loses its validity and justification. It must give way to a higher stage which will also in its turn decay and perish. Just as the bourgeoisie by large-scale industry, competition and the world market dissolves in practice all stable time-honoured institutions, so this dialectical philosophy dissolves all conceptions of final, absolute truth and of absolute states of humanity corresponding to it. For it [dialectical philosophy] nothing is final, absolute, sacred. It reveals the transitory character of everything and in everything; nothing can endure before it except the uninterrupted process of becoming and of passing away, of endless ascendancy from the lower to the higher. And dialectical philosophy itself is nothing more than the mere reflection of this process in the thinking brain. It has, of course, also a conservative side: it recognizes that definite stages of knowledge and society are justified for their time and circumstances; but only so far. The conservatism of this mode of outlook is relative; its revolutionary character is absolute—the only absolute dialectical philosophy admits.

It is not necessary, here, to go into the question of whether this mode of outlook is thoroughly in accord with the present state of natural science, which predicts a possible end even for the earth, and for its habitability a fairly certain one; which therefore recognizes that for the history of mankind, too, there is not only an ascending but also a descending branch. At any rate we still find ourselves a considerable distance from the turning-point at which the historical course of society becomes one of descent and we cannot expect Hegelian philosophy to be concerned with a subject which natural science, in its time, had not at all placed upon the agenda as yet.

But what must, in fact, be said here is this: that in Hegel the views developed above are not so sharply delineated. They are a necessary conclusion from his method, but one which he himself never drew with such explicitness. And this, indeed, for the simple reason that he was compelled to make a system and, in accordance with traditional requirements, a system of philosophy must conclude with some sort of absolute truth. Therefore, however much Hegel, especially in his *Logic*, emphasized that this eternal truth is nothing but the logical, or the historical, process itself, he nevertheless finds himself compelled to supply this process with an end, just because he has to bring his system to a termination at some point or other. In his *Logic* he can make this end a beginning again, since here the point of conclusion, the absolute idea—which is only absolute in so far as he has absolutely nothing to say about it—"alienates," that is, transforms, itself into nature and comes to itself again later in the mind, that is, in thought and in history. But at the end of the whole philosophy a similar return to the beginning is possible only in one way. Namely, by conceiving the end of history as follows; mankind arrives at the cognition of this selfsame absolute idea, and declares that this cognition of the absolute idea is reached in Hegelian philosophy. In this way, however, the whole dogmatic content of the Hegelian system is declared to be absolute truth, in contradiction to his dialectical method, which dissolves all dogmatism. Thus the revolutionary side is smothered beneath the overgrowth of the conservative side. And what applies to philosophical cognition applies also to historical practice. Mankind, which, in the person of Hegel, has reached the point of working out the absolute idea, must also in practice have got so far that it can carry out this absolute idea in reality. Hence the practical political demands of the absolute idea on contemporaries may not be stretched too far. And so we find at the conclusion of the *Philosophy of Right* that the absolute idea is to be realized in that monarchy based on social Estates which Frederick-William III so persistently but vainly promised to his subjects, that is, in a limited, moderate, indirect rule of the propertied classes suited to the petty-bourgeois German conditions of that time; and, moreover, the necessity of the nobility is demonstrated to us in a speculative fashion.

The inner necessities of the system are, therefore, of themselves sufficient to explain why a thoroughly revolutionary method of thinking produced an extremely tame political conclusion. As a matter of fact the specific form of this conclusion springs from this, that Hegel was a German, and like his contemporary Goethe had a bit of the philistine's queue dangling behind. Each of them was an Olympian Zeus in his own sphere, yet neither of them ever quite freed himself from German philistinism.

But all this did not prevent the Hegelian system from covering an incomparably greater domain than any earlier system, nor from developing in this domain a wealth of thought which is astounding even today. The phenomenology of mind (which one may call a parallel of the embryology and palaeontology of the mind, a development of individual consciousness through its different stages, set in the form of an abbridged reproduction of the stages through which the consciousness of man has passed in the course of history), logic, natural philosophy, philosophy of mind, and the latter worked out in its separate, historical subdivisions: philosophy of history, of right, of religion, history of philosophy, aesthetics, etc.—in all these different historical fields Hegel laboured to discover and demonstrate the pervading thread of development. And as he was not only a creative genius but also a man of encyclopaedic erudition, he played an epoch-making role in every sphere. It is self-evident that owing to the needs of the "system" he very often had to resort to those forced constructions about which his pigmy opponents make such a terrible fuss even today. But these constructions are only the frame and scaffolding of his work. If one does not loiter here needlessly, but presses on farther into the immense building, one finds innumerable treasures which today still possess undiminished value. With all philosophers it is precisely the "system" which is perishable; and for the simple reason that it springs from an imperishable desire of the human mind—the desire to overcome all contradictions. But if all contradictions are once for all disposed of, we shall have arrived at so-called absolute truth—world history will be at an end. And yet it has to continue, although there is nothing left for it to do—hence, a new, insoluble contradiction. As soon as we have once realized—and in the long run no one has helped us to realize it more than Hegel himself—that the task of philosophy thus stated means nothing but that a single philosopher should accomplish that which can only be accomplished by the entire human race in its progressive development—as soon as we realize that, there is an end to all philosophy in the hitherto accepted sense of the word. One leaves alone "absolute truth," which is unattainable along this path or by any single individual; instead, one pursues attainable relative truths along the path of the positive sciences, and the summation of their results by means of dialectical thinking. At any rate, with Hegel philosophy comes to an end: on the one hand, because in his system he summed up its whole development in the most splendid fashion; and on the other hand, because, even though unconsciously, he showed us the way out of the labyrinth of systems to real positive knowledge of the world.

One can imagine what a tremendous effect this Hegelian system must have produced in the philosophy-tinged atmosphere of Germany. It was a triumphal procession which lasted for decades and which by no means came to a standstill on the death of Hegel. On the contrary, it was precisely from 1830 to 1840 that "Hegelianism" reigned most exclusively, and to a greater or lesser extent infected even its opponents. It was precisely in this period that Hegelian views, consciously or unconsciously, most extensively penetrated the most diversified sciences and leavened even popular literature and the daily press, from which the average "educated consciousness" derives its mental pabulum. But this victory along the whole front was only the prelude to an internal struggle.

As we have seen, the doctrine of Hegel, taken as a whole, left plenty of room for the most diverse practical party views. And in the theoretical Germany of that time, two things above all were practical: religion and politics. Whoever placed the chief emphasis on the Hegelian *system* could be fairly conservative in both spheres; whoever regarded the dialectical *method* as the main thing could belong to the most extreme opposition, both in politics and religion. Hegel himself, despite the fairy frequent outbursts of revolutionary wrath in his works, seemed on the whole to be more inclined to the conservative side. Indeed, his system had cost him much more "hard mental plugging" than his method. Towards the end of the thirties, the cleavage in the school became more and more apparent. The Left wing, the so-called Young Hegelians, in their fight with the pietist orthodox and the feudal reactionaries, abandoned bit by bit that philosophical-genteel reserve in regard to the burning questions of the day which up to that time had secured state toleration and even protection for their teachings. And when, in 1840, orthodox pietism and absolutist feudal reaction ascended the throne with Frederick-William IV, open partisanship became unavoidable. The fight was still carried on with philosophical weapons, but no longer for abstract philosophical aims. It turned directly on the destruction of traditional religion and of the existing state. And while in *Deutsche Jahrbücher* the practical ends were still put forward predominantly in philosophical disguise, in *Rheinische Zeitung* of 1842 the Young Hegelian school revealed itself directly as the philosophy of the aspiring radical bourgeoisie and used the meagre cloak of philosophy only to deceive the censorship.

At that time, however, politics was a very thorny field, and hence the main fight came to be directed against religion; this fight, particularly since 1840, was indirectly also political. Strauss's *Life of Jesus*, published in 1835, had provided the first impulse. The theory therein developed of the formation of the Gospel myths was combated later by Bruno Bauer with proof that a whole series of evangelic stories had been fabricated by the authors themselves. The controversy between these two was carried out in the philosophical disguise of a battle between "self-consciousness" and "substance." The question whether the miracle stories of the Gospels came into being through unconscious traditional myth-creation within the bosom of the community or whether they were fabricated by the evangelists themselves was magnified into the question whether, in world history, "substance" or "self-consciousness" was the decisive operative force. Finally came Stirner, the prophet of contemporary anarchism—Bakunin has taken a great deal from him—and capped the sovereign "self-consciousness" by his sovereign "ego."[80]

We will not go further into this side of the decomposition process of the Hegelian school. More important for us is the following: the main body of the most determined Young Hegelians was, by the practical necessities of its fight against positive religion, driven back to Anglo-French materialism. This brought them into conflict with their school system. While materialism conceives nature as the sole reality, nature in the Hegelian system represents merely the "alienation" of the absolute idea, so to say, a degradation of the idea. At all events, thinking and its thought-product, the idea, is here the primary, nature the derivative, which only exists at all by the condescension of the idea. And in this contradiction they floundered as well or as ill as they could.

Then came Feuerbach's *Essence of Christianity*.[81] With one blow it pulverized the contradiction in that without circumlocutions it placed materialism on the throne again. Nature exists independently of all philosophy. It is the foundation upon which we human beings, ourselves products of nature, have grown up. Nothing exists outside nature and man, and the higher beings our religious fantasies have created are only the fantastic reflection of our own essence. The spell was broken; the "system" was exploded and cast aside, and the contradiction, shown to exist only in our imagination, was dissolved. One must oneself have experienced the liberating effect of this book to get an idea of it. Enthusiasm was general; we all became at once Feuerbachians. How enthusiastically Marx greeted the new conception and how much—in spite of all critical reservations—he was influenced by it, one may read in *The Holy Family*.

Even the shortcomings of the book contributed to its immediate effect. Its literary, sometimes even high-flown, style secured for it a large public and was at any rate refreshing after long years of abstract and abstruse Hegelianizing. The same is true of its extravagant deification of love, which, coming after the now intolerable sovereign rule of "pure reason," had its excuse, if not justification. But what we must not forget is that it was precisely these two weaknesses of Feuerbach that "true socialism," which had been spreading like a plague in "educated" Germany since 1844, took as its starting-point, putting literary phrases in the place of scientific knowledge, the liberation of mankind by means of "love" in place of the emancipation of the proletariat through the economic transformation of production—in short, losing itself in the nauseous fine writing and ecstasies of love typified by Herr Karl Grün.

Another thing we must not forget is this: the Hegelian school disintegrated, but Hegelian philosophy was not overcome through criticism; Strauss and Bauer each took one of its sides and set it polemically against the other. Feuerbach broke through the system and simply discarded it. But a philosophy is not disposed of by the mere assertion that it is false. And so powerful a work as Hegelian philosophy, which had exercised so enormous an influence on the intellectual development of the nation, could not be disposed of by simply being ignored. It had to be "sublated" in its own sense, that is, in the sense that while its form had to be annihilated through criticism, the new content which had been won through it had to be saved. How this was brought about we shall see below.

But in the meantime the Revolution of 1848 thrust the whole of philosophy aside as unceremoniously as Feuerbach had thrust aside Hegel. And in the process Feuerbach himself was also pushed into the background.

II

The great basic question of all philosophy, especially of more recent philosophy, is that concerning the relation of thinking and being. From the very early times when men, still completely ignorant of the structure of their own bodies, under the stimulus of dream apparitions* came to believe that their thinking and sensation were not activities of their bodies, but of a distinct soul which inhabits the body and leaves it at death—from this time men have been driven to reflect about the relation between this soul and the outside world. If upon death it took leave of the body and lived on, there was no occasion to invent yet another distinct death for it. Thus arose the idea of its immortality, which at that stage of development appeared not at all as a consolation but as a fate against which it was no use fighting, and often enough, as among the Greeks, as a positive misfortune. Not religious desire for consolation, but the quandary arising from the common universal ignorance of what to do with this soul, once its existence had been accepted, after the death of the body, led in a general way to the tedious notion of personal immortality. In an exactly similar manner the first gods arose through the personification of natural forces. And these gods in the further development of religions assumed more and more an extramundane form, until finally by a process of abstraction, I might almost say of distillation, occurring naturally in the course of man's intellectual development, out of the many more or less limited and mutually limiting gods there arose

* Among savages and lower barbarians the idea is still universal that the human forms which appear in dreams are souls which have temporarily left their bodies; the real man is, therefore, held responsible for acts committed by his dream apparition against the dreamer. Imthurn found this belief current, for example, among the Indians of Guiana in 1884. [*Note by Engels.*]

in the minds of men the idea of the one exclusive God of the monotheistic religions.

Thus the question of the relation of thinking to being, the relation of the spirit to nature—the paramount question of the whole of philosophy—has, no less than all religion, its roots in the narrow-minded and ignorant notions of savagery. But this question could for the first time be put forward in its whole acuteness, could achieve its full significance, only after humanity in Europe had awakened from the long hibernation of the Christian Middle Ages. The question of the position of thinking in relation to being, a question which, by the way, had played a great part also in the scholasticism of the Middle Ages, the question: Which is primary, spirit or nature—that question, in relation to the Church, was sharpened into this: Did God create the world or has the world been in existence eternally?

The answers which the philosophers gave to this question split them into two great camps. Those who asserted the primacy of spirit to nature and, therefore, in the last instance, assumed world creation in some form or other—and among the philosophers, Hegel, for example, this creation often becomes still more intricate and impossible than in Christianity—formed the camp of idealism. The others, who regarded nature as primary, belong to the various schools of materialism.

These two expressions, idealism and materialism, originally signify nothing else than this; and here too they are not used in any other sense. What confusion arises when some other meaning is put into them will be seen below.

But the question of the relation of thinking and being has yet another side: in what relation do our thoughts about the world surrounding us stand to this world itself? Is our thinking capable of cognition of the real world? Are we able in our ideas and notions of the real world to produce a correct reflection of reality? In philosophical language this question is called the question of the identity of thinking and being, and the overwhelming majority of philosophers give an affirmative answer to this question. With Hegel, for example, its affirmation is self-evident; for what we cognize in the real world is precisely its thought-content—that which makes the world a gradual realization of the absolute idea, which absolute idea has existed somewhere from eternity, independent of the world and before the world. But it is evident without further proof that thought can know a content which is from the outset a thought-content. It is equally evident that what is to be proved here is already tacitly contained in the premise. But that in no way prevents Hegel from drawing the further conclusion from his proof of the identity of thinking and being that his philosophy, because it is correct for his thinking, is therefore the only correct one, and that the identity of thinking and being must prove its validity by mankind immediately translating his philosophy from theory into practice and transforming the whole world according to Hegelian principles. This is an illusion which he shares with well-nigh all philosophers.

In addition there is yet a set of different philosophers—those who question the possibility of any cognition, or at least of an exhaustive cognition, of the world. To them, among the more modern ones, belong Hume and Kant, and they have played a very important role in philosophical development. What is decisive in the refutation of this view has already been said by Hegel, in so far as this was possible from an idealistic standpoint. The materialistic additions made by Feuerbach are more ingenious than profound. The most telling refutation of this as of all other philosophical crotchets is practice, namely, experiment and industry. If we are able to prove the correctness of our conception of a natural process by making it ourselves, bringing it into being out of its conditions and making it serve our own purposes into the bargain, then there is an end to the Kantian ungraspable "thing-in-itself." The chemical substances produced in the bodies of plants and animals remained just such "things-in-themselves" until organic chemistry began to produce them one after another, whereupon the "thing-in-itself" became a thing for us, as, for instance, alizarin, the colouring matter of the madder, which we no longer trouble to grow in the madder roots in the field but produce much more cheaply and simply from coal tar. For three hundred years the Copernican solar system was a hypothesis with a hundred, a thousand or ten thousand chances to one in its favour, but still always a hypothesis. But when Leverrier, by means of the data provided by this system, not only deduced the necessity of the existence of an unknown planet, but also calculated the position in the heavens which this planet must necessarily occupy, and when Galle really found this planet,[82] the Copernican system was proved. If, nevertheless, the Neo-Kantians are attempting to resurrect the Kantian conception in Germany and the agnostics that of Hume in England (where in fact it never became extinct), this is, in view of their theoretical and practical refutation accomplished long ago, scientifically a regression and practically merely a shamefaced way of surreptitiously accepting materialism, while denying it before the world.

But during this long period from Descartes to Hegel and from Hobbes to Feuerbach, the philosophers were by no means impelled, as they thought they were, solely by the force of pure reason. On the contrary, what really pushed them forward most was the powerful and ever more rapidly onrushing progress of natural science and industry. Among the materialists this was plain on the surface, but the idealist systems also filled themselves more and more with a materialist content and attempted pantheistically to reconcile the antithesis between mind and matter. Thus, ultimately, the Hegelian system represents merely a materialism idealistically turned upside down in method and content.

It is, therefore, comprehensible that Starcke in his characterization of Feuerbach first of all investigates the latter's position in regard to this fundamental question of the relation of thinking and being. After a short introduction, in which the views of the preceding philosophers, particularly since Kant, are described in unnecessarily ponderous philosophical language, and in which Hegel, by an all too formalistic adherence to certain passages of his works, gets far less than his due, there follows a detailed description of the course of development of Feuerbach's "metaphysics" itself, as this course was successively reflected in those writings of this philosopher which have a bearing here. This description is industriously and lucidly elaborated; only, like the whole book, it is loaded with a ballast of philosophical phraseology, by no means everywhere unavoidable, which is the more disturbing in its effect the less the author keeps to the manner of expression of one and the same school, or even of Feuerbach himself, and the more he interjects expressions of very different tendencies, especially of the tendencies now rampant and calling themselves philosophical.

The course of Feuerbach's evolution is that of a Hegelian—a never quite orthodox Hegelian, it is true—into a materialist; an evolution which at a definite stage necessitates a complete rupture with the idealist system of his predecessor. With irresistible force Feuerbach is finally driven to the realization that the Hegelian premundane existence of the "absolute idea," the "pre-existence of the logical categories" before the world existed, is nothing more than the fantastic survival of the belief in the existence of an extramundane creator; that the material, sensuously perceptible world to which we ourselves belong is the only reality; and that our consciousness and thinking, however suprasensuous they may seem, are the product of a material, bodily organ, the brain. Matter is not a product of mind, but mind itself is merely the highest product of matter. This is, of course, pure materialism. But, having got so far, Feuerbach stops short. He cannot overcome the customary philosophical prejudice, prejudice not against the thing but against the name materialism. He says:

"To me materialism is the foundation of the edifice of human essence and knowledge; but to me it is not what it is to the physiologist, to the natural scientist in the narrower sense, for example, to Moleschott, and necessarily is from their standpoint and profession, namely, the edifice itself. Backwards I fully agree with the materialists; but not forwards."

Here Feuerbach lumps together the materialism that is a general world outlook resting upon a definite conception of the relation between matter and mind, and the special form in which this world outlook was expressed at a definite historical stage, namely, in the eighteenth century. More than that, he lumps it with the shallow, vulgarized form in which the materialism of the eighteenth century continues to exist today in the heads of naturalists and physicians, the form which was preached on their tours in the fifties by Büchner, Vogt and Moleschott. But just as idealism underwent a series of stages of development, so also did materialism. With each epoch-making discovery even in the sphere of natural science it has to change its form; and after history also, was subjected to materialistic treatment, a new avenue of development opened here too.

The materialism of the last century was predominantly mechanical, because at that time of all natural sciences only mechanics, and indeed only the mechanics of solid bodies—celestial and terrestrial—in short, the mechanics of gravity, had come to any definite close. Chemistry at that time existed only in its infantile, phlogistic form. Biology still lay in swaddling clothes; vegetable and animal organisms had been only roughly examined and were explained as the result of purely mechanical causes. To the materialists of the eighteenth century man was what the animal was to Descartes—a machine. This exclusive application of the standards of mechanics to processes of a chemical and organic nature—in which processes the laws of mechanics are, indeed, also valid but are pushed into the background by other, higher laws—constitutes the first specific but at that time inevitable limitation of classical French materialism.

The second specific limitation of this materialism lay in its inability to comprehend the universe as a process, as matter undergoing uninterrupted historical development. This was in accordance with the level of the natural science of that time and with the metaphysical, that is, anti-dialectical manner of philosophizing connected with it. Nature, so much was known, was in eternal motion. But according to the ideas of that time, this motion turned, also eternally, in a circle and therefore never moved from the spot; it produced the same results over and over again. This conception was at that time inevitable. The Kantian theory of the origin of the solar system had been put forward but recently and was still regarded merely as a curiosity. The history of the development of the earth, geology, was still totally unknown, and the conception that the animate natural beings of today are the result of a long sequence of development from the simple to the complex could not at that time scientifically be put forward at all. The unhistorical view of nature was therefore inevitable. We have the less reason to reproach the philosophers of the eighteenth century on this account since the same thing is found in Hegel. According to him, nature, as a mere "alienation" of the idea, is incapable of development in time—capable only of extending its manifoldness in space, so that it displays simultaneously and alongside of one another all the stages of development comprised in it, and is condemned to an eternal repetition of the same processes. This absurdity of a development in space but outside of time—the fundamental condition of all development—Hegel imposed upon nature just at the very time when geology, embryology, the physiology of plants and animals, and organic chemistry were being built up, and when everywhere on the basis of these new sciences brilliant foreshadowings of the later theory of evolution were appearing (for instance, Goethe and Lamarck). But the system demanded it; hence the method, for the sake of the system, had to become untrue to itself.

This same unhistorical conception prevailed also in the domain of history. Here the struggle against the remnants of the Middle Ages blurred the view. The Middle Ages were regarded as a mere interruption of history by a thousand years of universal barbarism. The great progress made in the Middle Ages—the extension of the area of European culture, the viable great nations taking form there next to each other, and finally the enormous technical progress of the fourteenth and fifteenth centuries—all this was not seen. Thus a rational insight into the great historical interconnections was made impossible, and history served at best as a collection of examples and illustrations for the use of philosophers.

The vulgarizing pedlars who dabbled in materialism in Germany in the fifties by no means overcame this limitation of their teachers. All the advances of natural science which had been made in the meantime served them only as new proofs against the existence of a creator of the world; and, indeed, they did not in the least make it their business to develop the theory any further. Though idealism was at the end of its tether and was dealt a death-blow by the Revolution of 1848, it had the satisfaction of seeing that materialism had for the moment fallen lower still. Feuerbach was unquestionably right when he refused to take responsibility for this materialism; only he should not have confused the doctrines of these itinerant preachers with materialism in general.

Here, however, there are two things to be pointed out. First, even during Feuerbach's life-time, natural science was still in that process of violent fermentation which only during the last fifteen years had reached a clarifying, relative conclusion. New scientific data were acquired to a hitherto unheard-of extent, but the establishing of interrelations, and thereby the bringing of order into this chaos of discoveries following closely upon each other's heels, has only quite recently become possible. It is true that Feuerbach had lived to see all three of the decisive discoveries—that of the cell, the transformation of energy and the theory of evolution named after Darwin. But how could the lonely philosopher, living in rural solitude, be able sufficiently to follow scientific developments in order to appreciate at their full value discoveries which natural scientists themselves at that time either still contested or did not know how to make adequate use of? The blame for this falls solely upon the wretched conditions in Germany, in consequence of which cobweb-spinning eclectic flea-crackers had taken possession of the chairs of philosophy, while Feuerbach, who towered above them all, had to rusticate and grow sour in a little village. It is therefore not Feuerbach's fault that the historical conception of nature, which had now become possible and which removed all the one-sidedness of French materialism, remained inaccessible to him.

Secondly, Feuerbach is quite correct in asserting that exclusively natural-scientific materialism is indeed "the foundation of the edifice of human knowledge, but not the edifice itself." For we live not only in nature but also in human society, and this also no less than nature has its history of development and its science. It was therefore a question of bringing the science of society, that is, the sum total of the so-called historical and philosophical sciences, into harmony with the materialist foundation, and of reconstructing it thereupon. But it did not fall to Feuerbach's lot to do this. In spite of the "foundation," he remained here bound by the traditional idealist fetters, a fact which he recognizes in these words: "Backwards I agree with the materialists, but not forwards." But it was Feuerbach himself who did not go "forwards" here, in the social domain, who did not get beyond his standpoint of 1840 or 1844. And this was again chiefly due to his reclusion which compelled him, who, of all philosophers, was the most inclined to social intercourse, to produce thoughts out of his solitary head instead of in amicable or hostile encounters with other men of his calibre. Later we shall see in detail how much he remained an idealist in this sphere.

It need only be added here that Starcke looks for Feuerbach's idealism in the wrong place.

"Feuerbach is an idealist; he believes in the progress of mankind" (p. 19). "The foundation, the substructure of the whole, remains nevertheless idealism. Realism for us is nothing more than a protection against aberrations, while we follow our ideal tendencies. Are not compassion, love and enthusiasm for truth and justice ideal forces?" (P. viii.)

In the first place, idealism here means nothing but the pursuit of ideal aims. But these necessarily have to do at the most with Kantian idealism and its "categorical imperative"; however, Kant himself called his philosophy "transcendental idealism"; by no means because he dealt therein also with ethical ideals, but for quite other reasons, as Starcke will remember. The superstition that philosophical idealism is pivoted round a belief in ethical, that is, social, ideals, arose outside philosophy, among the German philistines, who learned by heart from Schiller's poems the few morsels of philosophical culture they needed. No one has criticized more severely the impotent "categorical imperative" of Kant—impotent because it demands the impossible, and therefore never attains to any reality—no one has more cruelly derided the philistine sentimental enthusiasm for unrealizable ideals purveyed by Schiller than precisely the complete idealist Hegel. (See, for example, his *Phenomenology*.)

In the second place, we simply cannot get away from the fact that everything that sets men acting must find its way through their brain—even eating and drinking, which begins as a consequence of the sensation of hunger or thirst transmitted through the brain, and ends as a result of the sensation of satisfaction likewise transmitted through the brain. The influences of the external world upon man express themselves in his brain, are reflected therein as feelings, thoughts, impulses, volitions—in short, as "ideal tendencies," and in this form become "ideal powers." If, then, a man is to be deemed an idealist because he follows "ideal tendencies" and admits that "ideal powers" have an influence over him, then every person who is at all normally developed is a born idealist and how, in that case, can there still be any materialists?

In the third place, the conviction that humanity, at least at the present moment, moves on the whole in a progressive direction has absolutely nothing to do with the antagonism between materialism and idealism. The French materialists no less than the deists Voltaire and Rousseau held this conviction to an almost fanatical degree and often enough made the greatest personal sacrifices for it. If ever anybody dedicated his whole life to the "enthusiasm for truth and justice"—using this phrase in the good sense—it was Diderot, for instance. If, therefore, Starcke declares all this to be idealism, this merely proves that the word materialism, and the whole antagonism between the two trends, has lost all meaning for him here.

The fact is that in this Starcke, although perhaps unconsciously, makes an unpardonable concession to the traditional philistine prejudice against the word materialism resulting from its long-continued defamation by the priests. By the word materialism the philistine understands gluttony, drunkenness, lust of the eye, lust of the flesh, arrogance, cupidity, avarice, covetousness, profit-hunting and stock-exchange swindling—in short, all the filthy vices in which he himself indulges in private. By the word idealism he understands the belief in virtue, universal philanthropy and in a general way a "better world," of which he boasts before others but in which he himself at the utmost believes only so long as he is in the blues or is going through the bankruptcy consequent upon his customary "materialist" excesses. It is then that he sings his favourite song. What is man?—Half beast, half angel.

For the rest, Starcke takes great pains to defend Feuerbach against the attacks and doctrines of the vociferous assistant professors who today go by the name of philosophers in Germany. For people who are interested in this afterbirth of classical German philosophy this is, of course, a matter of importance; for Starcke himself it may have appeared necessary. We, however, will spare the reader this.

III

The real idealism of Feuerbach becomes evident as soon as we come to his philosophy of religion and ethics. He by no means wishes to abolish religion; he wants to perfect it. Philosophy itself must be absorbed in religion.

"The periods of humanity are distinguished only by religious changes. A historical movement is fundamental only when it is rooted in the hearts of men. The heart is not a form of religion, so that the latter should exist *also* in the heart; the heart is the essence of religion." (Quoted by Starcke, p. 168.)

According to Feuerbach, religion is the relation between human beings based on the affections, the relation based on the heart, which relation until now has sought its truth in a fantastic mirror image of reality—in the mediation of one or many gods, the fantastic mirror images of human qualities—but now finds it directly and without any mediation in the love between "I" and "Thou." Thus, finally, with Feuerbach sex love becomes one of the highest forms, if not the highest form, of the practice of his new religion.

Now relations between human beings, based on affection, and especially between the two sexes, have existed as long as mankind has. Sex love in particular has undergone a development and won a place during the last eight hundred years which has made it a compulsory pivotal point of all poetry during this period. The existing positive religions have limited themselves to the bestowal of a higher consecration upon state-regulated sex love, that is, upon the marriage laws, and they could all disappear tomorrow without changing in the slightest the practice of love and friendship. Thus the Christian religion in France, as a matter of fact, so completely disappeared in the years 1793-98 that even Napoleon could not re-introduce it without opposition and difficulty; and this without any need for a substitute, in Feuerbach's sense, making itself felt in the interval.

Feuerbach's idealism consists here in this: he does not simply accept mutual relations based on reciprocal inclination between human beings, such as sex love, friendship, compassion, self-sacrifice, etc., as what they are in themselves—without associating them with any particular religion which to him, too, belongs to the past; but instead he asserts that they will attain their full value only when consecrated by the name of religion. The chief thing for him is not that these purely human relations exist, but that they shall be conceived as the new, true religion. They are to have full value only after they have been marked with a religious stamp. Religion is derived from *religare* and meant originally a bond. Therefore, every bond between two people is a religion. Such etymological tricks are the last resort of idealist philosophy. Not what the word means according to the historical development of its actual use, but what it ought to mean according to its derivation is what counts. And so sex love and the intercourse between the sexes is apotheosized to a *religion*, merely in order that the word religion, which is so dear to idealistic memories, may not disappear from the language. The Parisian reformers of the Louis Blanc trend used to speak in precisely the same way in the forties. They likewise could conceive a man without religion only as a monster, and used to say to us: "*Donc, l'athéisme c'est votre religion!*" If Feuerbach wishes to establish a true religion upon the basis of an essentially materialist conception of nature, that is the same as regarding modern chemistry as true alchemy. If religion can exist without its god, alchemy can exist without its philosopher's stone. By the way, there exists a very close connection between alchemy and religion. The philosopher's stone has many godlike properties and the Egypto-Greek alchemists of the first two centuries of our era had a hand in the development of Christian doctrines, as the data given by Kopp and Berthelot have proved.

Feuerbach's assertion that "the periods of humanity are distinguished only by religious changes" is decidedly false. Great historical turning-points have been *accompanied* by religious changes only so far as the three world religions which have existed up to the present—Buddhism, Christianity and Islam—are concerned. The old tribal and national religions, which arose spontaneously, did not proselytize and lost all their power of resistance as soon as the independence of the tribe or people was lost. For the Germans it was sufficient to have simple contact with the decaying Roman world empire and with its newly adopted Christian world religion which fitted its economic, political and ideological conditions. Only with these world religions, arisen more or less artificially, particularly Christianity and Islam, do we find that the more general historical movements acquire a religious imprint. Even in regard to Christianity the religious stamp in revolutions of really universal significance is restricted to the first stages of the bourgeoisie's struggle for emancipation—from the thirteenth to the seventeenth century—and is to be accounted for, not as Feuerbach thinks by the hearts of men and their religious needs, but by the entire previous history of the Middle Ages, which knew no other form of ideology than precisely religion and theology. But when the bourgeoisie of the eighteenth century had become strong enough likewise to possess an ideology of its own, suited to its own class standpoint, it made its great and conclusive revolution, the French, appealing exclusively to juristic and political ideas, and troubling itself with religion only in so far as it stood in its way. But it never occurred to it to put a new religion in place of the old. Everyone knows how Robespierre failed in his attempt.[83]

The possibility of purely human sentiments in our intercourse with other human beings has nowadays been sufficiently curtailed by the society in which we must live, which is based upon class antagonism and class rule. We have no reason to curtail it still more by exalting these sentiments to a religion. And similarly the understanding of the great historical class struggles has already been sufficiently obscured by current historiography, particularly in Germany, so that there is also no need for us to make such an understanding totally impossible by transforming the history of these struggles into a mere appendix of ecclesiastical history. Already here it becomes evident how far today we have moved beyond Feuerbach. His "finest passages" in glorification of his new religion of love are totally unreadable today.

The only religion which Feuerbach examines seriously is Christianity, the world religion of the Occident, based upon monotheism. He proves that the Christian god is only a fantastic reflection, a mirror image, of man. Now, this god is, however, himself the product of a tedious process of abstraction, the concentrated quintessence of the numerous earlier tribal and national gods. And man, whose image this god is, is therefore also not a real man, but likewise the quintessence of the numerous real men, man in the abstract, therefore himself again a mental image. Feuerbach, who on every page preaches sensuousness, absorption in the concrete, in actuality, becomes thoroughly abstract as soon as he begins to talk of any relations other than mere sex relations between human beings.

Of these relations only one aspect appeals to him: morality. And here we are again struck by Feuerbach's astonishing poverty when compared with Hegel. The latter's ethics, or doctrine of moral conduct, is the philosophy of right and embraces: 1) abstract right; 2) morality; 3) social ethics [*Sittlichkeit*], under which again are comprised: the family, civil society and the state. Here the content is as realistic as the form is idealistic. Besides morality the whole sphere of law, economy, politics is here included. With Feuerbach it is just the reverse. In form he is realistic since he takes his start from man; but there is absolutely no mention of the world in which this man lives;

hence, this man remains always the same abstract man who occupied the field in the philosophy of religion. For this man is not born of woman; he issues, as from a chrysalis, from the god of the monotheistic religions. He therefore does not live in a real world historically come into being and historically determined. True, he has intercourse with other men; however, each one of them is just as much an abstraction as he himself. In his philosophy of religion we still had men and women, but in his ethics even this last distinction disappears. Feuerbach, to be sure, at long intervals makes such statements as:

"Man thinks differently in a palace and in a hut." "If because of hunger, of misery, you have no stuff in your body, you likewise have no stuff for morality in your head, in your mind or heart." "Politics must become our religion," etc.

But Feuerbach is absolutely incapable of achieving anything with these maxims. They remain mere phrases, and even Starcke has to admit that for Feuerbach politics constituted an impassable frontier and the "science of society, sociology, was *terra incognita* to him."

He appears just as shallow, in comparison with Hegel, in his treatment of the antithesis of good and evil.

"One believes one is saying something great," Hegel remarks, "if one says that 'man is naturally good.' But one forgets that one says something far greater when one says 'man is naturally evil.' "

With Hegel evil is the form in which the motive force of historical development presents itself. This contains the twofold meaning that, on the one hand, each new advance necessarily appears as a sacrilege against things hallowed, as a rebellion against conditions, though old and moribund, yet sanctified by custom; and that, on the other hand, it is precisely the wicked passions of man—greed and lust for power—which, since the emergence of class antagonisms, serve as levers of historical development—a fact of which the history of feudalism and of the bourgeoisie, for example, constitutes a single continual proof. But it does not occur to Feuerbach to investigate the historical role of moral evil. To him history is altogether an uncanny domain in which he feels ill at ease. Even his dictum: "Man as he sprang originally from nature was only a mere creature of nature, not a man. Man is a product of man, of culture, of history"—with him even this dictum remains absolutely sterile.

What Feuerbach has to tell us about morals can, therefore, only be extremely meagre. The urge towards happiness is innate in man, and must therefore form the basis of all morality. But the urge towards happiness is subject to a double correction. First, by the natural consequences of our actions: after the debauch come the "blues," and habitual excess is followed by illness. Secondly, by its social consequences; if we do not respect the similar urge of other people towards happiness they will defend themselves, and so interfere with our own urge towards happiness. Consequently, in order to satisfy our urge, we must be in a position to appreciate rightly the results of our conduct and must likewise allow others an equal right to seek happiness. Rational self-restraint with regard to ourselves, and love—again and again love—in our intercourse with others—these are the basic laws of Feuerbach's morality; from them all others are derived. And neither the most spirited utterances of Feuerbach nor the strongest eulogies of Starcke can hide the tenuity and banality of these few propositions.

Only very exceptionally, and by no means to his and other people's profit, can an individual satisfy his urge towards happiness by preoccupation with himself. Rather it requires preoccupation with the outside world, means to satisfy his needs, that is to say, food, an individual of the opposite sex, books, conversation, argument, activities, objects for use and working up. Feuerbach's morality either presupposes that these means and objects of satisfaction are given to every individual as a matter of course, or else it offers only inapplicable good advice and is, therefore, not worth a brass farthing to people who are without these means. And Feuerbach himself states this in plain terms:

"Man thinks differently in a palace and in a hut. If because of hunger, of misery, you have no stuff in your body, you likewise have no stuff for morality in your head, in your mind or heart."

Do matters stand any better in regard to the equal right of others to satisfy their urge towards happiness? Feuerbach posed this claim as absolute, as holding good for all times and circumstances. But since when has it been valid? Was there ever in antiquity between slaves and masters, or in the Middle Ages between serfs and barons, any talk about an equal right to the urge towards happiness? Was not the urge of the oppressed class towards happiness sacrificed ruthlessly and "by right of law" to that of the ruling class? Yes, that was indeed immoral; nowadays, however, equality of rights is recognized. Recognized in words ever since and inasmuch as the bourgeoisie, in its fight against feudalism and in the development of capitalist production, was compelled to abolish all privileges of Estate, that is, personal privileges, and to introduce the equality of all individuals before the law, first in the sphere of private law, then gradually also in the sphere of public law. But the urge towards happiness thrives only to a trivial extent on ideal rights. To the greatest extent of all it thrives on material means; and capitalist production takes care to ensure that the great majority of those with equal rights shall get only what is essential for bare existence. Capitalist production has, therefore, little more respect, if indeed any more, for the equal right to the urge towards happiness of the majority than had slavery or serfdom. And are we better off in regard to the mental means of happiness, the educational means? Is not even "the schoolmaster of Sadowa"[84] a mythical person?

More. According to Feuerbach's theory of morals the Stock Exchange is the highest temple of moral conduct, provided only that one always speculates right. If my urge towards happiness leads me to the Stock Exchange, and if there I correctly gauge the consequences of my actions so that only agreeable results and no disadvantages ensue, that is, if I always win, then I am fulfilling Feuerbach's precept. Moreover, I do not thereby interfere with the equal right of another person to pursue his happiness; for that other man went to the Exchange just as voluntarily as I did and in concluding the speculative transaction with me he has followed his urge towards happiness as I have followed mine. If he loses his money, his action is *ipso facto* proved to have been unethical, because of his bad reckoning, and since I have given him the punishment he deserves, I can even slap my chest proudly, like a modern Rhadamanthus.[85] Love, too, rules on the Stock Exchange, in so far as it is not simply a sentimental figure of speech, for each finds in others the satisfaction of his own urge towards happiness, which is just what love ought to achieve and how it acts in practice. And if I gamble with correct prevision of the consequences of my operations, and therefore with success, I fulfil all the strictest injunctions of Feuerbachian morality—and become a rich man into the bargain. In other words, Feuerbach's morality is cut exactly to the pattern of modern capitalist society, little as Feuerbach himself might desire or imagine it.

But love!—yes, with Feuerbach love is everywhere and at all times the wonder-working god who should help to surmount all difficulties of practical life—and at that in a society which is split into classes with diametrically opposite interests. At this point the last relic of its revolutionary character disappears from his philosophy, leaving only the old cant: Love one another—fall into each other's arms regardless of distinctions of sex or status—a universal orgy of reconciliation!

In short, the Feuerbachian theory of morals fares like all its predecessors. It is designed to suit all periods, all peoples and all conditions, and precisely for that reason it is never and nowhere applicable. It remains, as regards the real world, as powerless as Kant's categorical imperative. In reality every class, even every profession, has its own morality, and even this it violates whenever it can do so with impunity. And love, which is to unite all, manifests itself in wars, altercations, lawsuits, domestic broils, divorces and every possible exploitation of one by another.

Now how was it possible that the powerful impetus given by Feuerbach turned out to be so unfruitful for himself? For the simple reason that Feuerbach himself never contrives to escape from the realm of abstraction—for which he has a deadly hatred—into that of living reality. He clings fiercely to nature and man; but nature and man remain mere words with him. He is incapable of telling us anything definite either about real nature or real man. But from the abstract man of Feuerbach one arrives at real living men only when one considers them as participants in history. And that is what Feuerbach resisted, and therefore the year 1848, which he did not understand, meant to him merely the final break with the real world, retirement into solitude. The blame for this again falls chiefly on the conditions then obtaining in Germany, which condemned him to rot away miserably.

But the step which Feuerbach did not take had nevertheless to be taken. The cult of abstract man, which formed the kernel of Feuerbach's new religion, had to be replaced by the science of real men and of their historical development. This further development of Feuerbach's standpoint beyond Feuerbach was inaugurated by Marx in 1845 in *The Holy Family*.

IV

Strauss, Bauer, Stirner, Feuerbach—these were the offshoots of Hegelian philosophy, in so far as they did not abandon the field of philosophy. Strauss, after his *Life of Jesus* and *Dogmatics*, produced only literary studies in philosophy and ecclesiastical history after the fashion of Renan. Bauer only achieved anything in the field of the history of the origin of Christianity, though what he did here was important. Stirner remained a curiosity, even after Bakunin blended him with Proudhon and labelled the blend "anarchism." Feuerbach alone was of significance as a philosopher. But not only did philosophy—claimed to soar above all special sciences and to be the science of sciences connecting them—remain to him an impassable barrier, an inviolable holy thing, but as a philosopher, too, he stopped halfway, was a materialist below and an idealist above. He was incapable of disposing of Hegel through criticism; he simply threw him aside as useless, while he himself, compared with the encyclopaedic wealth of the Hegelian system, achieved nothing positive beyond a turgid religion of love and a meagre, impotent morality.

Out of the dissolution of the Hegelian school, however, there developed still another tendency, the only one which has borne real fruit. And this tendency is essentially connected with the name of Marx.*

---

* Here I may be permitted to make a personal explanation. Lately repeated reference has been made to my share in this theory, and so I can hardly avoid saying a few words here to settle this

The separtion from Hegelian philosophy was here also the result of a return to the materialist standpoint. That means it was resolved to comprehend the real world—nature and history—just as it presents itself to everyone who approaches it free from preconceived idealist crotchets. It was decided mercilessly to sacrifice every idealist crotchet which could not be brought into harmony with the facts conceived in their own and not in a fantastic interconnection. And materialism means nothing more than this. But here the materialistic world outlook was taken really seriously for the first time and was carried through consistently—at least in its basic features—in all domains of knowledge concerned.

Hegel was not simply put aside. On the contrary, one started out from his revolutionary side, described above, from the dialectical method. But in its Hegelian form this method was unusable. According to Hegel, dialectics is the self-development of the concept. The absolute concept does not only exist—unknown where—from eternity, it is also the actual living soul of the whole existing world. It develops into itself through all the preliminary stages which are treated at length in the *Logic* and which are all

---

point. I cannot deny that both before and during my forty years' collaboration with Marx I had a certain independent share in laying the foundations of the theory, and more particularly in its elaboration. But the greater part of its leading basic principles, especially in the realm of economics and history, and, above all, their final trenchant formulation, belong to Marx. What I contributed—at any rate with the exception of my work in a few special fields—Marx could very well have done without me. What Marx accomplished I would not have achieved. Marx stood higher, saw further, and took a wider and quicker view than all the rest of us. Marx was a genius; we others were at best talented. Without him the theory would not be by far what it is today. It therefore rightly bears his name. [*Note by Engels.*]

included in it. Then it "alienates" itself by changing into nature, where, without consciousness of itself, disguised as the necessity of nature, it goes through a new development and finally comes again to self-consciousness in man. This self-consciousness then elaborates itself again in history from the crude form until finally the absolute concept again comes to itself completely in the Hegelian philosophy. According to Hegel, therefore, the dialectical development apparent in nature and history, that is, the causal interconnection of the progressive movement from the lower to the higher, which asserts itself through all zigzag movements and temporary retrogressions, is only a copy [*Abklatsch*] of the self-movement of the concept going on from eternity, no one knows where, but at all events independently of any thinking human brain. This ideological perversion had to be done away with. We comprehended the concepts in our heads once more materialistically—as images [*Abbilder*] of real things instead of regarding the real things as images of this or that stage of the absolute concept. Thus dialectics reduced itself to the science of the general laws of motion, both of the external world and of human thought—two sets of laws which are identical in substance, but differ in their expression in so far as the human mind can apply them consciously, while in nature and also up to now for the most part in human history these laws assert themselves unconsciously, in the form of external necessity, in the midst of an endless series of seeming accidents. Thereby the dialectic of concepts itself became merely the conscious reflex of the dialectical motion of the real world and thus the dialectic of Hegel was placed upon its head; or rather, turned off its head, on which it was standing, and placed upon its feet. And this materialist dialectic, which for years has been our best working tool and our sharpest weapon, was, remarkably enough, discovered not only by us but also, independently of us and even of Hegel, by a German worker, Joseph Dietzgen.*

In this way, however, the revolutionary side of Hegelian philosophy was again taken up and at the same time freed from the idealist trimmings which with Hegel had prevented its consistent execution. The great basic thought that the world is not to be comprehended as a complex of ready-made *things*, but as a complex of *processes*, in which the things apparently stable no less than their mind images in our heads, the concepts, go through an uninterrupted change of coming into being and passing away, in which, in spite of all seeming accidentality and all temporary retrogression, a progressive development asserts itself in the end—this great fundamental thought has, especially since the time of Hegel, so thoroughly permeated ordinary consciousness that in this generality it is now scarcely ever contradicted. But to acknowledge this fundamental thought in words and to apply it in reality in detail to each domain of investigation are two different things. If, however, investigation always proceeds from this standpoint, the demand for final solutions and eternal truths ceases once for all; one is always conscious of the necessary limitation of all acquired knowledge, of the fact that it is conditioned by the circumstances in which it was acquired. On the other hand, one no longer permits oneself to be imposed upon by the antitheses, insuperable for the still common old metaphysics, between true and false, good and bad, identical and different, necessary and accidental. One knows that these antitheses have only a relative validity; that what is recognized now as true has also its latent false side which will later manifest itself, just as what is

* See *Das Wesen der menschlichen Kopfarbeit, dargestellt von einem Handarbeiter* [*The Nature of Human Brainwork, Described by a Manual Worker*]. Hamburg, Meissner, 1869. [*Note by Engels.*]

now regarded as false has also its true side by virtue of which it could previously be regarded as true. One knows that what is maintained to be necessary is composed of sheer accidents and that the so-called accidental is the form behind which necessity hides itself—and so on.

The old method of investigation and thought which Hegel calls "metaphysical," which preferred to investigate *things* as given, as fixed and stable, a method the relics of which still strongly haunt people's minds, had a great deal of historical justification in its day. It was necessary first to examine things before it was possible to examine processes. One had first to know what a particular thing was before one could observe the changes it was undergoing. And such was the case with natural science. The old metaphysics, which accepted things as finished objects, arose from a natural science which investigated dead and living things as finished objects. But when this investigation had progressed so far that it became possible to take the decisive step forward of transition to the systematic investigation of the changes which these things undergo in nature itself, then the last hour of the old metaphysics struck in the realm of philosophy too. And in fact, while natural science up to the end of the last century was predominantly a *collecting* science, a science of finished things, in our century it is essentially a *systematizing* science, a science of the processes, of the origin and development of these things and of the interconnection which binds all these natural processes into one great whole. Physiology, which investigates the processes occurring in plant and animal organisms; embryology, which deals with the development of individual organisms from germ to maturity; geology, which investigates the gradual formation of the earth's surface—all these are the offspring of our century.

But, above all, there are three great discoveries which

have enabled our knowledge of the interconnection of natural processes to advance by leaps and bounds: first, the discovery of the cell as the unit from whose multiplication and differentiation the whole plant and animal body develops, so that not only is the development and growth of all higher organisms recognized to proceed according to a single general law, but also, in the capacity of the cell to change, the way is pointed out by which organisms can change their species and thus go through a more than individual development.

Second, the transformation of energy, which has demonstrated to us that all the so-called forces operative in the first instance in inorganic nature—mechanical force and its complement, so-called potential energy, heat, radiation (light, or radiant heat), electricity, magnetism and chemical energy—are different forms of manifestation of universal motion, which pass into one another in definite proportions so that in place of a certain quantity of the one which disappears, a certain quantity of another makes its appearance and thus the whole motion of nature is reduced to this incessant process of transformation from one form into another.

Finally, the proof, which Darwin first developed in connected form, that the stock of organic products of nature environing us today, including man, is the result of a long process of evolution from a few originally unicellular germs, and that these again have arisen from protoplasm or albumen, which came into existence by chemical means.

Thanks to these three great discoveries and the other immense advances in natural science, we have now arrived at the point where we can demonstrate the interconnection between the processes in nature not only in particular spheres but also the interconnection of these particular spheres on the whole, and so can present in an approximately systematic form a comprehensive view of the interconnection in nature by means of the facts provided by empirical natural science itself. To furnish this comprehensive view was formerly the task of so-called natural philosophy. It could do this only by putting in place of the real but as yet unknown interconnections ideal, fancied ones, filling in the missing facts by figments of the mind and bridging the actual gaps merely in imagination. In the course of this procedure it conceived many brilliant ideas and foreshadowed many later discoveries, but it also produced a considerable amount of nonsense, which indeed could not have been otherwise. Today, when one needs to comprehend the results of natural scientific investigation only dialectically, that is, in the sense of their own interconnection, in order to arrive at a "system of nature" sufficient for our time; when the dialectical character of this interconnection is forcing itself against their will even into the metaphysically-trained minds of the natural scientists, today natural philosophy is finally disposed of. Every attempt at resurrecting it would be not only superfluous but a *step backwards.*

But what is true of nature, which is hereby recognized also as a historical process of development, is likewise true of the history of society in all its branches and of the totality of all sciences which occupy themselves with things human (and divine). Here, too, the philosophy of history, of right, of religion, etc., has consisted in the substitution of an interconnection fabricated in the mind of the philosopher for the real interconnection to be demonstrated in the events; has consisted in the comprehension of history as a whole as well as in its separate parts, as the gradual realization of ideas—and naturally always only the pet ideas of the philosopher himself. According to this, history worked unconsciously but of necessity towards a certain ideal goal set in advance—as, for example, in Hegel, towards the realization of his absolute idea—and the unalterable trend towards this absolute idea formed the inner interconnection in the events of history. A new mysterious providence—unconscious or gradually coming into consciousness—was thus put in the place of the real, still unknown interconnection. Here, therefore, just as in the realm of nature, it was necessary to do away with these fabricated, artificial interconnections by the discovery of the real ones—a task which ultimately amounts to the discovery of the general laws of motion which assert themselves as the ruling ones in the history of human society.

In one point, however, the history of the development of society proves to be essentially different from that of nature. In nature—in so far as we ignore man's reaction upon nature—there are only blind, unconscious agencies acting upon one another, out of whose interplay the general law comes into operation. Nothing of all that happens—whether in the innumerable apparent accidents observable upon the surface, or in the ultimate results which confirm the regularity inherent in these accidents—happens as a consciously desired aim. In the history of society, on the contrary, the actors are all endowed with consciousness, are men acting with deliberation or passion, working towards definite goals; nothing happens without a conscious purpose, without an intended aim. But this distinction, important as it is for historical investigation, particularly of single epochs and events, cannot alter the fact that the course of history is governed by inner general laws. For here, also, on the whole, in spite of the consciously desired aims of all individuals, accident apparently reigns on the surface. That which is willed happens but rarely; in the majority of instances the numerous desired ends cross and conflict with one another, or these ends themselves are from the outset incapable of realization or the means of attaining them are insufficient. Thus the conflicts of innumerable individual wills and individual actions in the domain of history produce a state of affairs entirely analogous to that prevailing in the realm of unconscious nature. The ends of the actions are intended, but the results which actually follow from these actions are not intended; or when they do seem to correspond to the end intended, they ultimately have consequences quite other than those intended. Historical events thus appear on the whole to be likewise governed by chance. But where on the surface accident holds sway, actually it is always governed by inner, hidden laws and it is only a matter of discovering these laws.

Men make their own history, whatever its outcome may be, in that each person follows his own consciously desired end, and it is precisely the resultant of these many wills operating in different directions and of their manifold effects upon the outer world that constitutes history. Thus it is also a question of what the many individuals desire. The will is determined by passion or deliberation. But the levers which immediately determine passion or deliberation are of very different kinds. Partly they may be external objects, partly ideal motives, ambition, "enthusiasm for truth and justice," personal hatred or even purely individual whims of all kinds. But, on the one hand, we have seen that the many individual wills active in history for the most part produce results quite other than those intended—often quite the opposite; that their motives, therefore, in relation to the total result, are likewise of only secondary importance. On the other hand, the further question arises: What driving forces in turn stand behind these motives? What are the historical causes which transform themselves into these motives in the brains of the actors?

The old materialism never put this question to itself. Its conception of history, in so far as it has one at all, is therefore essentially pragmatic; it judges everything according to the motives of the action; it divides men who act in history into noble and ignoble and then finds that as a rule the noble are defrauded and the ignoble are victorious. Hence, it follows for the old materialism that nothing very edifying is to be got from the study of history, and for us that in the realm of history the old materialism becomes untrue to itself because it takes the ideal driving forces which operate there as ultimate causes, instead of investigating what is behind them, what are the driving forces of these driving forces. The inconsistency does not lie in the fact that *ideal* driving forces are recognized, but in the investigation not being carried further back behind these into their motive causes. On the other hand, the philosophy of history, particularly as represented by Hegel, recognizes that the ostensible and also the really operating motives of men who act in history are by no means the ultimate causes of historical events; that behind these motives are other motive powers, which have to be discovered. But it does not seek these powers in history itself, it imports them rather from outside, from philosophical ideology, into history. Hegel, for example, instead of explaining the history of Ancient Greece out of its own inner interconnections, simply maintains that it is nothing more than the working out of "forms of beautiful individuality," the realization of a "work of art" as such. He says much in this connection about the old Greeks that is fine and profound, but that does not prevent us today from refusing to be put off with such an explanation, which is a mere manner of speech.

When, therefore, it is a question of investigating the driving powers which—consciously or unconsciously, and indeed very often unconsciously—lie behind the motives of men who act in history and which constitute the real ultimate driving forces of history, then it is not a question so much of the motives of single individuals, however eminent, as of those motives which set in motion great masses, whole peoples, and again whole classes of the people in each people; and this, too, not momentarily, for the transient flaring up of a straw-fire which quickly dies down, but for a lasting action resulting in a great historical transformation. To ascertain the driving causes which here in the minds of acting masses and their leaders—the so-called great men—are reflected as conscious motives, clearly or unclearly, directly or in ideological, even glorified form—that is the only path which can put us on the track of the laws holding sway both in history as a whole and at particular periods and in particular lands. Everything which sets men in motion must go through their minds; but what form it will take in the mind will depend very much upon the circumstances. The workers have by no means become reconciled to capitalist machine industry, even though they no longer simply break the machines to pieces as they still did in 1848 on the Rhine.

But while in all earlier periods the investigation of these driving causes of history was almost impossible—on account of the complicated and concealed interconnections between them and their effects—our present period has so far simplified these interconnections that the riddle could be solved. Since the establishment of large-scale industry, that is, at least since the European peace of 1815, it has been no longer a secret to any man in England that the whole political struggle there turned on the claims to supremacy of two classes: the landed aristocracy and the bourgeoisie (middle class). In France, with the return of the Bourbons, the same fact was percevied; the historians of the Restoration period, from Thierry to Guizot, Mignet and Thiers, speak of it everywhere as the key to the understanding of all French history since the Middle Ages. And since 1830 the working class, the proletariat, has been recognized in both countries as a third competitor for power. Conditions had become so simplified that one would have had to close one's eyes deliberately not to see in the fight of these three great classes and in the conflict of their interests the driving force of modern history—at least in the two most advanced countries.

But how did these classes come into existence? If it was possible at first glance still to ascribe the origin of the great, formerly feudal landed property—at least in the first instance—to political causes, to taking possession by force, this could not be done in regard to the bourgeoisie and the proletariat. Here the origin and development of two great classes was seen to lie clearly and palpably in purely economic causes. And it was just as clear that in the struggle between landed property and the bourgeoisie, no less than in the struggle between the bourgeoisie and the proletariat, it was a question, first and foremost, of economic interests, to the furtherance of which political power was intended to serve merely as a means. Bourgeoisie and proletariat both arose in consequence of a transformation of the economic conditions, more precisely, of the mode of production. The transition, first from guild handicrafts to manufacture, and then from manufacture to large-scale industry, with steam and mechanical power, caused the development of these two classes. At a certain stage the new productive forces set in motion by the bourgeoisie—in the first place the division of labour and the combination of many detail labourers [*Teilarbeiter*] in one general manufactory—and the conditions and requirements of exchange, developed through these productive forces, became incompatible with the existing order of production handed down by history and sanctified by law, that is to say, incompatible with the privileges of the guild and the numerous other personal and local privileges (which were only so many fetters to the unprivileged estates) of the feudal order of society. The productive forces represented by the bourgeoisie rebelled against the order of production represented by the feudal landlords and the guild-masters. The result is known: the feudal fetters were smashed, gradually in England, at one blow in France. In Germany the process is not yet finished. But just as, at a definite stage of its development, manufacture came into conflict with the feudal order of production, so now large-scale industry has already come into conflict with the bourgeois order of production established in its place. Tied down by this order, by the narrow limits of the capitalist mode of production, this industry produces, on the one hand, an ever-increasing proletarianization of the great mass of the people, and on the other hand, an ever greater mass of unsaleable products. Overproduction and mass misery, each the cause of the other—that is the absurd contradiction which is its outcome, and which of necessity calls for the liberation of the productive forces by means of a change in the mode of production.

In modern history at least it is, therefore, proved that all political struggles are class struggles, and all class struggles for emancipation, despite their necessarily political form—for every class struggle is a political struggle—turn ultimately on the question of *economic* emancipation. Therefore, here at least, the state—the political order—is the subordinate, and civil society—the realm of economic relations—the decisive element. The traditional conception, to which Hegel, too, pays homage, saw in the state the determining element, and in civil society the element determined by it. Appearances correspond to this. As all the driving forces of the actions of any individual person must pass through his brain, and transform themselves into motives of his will in order to set him into action, so also all the needs of civil society—no matter which class happens to be the ruling one—must pass through the will of the state in order to secure general validity in the form of laws. That is the formal aspect of the matter—the one which is self-evident. The question arises, however: what is the content of this merely formal will—of the individual as well as of the state—and whence is this content derived? Why is just this willed and not something else? If we inquire into this we discover that in modern history the will of the state is, on the whole, determined by the changing needs of civil society, by the supremacy of this or that class, in the last resort, by the development of the productive forces and relations of exchange.

But if even in our modern era, with its gigantic means of production and communication, the state is not an independent domain with an independent development, but one whose existence as well as development is to be explained in the last resort by the economic conditions of life of society, then this must be still more true of all earlier times when the production of the material life of man was not yet carried on with these abundant auxiliary means, and when, therefore, the necessity of such production must have exercised a still greater mastery over men. If the state even today, in the era of big industry and of railways, is on the whole only a reflexion, in concentrated form, of the economic needs of the class controlling production, then this must have been much more so in an epoch when each generation of men was forced to spend a far greater part of its aggregate life-time in satisfying material needs, and was therefore much more dependent on them than we are today. An examination of the history of earlier periods, as soon as it is seriously undertaken from this angle, abundantly confirms this. But, of course, this cannot be gone into here.

If the state and public law are determined by economic relations, so too, of course, is private law, which indeed in essence only sanctions the existing economic relations between individuals which are normal in the given circumstances. The form in which this happens can, however, vary considerably. It is possible, as happened in England in harmony with the whole national development, to retain in the main the forms of the old feudal laws while giving them a bourgeois content; in fact, directly reading a bourgeois meaning into the feudal name. But, also, as happened in western continental Europe, Roman Law, the first world law of a commodity-producing society, with its unsurpassably fine elaboration of all the essential legal relations of simple commodity owners (of buyers and sellers, debtors and creditors, contracts, obligations, etc.) can be taken as the foundation. In which case, for the benefit of a still petty-bourgeois and semi-feudal society, it can either be reduced to the level of such a society simply through judicial practice (common law) or, with the help of allegedly enlightened, moralizing jurists it can be worked into a special code of law to correspond with such social level—a code which in these circumstances will be a bad one also from the legal standpoint (for instance, Prussian *Landrecht*). In this case, however, after a great bourgeois revolution it is also possible for such a classic law code of bourgeois society as the French *Code Civil* to be worked out upon the basis of this same Roman Law. If, therefore, bourgeois legal rules merely express the economic life conditions of society in legal form, then they can do so well or ill according to circumstances.

The state presents itself to us as the first ideological power over man. Society creates for itself an organ for the safeguarding of its common interests against internal and external attacks. This organ is the state power. Hardly come into being, this organ makes itself independent vis-à-vis society; and, indeed, the more it becomes the organ of a definite class, the more it directly enforces the supremacy of that class. The fight of the oppressed class against the ruling class becomes necessarily a political fight, a fight first of all against the political domination of that class. The consciousness of the interconnection between this political struggle and its economic basis becomes dulled and can be lost altogether. While this is not wholly the case with the participants, it almost always happens with the historians. Of the ancient sources on the struggles within the Roman Republic only Appian tells us clearly and distinctly what was at issue in the last resort—namely, landed property.

But once the state has become an independent power vis-à-vis society, it produces forthwith a further ideology. It is indeed among professional politicians, theorists of public law and jurists of private law that the connection with economic facts gets lost for fair. Since in each particular case the economic facts must assume the form of juristic motives in order to receive legal sanction; and since, in so doing, consideration, of course, has to be given to the whole legal system already in operation, the juristic form is, in consequence, made everything and the economic content nothing. Public law and private law are treated as independent spheres, each having its own independent historical development, each being capable of and needing a systematic presentation by the consistent elimination of all inner contradictions.

Still higher ideologies, that is, such as are still further removed from the material, economic basis, take the form of philosophy and religion. Here the interconnection between conceptions and their material conditions of existence becomes more and more complicated, more and more obscured by intermediate links. But the interconnection exists. Just as the whole Renaissance period, from the middle of the fifteenth century, was an essential product of the towns and, therefore, of the burghers, so also was the subsequently newly awakened philosophy. Its content was in essence only the philosophical expression of the thoughts corresponding to the development of the small and middle burghers into a big bourgeoisie. Among last century's Englishmen and Frenchmen, who in many cases were just as much political economists as philosophers, this is clearly evident; and we have proved it above in regard to the Hegelian school.

We will now in addition deal only briefly with religion, since the latter stands furthest away from material life and seems to be most alien to it. Religion arose in very primitive times from erroneous, primitive conceptions of men about their own nature and external nature surrounding them. Every ideology, however, once it has arisen, develops in connection with the given concept-material, and develops this material further; otherwise it would not be an ideology, that is, occupation with thoughts as with independent entities, developing independently and subject only to their own laws. That the material life conditions of the persons inside whose heads this thought process goes on in the last resort determine the course of this process remains of necessity unknown to these persons, for otherwise there would be an end to all ideology. These original religious notions, therefore, which in the main are common to each group of kindred peoples, develop, after the group is divided, in a manner peculiar to each people, according to the conditions of life falling to their lot. For a number of groups of peoples, and particularly for the Aryans (so-called Indo-Europeans) this process has been shown in detail by comparative mythology. The gods thus fashioned within each people were national gods whose domain extended no farther than the national territory which they were to protect; on the other side of its boundaries other gods held undisputed sway. They could continue to exist, in imagination, only as long as the nation existed; they fell with its fall. The Roman world empire, the economic conditions of whose origin we do not need to examine here, brought about this downfall of the old nationalities. The old national gods decayed, even those of the Romans, which also were patterned to suit only the narrow confines of the city of Rome. The need to complement the world empire by means of a world religion was clearly revealed in the attempts made to provide in Rome recognition and altars for all the foreign gods to the slightest degree respectable alongside of the indigenous ones. But a new world religion is not to be made in this fashion, by imperial decree. The new world religion, Christianity, had already quietly come into being, out of a mixture of generalized Oriental, particularly Jewish, theology, and vulgarized Greek, particularly Stoic, philosophy. What it originally looked like has to be first laboriously discovered, since its official form, as it has been handed down to us, is merely that in which it became the state religion to which purpose it was adapted by the Council of Nicaea. The fact that after no more than 250 years it became the state religion suffices to show that it was the religion corresponding to the conditions of the time. In the Middle Ages, in the same measure as feudalism developed, Christianity grew into the religious counterpart to it, with a corresponding feudal hierarchy. And when the burghers began to thrive, there developed, in opposition to feudal Catholicism, the Protestant heresy, which first appeared in Southern France, among the Albigenses,[86] at the time the cities there reached the highest point of their florescence. The Middle Ages had attached to theology all the other forms of ideology—philosophy, politics, jurisprudence—and made them subdivisions of theology. It thereby constrained every social and political movement to take on a theological form. The sentiments of the masses were fed with religion to the exclusion of all else; it was therefore necessary to put forward their own interests in a religious guise in order to produce an impetuous movement. And just as the burghers from the beginning brought into being an appendage of propertyless urban plebeians, day labourers and servants of all kinds, belonging to no recognized social Estate, precursors of the later proletariat, so likewise heresy soon became divided into a burgher-moderate heresy and a plebeian-revolutionary one, the latter an abomination to the burgher heretics themselves.

The ineradicability of the Protestant heresy corresponded to the invincibility of the rising burghers. When these burghers had become sufficiently strengthened, their struggle against the feudal nobility, which till then had been predominantly local, began to assume national dimensions. The first great action occurred in Germany—the so-called Reformation. The burghers were neither powerful enough nor sufficiently developed to be able to unite under their banner the remaining rebellious estates—the plebeians of the towns, the lower nobility and the peasants on the land. At first the nobles were defeated; the peasants rose in a revolt which formed the peak of the whole revolutionary struggle; the cities left them in the lurch, and thus the revolution succumbed to the armies of the secular princes who reaped the whole profit. Thenceforward Germany disappears for three centuries from the ranks of countries playing an independent active part in history. But beside the German Luther appeared the Frenchman Calvin. With true French acuity he put the bourgeois character of the Reformation in the forefront, republicanized and democratized the Church. While the Lutheran Reformation in Germany degenerated and brought the country to rack and ruin, the Calvinist Reformation served as a banner for the republicans in Geneva, in Holland and in Scotland, freed Holland from Spain and from the German Empire and provided the ideological costume for the second act of the bourgeois revolution, which was taking place in England. Here Calvinism justified itself as the true religious disguise of the interests of the bourgeoisie of that time, and on this account did not attain full recognition when the revolution ended in 1689 in a compromise between one part of the nobility and the bourgeoisie. The English state church was re-established, not in its earlier form of a Catholicism which had the king for its pope, but, instead, strongly Calvinized. The old state church had celebrated the merry Catholic Sunday and had fought against the dull Calvinist one. The new, bourgeoisified church introduced the latter, which adorns England to this day.

In France, the Calvinist minority was suppressed in 1685 and either Catholicized or driven out of the country. But what was the good? Already at that time the free-thinker Pierre Bayle was at the height of his activity, and in 1694 Voltaire was born. The forcible measures of Louis XIV only made it easier for the French bourgeoisie to carry through its revolution in the irreligious, exclusively political form which alone was suited to a developed bourgeoisie. Instead of Protestants, free-thinkers took their seats in the national assemblies. Thereby Christianity entered into its final stage. It had become incapable for the future of serving any progressive class as the ideological garb of its aspirations. It became more and more the exclusive possession of the ruling classes and these apply it as a mere means of government, to keep the lower classes within bounds. Moreover, each of the different classes uses its own appropriate religion: the landed nobility—Catholic Jesuitism or Protestant orthodoxy; the liberal and radical bourgeoisie—rationalism; and it makes little difference whether these gentlemen themselves believe in their respective religions or not.

We see, therefore: religion, once formed, always contains traditional material, just as in all ideological domains tradition forms a great conservative force. But the transformations which this material undergoes spring from class relations, that is to say, out of the economic relations of the people who execute these transformations. And here that is sufficient.

In the above it could only be a question of giving a general sketch of the Marxist conception of history, at most with a few illustrations. The proof must be derived from history itself; and in this regard I may be permitted to say that it has been sufficiently furnished in other writings. This conception, however, puts an end to philosophy in the realm of history, just as the dialectical conception of nature makes all natural philosophy both unnecessary and impossible. It is no longer a question anywhere of inventing interconnections out of our brain, but of discovering them in the facts. For philosophy, which has been expelled from nature and history, there remains only the realm of pure thought, so far as it is left: the theory of the laws of the thought process itself, logic and dialectics.

* * *

With the Revolution of 1848, "educated" Germany said farewell to theory and went over to the field of practice. Small production and manufacture, based upon manual labour, were superseded by real large-scale industry. Germany again appeared on the world market. The new little German Empire[87] abolished at least the most crying of the abuses with which this development had been obstructed by the system of petty states, the relics of feudalism, and bureaucratic management. But to the same degree that speculation abandoned the philosopher's study in order to set up its temple in the Stock Exchange, educated Germany lost the great aptitude for theory which had been the glory of Germany in the days of its deepest political humiliation —the aptitude for purely scientific investigation, irrespective of whether the result obtained was practically applicable or not, whether likely to offend the police authorities or not. Official German natural science, it is true, maintained its position in the front rank, particularly in the field of specialized research. But even the American journal *Science* rightly remarks that the decisive advances in the sphere of the comprehensive correlation of particular facts and their generalization into laws are now being made much more in England, instead of, as formerly, in Germany. And in the sphere of the historical sciences, philosophy included, the old fearless zeal for theory has now disappeared completely, along with classical philosophy. Inane eclecticism and an anxious concern for career and income, descending to the most vulgar job-hunting, occupy its place. The official representatives of these sciences have become the undisguised ideologists of the bourgeoisie and the existing state—but at a time when both stand in open antagonism to the working class.

Only among the working class does the German aptitude for theory remain unimpaired. Here it cannot be exterminated. Here there is no concern for careers, for profit-making, or for gracious patronage from above. On the contrary, the more ruthlessly and disinterestedly science proceeds the more it finds itself in harmony with the interests and aspirations of the workers. From the outset the new tendency, which recognized that the key to the understanding of the whole history of society lies in the history of the development of labour, addressed itself by preference to the working class and here found the response which it neither sought nor expected from officially recognized science. The German working-class movement is the heir of German classical philosophy.

FREDERICK ENGELS

JURISTIC SOCIALISM

The world outlook of the Middle Ages was substantially theological. The unity of the European world which actually did not exist internally, was established externally, against the common Saracen foe, by Christianity.

The unity of the West-European world, which consisted of a group of nations developing in continual intercourse, was welded in Catholicism. This theological welding was not only in ideas, it existed in reality, not only in the Pope, its monarchistic centre, but above all in the feudally and hierarchically organized Church, which, owning about a third of the land in every country, occupied a position of tremendous power in the feudal organization. The Church with its feudal landownership was the real link between the different countries; the feudal organization of the Church gave a religious consecration to the secular feudal state system. Besides, the clergy was the only educated class. It was therefore natural that Church dogma was the starting-point and basis of all thought. Jurisprudence, natural science, philosophy, everything was dealt with according to whether its content agreed or disagreed with the doctrines of the Church.

But in the womb of feudalism the power of the bourgeoisie was developing. A new class appeared in opposition to the big landowners. The city burghers were first and foremost and exclusively producers of and traders in commodities, while the feudal mode of production was based substantially on self-consumption of the product within a limited circle, partly by the producers and partly by the feudal lord. The Catholic world outlook, fashioned on the pattern of feudalism, was no longer adequate for this new class and its conditions of production and exchange. Nevertheless, this new class remained for a long time a captive in the bonds of almighty theology. From the thirteenth to the seventeenth century all the reformations and the struggles carried out under religious slogans that were connected with them were, on the theoretical side, nothing but repeated attempts of the burghers and plebeians in the towns and the peasants who had become rebellious by contact with both the latter to adapt the old theological world outlook to the changed economic conditions and the condition of life of the new class. But that could not be done. The flag of religion waved for the last time in England in the seventeenth century, and hardly fifty years later appeared undisguised in France the new world outlook which was to become the classical outlook of bourgeoisie, the *juristic world outlook.*

It was a secularization of the theological outlook. Human right took the place of dogma, of divine right, the state took the place of the church. The economic and social conditions, which had formerly been imagined to have been created by the Church and dogma because they were sanctioned by the Church, were now considered as founded on right and created by the state. Because commodity exchange on a social scale and in its full development, particularly through advance and credit, produces complicated mutual contract relations and therefore demands generally applicable rules that can be given only by the community—state-determined standards of right—it was imagined that these standards of right arose not from the economic facts but from formal establishment by the state. And because competition, the basic form of trade of free commodity producers, is the greatest equalizer, equality before the law became the main battle-cry of the bourgeoisie. The fact that this newly aspiring class's struggle against the feudal lords and the absolute monarchy then protecting them, like every class struggle, had to be a political struggle, a struggle for the mastery of the state, and had to be fought on *juridical demands* contributed to strengthen the juristic outlook.

But the bourgeoisie produced its negative double, the proletariat, and with it a new class struggle which broke out before the bourgeoisie had completed the conquest of political power. As the bourgeoisie in its time had by force of tradition dragged the theological outlook with it for a while in its fight against the nobility, so, too, the proletariat at first took over the juristic outlook from its opponent and sought in it weapons against the bourgeoisie. The first elements of the proletarian party as well as their theoretical representatives remained wholly on the juristic "ground of right," the only distinction being that they built up for themselves a different ground of "right" from that of the bourgeoisie. On one side the demand for equality was extended so that equality in right would be completed by social equality; on the other, from Adam Smith's proposition that labour is the source of all wealth but that the product of labour must be shared with the landowner and the capitalist the conclusion was drawn that this sharing was unjust and must be either abolished or modified in favour of the worker. But the feeling that to leave this question on the mere juristic "ground of right" in no way made possible the abolition of the evil conditions created by the bourgeois-capitalistic mode of production, i.e., the mode of production based on large-scale industry, already then led the major minds among the earlier socialists—Saint-Simon, Fourier and Owen—to abandon entirely the juristic-political field and to declare all political struggle fruitless.

Both these views were equally unsatisfactory to express adequately and embrace completely the working class's desire for emancipation created by economic conditions. The demand for the full product of labour and just as much the demand for equality lost themselves in unsolvable contradictions as soon as they were formulated juristically in detail and left the core of the question—the transformation of the mode of production—more or less untouched. The rejection of the political struggle by the great Utopians was at the same time the rejection of the class struggle, i.e., of the only form of activity of the class whose interests they represented. Both outlooks made abstraction of the historical background to which they owed their existence; both appealed to feeling: some to the feeling of justice, others to the feeling of humanity. Both attired their demands in the form of pious wishes of which one could not say why they had to be fulfilled at that very time and not a thousand years earlier or later.

The working class, who by the changing of the feudal mode of production into the capitalist mode was deprived of all ownership of the means of production and by the mechanism of the capitalist mode of production is continually engendered anew in that hereditary state of propertylessness, cannot find an exhaustive expression of its living condition in the juristic illusion of the bourgeoisie. It can only know that condition of life fully itself if it looks at things in their reality without juristically coloured glasses. But Marx helped it to do that with his materialist conception of history, by providing the proof that all man's juristic, political, philosophical, religious and other ideas are derived in the last resort from his economic conditions of life, from his mode of production and of exchanging the product. Thus he provided the world outlook corresponding to the conditions of the life and struggle of the proletariat; only lack of illusions in the heads of the workers could correspond to their lack of property. And this proletarian world outlook is now spreading over the world.

ENGELS TO BLOCH

London, September 21-22,1890

Dear Sir,

Your letter of 3rd inst. was forwarded to me at Folkestone, but as I had not the book in question there I could not answer it. On my return home on the 12th I found such a lot of urgent work waiting for me that I have not been able to find time to write you a few lines until today. Please accept this explanation and excuse me for the delay.

Ad. I. First, you conclude from page 19 of *The Origin*[88] that the process of the development of the Punalua family is presented as proceeding so gradually that even in this century marriages took place between brothers and sisters (*from the same mother*) in the royal family in Hawaii. And during the whole of antiquity we find examples of marriages between brothers and sisters, e.g., among the Ptolomies. But here, secondly, a difference must be made between brothers and sisters from the same *mother* and from the same *father*; ἀδελφὸς, ἀδελφὴ *brother*, *sister*, come from ἀδελφὸς —*womb* and therefore originally mean only brothers and sisters on the *mother's side*. The sentiment long remained prevalent from the matriarchy that children of the same mother, though of different fathers are more closely related than children of the same father but of different mothers. The Punalua form of the family excludes marriage only between the former, by no means between the latter, who according to the corresponding conception *are not even relatives* (since matriarchal right is in vigour). As far as I know the marriages between brothers and sisters which we find in Greek antiquity are confined to cases in which the parties had different mothers or cases in which it was not ascertained and, therefore not precluded, that they were of different mothers, and such marriages are therefore absolutely not contrary to Punalua customs. You have overlooked the fact that between the Punalua period and Greek monogamy there was the leap from matriarchy to patriarchy which considerably alters the situation.

According to Wachsmuth's *Hellenische Alterthümer*, in the heroic Greek age there is "no trace of scruples about too close affinity of the married couple, except the relation between parents and children" (III, p. 156). "Marriage to a full sister was not improper in Creta" (*ibid.*, p. 170). Finally, concerning Strabo, Book X, but I cannot find the passage at present owing to lack of division into chapters. —By *full* sister, until proof of the contrary, I understand sister on the father's side.

Ad. II. I qualify your first main statement as follows: According to the materialist conception of history, the *ultimately* determining element in history is the production and reproduction of real life. More than this neither Marx nor I have ever asserted. Hence if somebody twists this into saying that the economic element is the *only* determining one, he transforms that proposition into a meaningless, abstract, senseless phrase. The economic situation is the basis, but the various elements of the superstructure—political forms of the class struggle and its results, to wit: constitutions established by the victorious class after a successful battle, etc., juridical forms, and even the reflexes of all these actual struggles in the brain of the participants, political, juristic, philosophical theories, religious views and their further development into systems of dogmas—also exercise their influence upon the course of the historical struggles and in many cases preponderate in determining their *form*. There is an interaction of all these elements in which, amid all the endless host of accidents (that is, of things and events whose inner interconnection is so remote or so impossible of proof that we can regard it as non-existent, as negligible) the economic movement finally asserts itself as necessary. Otherwise the application of the theory to any period of history would be easier than the solution of a simple equation of the first degree.

We make our history ourselves, but, in the first place, under very definite assumptions and conditions. Among these the economic ones are ultimately decisive. But the political ones, etc., and, indeed, even the traditions which haunt human minds, also play a part, although not the decisive one. The Prussian state also arose and developed from historical, ultimately economic, causes. But it could scarcely be maintained without pedantry that among the many small states of North Germany, Brandenburg was specifically determined by economic necessity to become the great power embodying the economic, linguistic and, after the Reformation, also the religious difference between North and South, and not by other element as well (above all by its entanglement with Poland, owing to the possession of Prussia, and hence with international political relations—which were indeed also decisive in the formation of the Austrian dynastic power). Without making oneself ridiculous it would be a difficult thing to explain in terms of economics the existence of every small state in Germany, past and present, or the origin of the High German consonant shifts, which widened the geographic partition formed by the mountains from the Sudet range to the Taunus to form a regular fissure across all Germany.

In the second place, however, history is made in such a way that the final result always arises from conflicts between many individual wills, of which each in turn has been made what it is by a host of particular conditions of life. Thus there are innumerable intersecting forces, an infinite series of parallelograms of forces which give rise to one resultant—the historical event. This may again itself be viewed as the product of a power which works as a whole *unconsciously* and without volition. For what each individual wills is obstructed by everyone else, and what emerges is something that no one willed. Thus history has proceeded hitherto in the manner of a natural process and is essentially subject to the same laws of motion. But from the fact that the wills of individuals—each of whom desires what he is impelled to by his physical constitution and external, in the last resort economic, circumstances (either his own personal circumstances or those of society in general)—do not attain what they want, but are merged into an aggregate mean, a common resultant, it must not be concluded that they are equal to zero. On the contrary, each contributes to the resultant and is to this extent included in it.

I would furthermore ask you to study this theory from its original sources and not at second hand; it is really much easier. Marx wrote hardly anything in which it did not play a part. But especially *The Eighteenth Brumaire of Louis Bonaparte* is a most excellent example of its application. There are also many allusions to it in *Capital*. Then may I also direct you to my writings: *Herr Eugen Dühring's Revolution in Science* and *Ludwig Feuerbach and the End of Classical German Philosophy*, in which I have given the most detailed account of historical materialism which, as far as I know, exists.

Marx and I are ourselves partly to blame for the fact that the younger people sometimes lay more stress on the economic side than is due to it. We had to emphasize the main principle vis-à-vis our adversaries, who denied it, and we had not always the time, the place or the opportunity to give their due to the other elements involved in the interaction. But when it came to presenting a section of history, that is, to making a practical application, it was a different matter and there no error was permissible. Unfortunately, however, it happens only too often that people think they have fully understood a new theory and can apply it without more ado from the moment they have assimilated its main principles, and even those not always correctly. And I cannot exempt many of the more recent "Marxists" from this reproach, for thc most amazing rubbish has been produced in this quarter, too.

Ad. I. Yesterday (I am writing this on September 22) I found in Schoemann's *Griechische Alterthümer*, Berlin 1855, I. p. 52, another decisive passage which fully confirms the interpretation I gave above. It is the following: "It is known, however, that marriages between half-brothers and sisters having different mothers were not considered as incest in Ancient Greece."

I hope that the number of intercalations that I have made for the sake of brevity will not put you out too much, and remain

Your devoted

F. Engels

ENGELS TO C. SCHMIDT

London, October 27, 1890

I am taking advantage of the first free moments to reply to you. I think you would do very well to take the post in Zürich. You could always learn a good deal about economics there, especially if you bear in mind that Zürich is after all only a third-rate money and speculation market, so that the impressions which make themselves felt there are weakened by twofold or threefold reflection or are deliberately distorted. But you will get a practical knowledge of the mechanism and be obliged to follow the stock-exchange reports from London, New York, Paris, Berlin and Vienna at first hand, and thus the world market, in its reflex as money and stock market, will reveal itself to you. Economic, political and other reflections are just like those in the human eye: they pass through a condensing lens and therefore appear upside down, standing on their heads. Only the nervous apparatus which would put them on their feet again for presentation to us is lacking. The money-market man sees the movement of industry and of the world market only in the inverted reflection of the money and stock market and so effect becomes cause to him. I noticed that as early as in the forties in Manchester: the London stock-exchange reports were utterly useless for understanding the course of industry and its periodical maxima and minima because these gentry tried to explain everything by crises on the money market, which of course were themselves generally only symptoms. At that time the point was to disprove temporary over-production as the origin of industrial crises, so that the thing had in addition its tendentious side, provocative of distortion. This point now ceases to exist—for us, at any rate, for good and all—besides which it is indeed a fact that the money market can also have its own crises, in which direct disturbances of industry play only a subordinate part or no part at all. Here there is still much to be established and examined, especially in the history of the last twenty years.

Where there is division of labour on a social scale, there the separate labour processes become independent of each other. In the last instance production is the decisive factor. But as soon as trade in products becomes independent of production proper, it follows a movement of its own, which, while governed as a whole by that of production, still in particulars and within this general dependence again follows laws of its own inherent in the nature of this new factor; this movement has phases of its own and in its turn reacts on the movement of production. The discovery of America was due to the thirst for gold which had previously driven the Portuguese to Africa (cf. Soetbeer's *Production of Precious Metals*), because the enormously extended European industry of the fourteenth and fifteenth centuries and the trade corresponding to it demanded more means of exchange than Germany, the great silver country from 1450 to 1550, could provide. The conquest of India by the Portuguese, Dutch and English between 1500 and 1800 had *imports from* India as its object—nobody dreamt of exporting anything there. And yet what a colossal reaction these discoveries and conquests, brought about solely by trade interests, had upon industry: it was only the need for *exports to* these countries that created and developed modern large-scale industry.

So it is, too, with the money market. As soon as trade in money becomes separate from trade in commodities it has—under certain conditions imposed by production and commodity trade and within these limits—a development of its own, special laws determined by its own nature and separate phases. If to this is added that money trade, developing further, comes to include trade in securities and that these securities are not only government papers but also industrial and transport stocks, so that money trade gains direct control over a portion of the production by which, taken as a whole, it is itself controlled, then the reaction of money trading on production becomes still stronger and more complicated. The traders in money are the owners of railways, mines, iron works, etc. These means of production take on a double aspect: their operation has to be directed sometimes in the interests of direct production, but sometimes also according to the requirements of the shareholders, so far as they are money traders. The most striking example of this is furnished by the North American railways, whose operation is entirely dependent on the daily stock-exchange operations of a Jay Gould or a Vanderbilt, etc., which have nothing whatever to do with the particular railway and its interests as a means of communication. And even here in England we have seen contests lasting decades between different railway companies over the boundaries of their respective territories—contests on which an enormous amount of money was thrown away, not in the interests of production and communication but simply because of a rivalry whose sole object usually was to facilitate the stock-exchange transactions of the shareholding money traders.

With these few indications of my conception of the relation of production to commodity trade and of both to money trade, I have answered, in essence, your questions about historical materialism generally. The thing is easiest to grasp from the point of view of the division of labour. Society gives rise to certain common functions which it cannot dispense with. The persons appointed for this purpose form a new branch of the division of labour *within society*. This gives them a particular interest, distinct, too, from the interests of those who empowered them; they make themselves independent of the latter and —the state is in being. And now things proceed in a way similar to that in commodity trade and later in money trade: the new independent power, while having in the main to follow the movement of production, reacts in its turn, by virtue of its inherent relative independence—that is, the relative independence once transferred to it and gradually further developed—upon the conditions and course of production. It is the interaction of two unequal forces: on the one hand, the economic movement, on the other, the new political power, which strives for as much independence as possible, and which, having once been established, is endowed with a movement of its own. On the whole, the economic movement gets its way, but it has also to suffer reactions from the political movement which it itself established and endowed with relative independence, from the movement of the state power, on the one hand, and of the opposition simultaneously engendered, on the other. Just as the movement of the industrial market is, in the main and with the reservations already indicated, reflected in the money market and, of course, in *inverted* form, so the struggle between the classes already existing and fighting with one another is reflected in the struggle between government and opposition, but likewise in inverted form, no longer directly but indirectly, not as a class struggle but as a fight for political principles, and so distorted that it has taken us thousands of years to get behind it.

The reaction of the state power upon economic development can be of three kinds: it can run in the same direction, and then development is more rapid; it can oppose the line of development, in which case nowadays it will go to pieces in the long run in every great people; or it can prevent the economic development from proceeding along certain lines, and prescribe other lines. This case ultimately reduces itself to one of the two previous ones. But it is obvious that in cases two and three the political power can do great damage to the economic development and cause a great squandering of energy and material.

Then there is also the case of the conquest and brutal destruction of economic resources, by which, in certain circumstances, a whole local or national economic development could formerly be ruined. Nowadays such a case usually has the opposite effect, at least with great peoples: in the long run the vanquished often gains more economically, politically and morally than the victor.

Similarly with law. As soon as the new division of labour which creates professional lawyers becomes necessary, another new and independent sphere is opened up which, for all its general dependence on production and trade, has also a special capacity for reacting upon these spheres. In a modern state, law must not only correspond to the general economic condition and be its expression, but must also be an *internally coherent* expression which does not, owing to inner contradictions, reduce itself to nought. And in order to achieve this, the faithful reflection of economic conditions suffers increasingly. The more so as it more seldom happens that a code of law is the blunt, unmitigated, unadulterated expression of the domination of a class—this in itself would offend the "conception of right." Even in the *Code Napoléon* the pure, consistent conception of right held by the revolutionary bourgeoisie of 1792-96 is alrealy adulterated in many ways, and, in so far as it is embodied there, has daily to undergo all sorts of attenuations owing to the rising power of the proletariat. This does not prevent the *Code Napoléon* from being the statute book which serves as the basis of every new code of law in every part of the world. Thus to a great extent the course of the "development of right" consists only, first, in the attempt to do away with the contradictions arising from the direct translation of economic relations into legal principles, and to establish a harmonious system of law, and then in the repeated breaches made in this system by the influence and compulsion of further economic development, which involves it in further contradictions. (I am speaking here for the moment only of civil law.)

The reflection of economic relations as legal principles is necessarily also a topsy-turvy one: it goes on without the person who is acting being conscious of it; the jurist imagines he is operating with *a piori* propositions, whereas they are really only economic reflexes; so everything is upside down. And it seems to me obvious that this inversion, which, so long as it remains unrecognized, forms what we call *ideological outlook*, reacts in its turn upon the economic basis and may, within certain limits, modify it. The basis of the right of inheritance—assuming that the stages reached in the development of the family are the same—is an economic one. Nevertheless, it would be difficult to prove, for instance, that the absolute liberty of the testator in England and the severe restrictions in every detail imposed upon him in France are due to economic causes alone. Both react back, however, on the economic sphere to a very considerable extent, because they influence the distribution of property.

As to the realms of ideology which soar still higher in the air—religion, philosophy, etc.—these have a prehistoric stock, found already in existence and taken over by the historical period, of what we should today call bunk. These various false conceptions of nature, of man's own being, of spirits, magic forces, etc., have for the most part only a negative economic element as their basis; the low economic development of the prehistoric period is supplemented and also partially conditioned and even caused by the false conceptions of nature. And even though economic necessity was the main driving force of the progressive knowledge of nature and has become ever more so, it would surely be pedantic to try and find economic causes for all this primitive nonsense. The history of science is the history of the gradual clearing away of this nonsense or rather of its replacement by fresh but always less absurd nonsense. The people who attend to this belong in their turn to special spheres in the division of labour and appear to themselves to be working in an independent field. And to the extent that they form an independent group within the social division of labour, their productions, including their errors, react upon the whole development of society, even on its economic development. But all the same they themselves are in turn under the dominating influence of economic development. In philosophy, for instance, this can be most readily proved true for the bourgeois period. Hobbes was the first modern materialist (in the eighteenth-century sense) but he was an absolutist in a period when absolute monarchy was at its height throughout Europe and entered the lists against the people in England. Locke, both in religion and politics, was the child of the class compromise of 1688. The English deists and their more consistent continuators, the French materialists, were the true philosophers of the bourgeoisie, the French even of the bourgeois revolution. The German philistine runs through German philosophy from Kant to Hegel, sometimes positively and sometimes negatively. But as a definite sphere in the division of labour, the philosophy of every epoch presupposes certain definite thought material handed down to it by its predecessors, from which it takes its start. And that is why economically backward countries can still play first fiddle in philosophy: France in the eighteenth century as compared with England, on whose philosophy the French based themselves, and later Germany as compared with both. But in France as well as Germany philosophy and the general blossoming of literature at that time were the result of a rising economic development. I consider the ultimate supremacy of economic development established in these spheres too, but it comes to pass within the limitations imposed by the particular sphere itself: in philosophy, for instance, by the operation of economic influences (which again generally act only under political and other disguises) upon the existing philosophic material handed down by predecessors. Here economy creates nothing anew, but it determines the way in which the thought material found in existence is altered and further developed, and that too for the most part indirectly, for it is the political, legal and moral reflexes which exert the greatest direct influence on philosophy.

About religion I have said what was most necessary in the last section on Feuerbach.*

If therefore Barth supposes that we deny any and every reaction of the political and other reflexes of the economic movement upon the movement itself, he is simply tilting at windmills. He has only got to look at Marx's *Eighteenth Brumaire*, which deals almost exclusively with the *particular* part played by political struggles and events, of course within their *general* dependence upon economic conditions, or *Capital*,[89] the section on the working day, for instance, where legislation, which is surely a political

---

* See pp. 245-66 of this collection.—*Ed.*

act, has such a trenchant effect. Or the section on the history of the bourgeoisie. (Chapter XXIV.) Or why do we fight for the political dictatorship of the proletariat if political power is economically impotent? Force (that is, state power) is also economic power!

But I have no time to criticize the book[90] now. I must first get volume III* out and besides I think that Bernstein, for instance, could deal with it quite effectively.

What these gentlemen all lack is dialectics. They always see only here cause, there effect. That this is a hollow abstraction, that such metaphysical polar opposites exist in the real world only during crises, while the whole vast process goes on in the form of interaction—though of very unequal forces, the economic movement being by far the strongest, most primordial, most decisive—that here everything is relative and nothing absolute—this they never begin to see. As far as they are concerned Hegel never existed. . . .

* of Marx's *Capital.*—*Ed.*

FREDERICK ENGELS

INTRODUCTION TO THE ENGLISH EDITION OF *SOCIALISM: UTOPIAN AND SCIENTIFIC*

The present little book is, originally, a part of a larger whole. About 1875, Dr. E. Dühring, *privatdocent* at Berlin University, suddenly and rather clamorously announced his conversion to socialism, and presented the German public not only with an elaborate socialist theory, but also with a complete practical plan for the reorganization of society. As a matter of course, he fell foul of his predecessors; above all, he honoured Marx by pouring out upon him the full vials of his wrath.

This took place about the time when the two sections of the Socialist party in Germany—Eisenachers and Lassalleans—had just effected their fusion, and thus obtained not only an immense increase of strength, but, what was more, the faculty of employing the whole of this strength against the common enemy. The Socialist party in Germany was fast becoming a power. But to make it a power, the first condition was that the newly conquered unity should not be imperilled. And Dr. Dühring openly proceeded to form around himself a sect, the nucleus of a future separate party. It thus became necessary to take up the gauntlet thrown down to us and to fight out the struggle whether we liked it or not.

This, however, though it might not be an over-difficult, was evidently a long-winded business. As is well known, we Germans are of a terribly ponderous *Gründlichkeit*, radical profundity or profound radicality, whatever you may like to call it. Whenever anyone of us expounds what he considers a new doctrine, he has first to elaborate it into an all-comprising system. He has to prove that both the first principles of logic and the fundamental laws of the universe had existed from all eternity for no other purpose than to ultimately lead to this newly discovered, crowning theory. And Dr. Dühring, in this respect, was quite up to the national mark. Nothing less than a complete "System of Philosophy," mental, moral, natural, and historical; a complete "System of Political Economy and Socialism"; and, finally, a "Critical History of Political Economy"—three big volumes in octavo, heavy extrinsically and intrinsically, three army corps of arguments mobilized against all previous philosophers and economists in general, and against Marx in particular—in fact, an attempt at a complete "revolution in science"—these were what I should have to tackle. I had to treat of all and every possible subject, from the concepts of time and space to bimetallism; from the eternity of matter and motion to the perishable nature of moral ideas; from Darwin's natural selection to the education of youth in a future society. Anyhow the systematic comprehensiveness of my opponent gave me the opportunity of developing, in opposition to him, and in a more connected form than had previously been done, the views held by Marx and myself on this great variety of subjects. And that was the principal reason which made me undertake this otherwise ungrateful task.

My reply was first published in a series of articles in the Leipzig *Vorwärts,* the chief organ of the Socialist party,[91] and later on as a book: *Herrn Eugen Dührings Umwälzung der Wissenschaft (Mr. E. Dühring's Revolution in Science),* a second edition of which appeared in Zürich, 1886.

At the request of my friend, Paul Lafargue, now representative of Lille in the French Chamber of Deputies, I arranged three chapters of this book as a pamphlet, which he translated and published in 1880, under the title: *Socialisme utopique et Socialisme scientifique.* From this French text a Polish and a Spanish edition were prepared. In 1883, our German friends brought out the pamphlet in the original language. Italian, Russian, Danish, Dutch, and Roumanian translations, based upon the German text, have since been published. Thus, with the present English edition, this little book circulates in ten languages. I am not aware that any other socialist work, not even our *Communist Manifesto* of 1848 or Marx's *Capital,* has been so often translated. In Germany it has had four editions of about 20,000 copies in all.

The Appendix, "The Mark,"[92] was written with the intention of spreading among the German Socialist Party some elementary knowledge of the history and development of landed property in Germany. This seemed all the more necessary at a time when the assimilation by that party of the working people of the towns was in a fair way of completion, and when the agricultural labourers and peasants had to be taken in hand. This appendix has been included in the translation, as the original forms of tenure of land common to all Teutonic tribes, and the history of their decay, are even less known in England than in Germany. I have left the text as it stands in the original, without alluding to the hypothesis recently started by Maxim Kovalevsky, according to which the partition of the arable and meadow lands among the members of the Mark was preceded by their being cultivated for joint-account by a large patriarchal family community embracing several generations (as exemplified by the still existing South Slavonian Zadruga), and that the partition, later on, took place when the community had increased, so as to become too unwieldy for joint-account management. Kovalevsky is probably quite right, but the matter is still *sub judice.**

The economic terms used in this work, as far as they are new, agree with those used in the English edition of Marx's *Capital.* We call "production of commodities" that economic phase where articles are produced not only for the use of the producers, but also for purposes of exchange; that is, *as commodities,* not as use values. This phase extends from the first beginnings of production for exchange down to our present time; it attains its full development under capitalist production only, that is, under conditions where the capitalist, the owner of the means of production, employs, for wages, labourers, people deprived of all means of production except their own labour-power, and pockets the excess of the selling price of the products over his outlay. We divide the history of industrial production since the Middle Ages into three periods: (1) handicraft, small master craftsmen with a few journeymen and apprentices, where each labourer produces the complete article; (2) manufacture, where greater numbers of workmen, grouped in one large establishment, produce the complete article on the principle of division of labour, each workman performing only one partial operation so that the product is complete only after having passed succesively through the hands of all; (3) modern industry, where the product is produced by machinery driven by power, and where the work of the labourer is limited to superintending and correcting the performances of the mechanical agent.

I am perfectly aware that the contents of this work will meet with objection from a considerable portion of the British public. But if we Continentals had taken the slightest notice of the prejudices of British "respectability," we

* Under consideration.—*Ed.*

should be even worse off than we are. This book defends what we call "historical materialism," and the word materialism grates upon the ears of the immense majority of British readers. "Agnosticism"[93] might be tolerated, but materialism is utterly inadmissible.

And yet the original home of all modern materialism, from the seventeenth century onwards, is England.

"Materialism is the natural-born son of Great Britain. Already the British schoolman, Duns Scotus, asked, 'whether it was impossible for matter to think?'

"In order to effect this miracle, he took refuge in God's omnipotence, i.e., he made theology preach materialism. Moreover, he was a nominalist. Nominalism, the first form of materialism, is chiefly found among the English schoolmen.

"The real progenitor of English materialism is Bacon. To him natural philosophy is the only true philosophy, and physics based upon the experience of the senses is the chiefest part of natural philosophy. Anaxagoras and his homoiomeriae, Democritus and his atoms, he often quotes as his authorities. According to him the senses are infallible and the source of all knowledge. All science is based on experience, and consists in subjecting the data furnished by the senses to a rational method of investigation. Induction, analysis, comparison, observation, experiment, are the principal forms of such a rational method. Among the qualities inherent in matter, motion is the first and foremost, not only in the form of mechanical and mathematical motion, but chiefly in the form of an impulse, a vital spirit, a tension—or a 'qual,' to use a term of Jakob Böhme's*—of matter.

---

* "*Qual*" is a philosophical play upon words. Qual literally means torture, a pain which drives to action of some kind; at the same time the mystic Böhme puts into the German word something of the mean-

"In Bacon, its first creator, materalism still occludes within itself the germs of a many-sided development. On the one hand, matter, surrounded by a sensuous, poetic glamour, seems to attract man's whole entity by winning smiles. On the other, the aphoristically formulated doctrine pullulates with inconsistencies imported from theology.

"In its further evolution, materialism becomes one-sided. Hobbes is the man who systematizes Baconian materialism. Knowledge based upon the senses loses its poetic blossom, it passes into the abstract experience of the mathematician; geometry is proclaimed as the queen of sciences. Materialism takes to misanthropy. If it is to overcome its opponent, misanthropic, fleshless spiritualism, and that on the latter's own ground, materialism has to chastise its own flesh and turn ascetic. Thus, from a sensual, it passes into an intellectual, entity; but thus, too, it evolves all the consistency, regardless of consequences, characteristic of the intellect.

"Hobbes, as Bacon's continuator, argues thus: if all human knowledge is furnished by the senses, then our concepts and ideas are but the phantoms, divested of their sensual forms, of the real world. Philosophy can but give names to these phantoms. One name may be applied to more than one of them. There may even be names of names. It would imply a contradiction if, on the one hand, we maintained that all ideas had their origin in the world of sensation, and, on the other, that a word was more than a word; that besides the beings known to us by our senses, beings which are one and all individuals, there existed also beings of a general, not individual, nature. An un-

---

ing of the Latin *qualitas*; his "qual" was the activating principle arising from, and promoting in its turn, the spontaneous development of the thing, relation, or person subject to it, in contradistinction to a pain inflicted from without. [*Note by Engels to the English edition.*]

bodily substance is the same absurdity as an unbodily body. Body, being, substance, are but different terms for the same reality. *It is impossible to separate thought from matter that thinks.* This matter is the substratum of all changes going on in the world. The word infinite is meaningless, unless it states that our mind is capable of performing an endless process of addition. Only material things being perceptible to us, we cannot know anything about the existence of God. My own existence alone is certain. Every human passion is a mechanical movement which has a beginning and an end. The objects of impulse are what we call good. Man is subject to the same laws as nature. Power and freedom are identical.

"Hobbes had systematized Bacon, without, however, furnishing a proof for Bacon's fundamental principle, the origin of all human knowledge from the world of sensation. It was Locke who, in his 'Essay on the Human Understanding,' supplied this proof.

"Hobbes had shattered the theistic prejudices of Baconian materialism; Collins, Dodwell, Coward, Hartley, Priestley similarly shattered the last theological bars that still hemmed in Locke's sensationalism. At all events, for practical materialists, Deism is but an easy-going way of getting rid of religion."*

Thus Karl Marx wrote about the British origin of modern materialism. If Englishmen nowadays do not exactly relish the compliment he paid their ancestors, more's the pity. It is none the less undeniable that Bacon, Hobbes and Locke are the fathers of that brilliant school of French materialists which made the eighteenth century, in spite of all battles on land and sea won over Frenchmen by Germans and Englishmen, a pre-eminently French century,

* Marx and Engels, *Die Heilige Familie*, Frankfort a M. 1845, pp. 201-04. [*Note by Engels.*][94]

even before that crowning French Revolution, the results of which we outsiders, in England as well as in Germany, are still trying to acclimatize.

There is no denying it. About the middle of this century, what struck every cultivated foreigner who set up his residence in England, was what he was then bound to consider the religious bigotry and stupidity of the English respectable middle class. We, at that time, were all materialists, or, at least, very advanced free-thinkers, and to us it appeared inconceivable that almost all educated people in England should believe in all sorts of impossible miracles, and that even geologists like Buckland and Mantell should contort the facts of their science so as not to clash too much with the myths of the book of Genesis; while, in order to find people who dared to use their own intellectual faculties with regard to religious matters, you had to go amongst the uneducated, the "great unwashed," as they were then called, the working people, especially the Owenite Socialists.

But England has been "civilized" since then. The exhibition of 1851 sounded the knell of English insular exclusiveness. England became gradually internationalized, in diet, in manners, in ideas; so much so that I begin to wish that some English manners and customs had made as much headway on the Continent as other Continental habits have made here. Anyhow, the introduction and spread of salad-oil (before 1851 known only to the aristocracy) has been accompanied by a fatal spread of Continental scepticism in matters religious, and it has come to this, that agnosticism, though not yet considered "the thing" quite as much as the Church of England, is yet very nearly on a par, as far as respectability goes, with Baptism, and decidedly ranks above the Salvation Army. And I cannot help believing that under these circumstances it will be consoling to many who sincerely regret and condemn this progress of infidelity to learn that these "new-fangled notions" are not of foreign origin, are not "made in Germany," like so many other articles of daily use, but are undoubtedly Old English, and that their British originators two hundred years ago went a good deal further than their descendants now dare to venture.

What, indeed, is agnosticism but, to use an expressive Lancashire term, "shamefaced" materialism? The agnostic's conception of nature is materialistic throughout. The entire natural world is governed by law, and absolutely excludes the intervention of action from without. But, he adds, we have no means either of ascertaining or of disproving the existence of some Supreme Being beyond the known universe. Now, this might hold good at the time when Laplace, to Napoleon's question, why in the great astronomer's *Mécanique céleste* the Creator was not even mentioned, proudly replied: "*Je n'avais pas besoin de cette hypothèse.*" But nowadays, in our evolutionary conception of the universe, there is absolutely no room for either a Creator or a Ruler; and to talk of a Supreme Being shut out from the whole existing world, implies a contradiction in terms, and, as it seems to me, a gratuitous insult to the feelings of religious people.

Again, our agnostic admits that all our knowledge is based upon the information imparted to us by our senses. But, he adds, how do we know that our senses give us correct representations of the objects we perceive through them? And he proceeds to inform us that, whenever he speaks of objects or their qualities, he does in reality not mean these objects and qualities, of which he cannot know anything for certain, but merely the impressions which they have produced on his senses. Now, this line of reasoning seems undoubtedly hard to beat by mere argumentation. But before there was argumentation there was action. *Im Anfang war die Tat.** And human action had solved the difficulty long before human ingenuity invented it. The proof of the pudding is in the eating. From the moment we turn to our own use these objects, according to the qualities we perceive in them, we put to an infallible test the correctness or otherwise of our sense-perceptions. If these perceptions have been wrong, then our estimate of the use to which an object can be turned must also be wrong, and our attempt must fail. But if we succeed in accomplishing our aim, if we find that the object does agree with our idea of it, and does answer the purpose we intended it for, then that is positive proof that our perceptions of it and of its qualities, *so far,* agree with reality outside ourselves. And whenever we find ourselves face to face with a failure, then we generally are not long in making out the cause that made us fail; we find that the perception upon which we acted was either incomplete and superficial, or combined with the results of other perceptions in a way not warranted by them—what we call defective reasoning. So long as we take care to train and to use our senses properly, and to keep our action within the limits prescribed by perceptions properly made and properly used, so long we shall find that the result of our action proves the conformity of our perceptions with the objective nature of the things perceived. Not in one single instance, so far, have we been led to the conclusion that our sense-perceptions, scientifically controlled, induce in our minds ideas respecting the outer world that are, by their very nature, at variance with reality, or that there is an inherent incompatibility between the outer world and our sense-perceptions of it.

But then come the Neo-Kantian agnostics and say: We may correctly perceive the qualities of a thing, but we

---

* In the beginning was the deed. From Goethe's *Faust.—Ed.*

cannot by any sensible or mental process grasp the thing-in-itself. This "thing-in-itself" is beyond our ken. To this Hegel, long since, has replied: If you know all the qualities of a thing, you know the thing itself; nothing remains but the fact that the said thing exists without us; and when your senses have taught you that fact, you have grasped the last remnant of the thing-in-itself, Kant's celebrated unknowable *Ding an sich.* To which it may be added that in Kant's time our knowledge of natural objects was indeed so fragmentary that he might well suspect, behind the little we knew about each of them, a mysterious "thing-in-itself." But one after another these ungraspable things have been grasped, analyzed, and, what is more, *reproduced* by the giant progress of science; and what we can produce we certainly cannot consider as unknowable. To the chemistry of the first half of this century organic substances were such mysterious objects; now we learn to build them up one after another from their chemical elements without the aid of organic processes. Modern chemists declare that as soon as the chemical constitution of no matter what body is known it can be built up from its elements. We are still far from knowing the constitution of the highest organic substances, the albuminous bodies; but there is no reason why we should not, if only after centuries, arrive at the knowledge and, armed with it, produce artificial albumen. But if we arrive at that, we shall at the same time have produced organic life, for life, from its lowest to its highest forms, is but the normal mode of existence of albuminous bodies.

As soon, however, as our agnostic has made these formal mental reservations, he talks and acts as the rank materialist he at bottom is. He may say that, as far as *we* know, matter and motion, or as it is now called, energy can neither be created nor destroyed, but that we have no proof of their not having been created at some time or other.

But if you try to use this admission against him in any particular case, he will quickly put you out of court. If he admits the possibility of spiritualism *in abstracto,* he will have none of it *in concreto.* As far as we know and can know, he will tell you there is no Creator and no Ruler of the universe; as far as we are concerned, matter and energy can neither be created nor annihilated; for us, mind is a mode of energy, a function of the brain; all we know is that the material world is governed by immutable laws, and so forth. Thus, as far as he is a scientific man, as far as he *knows* anything, he is a materialist; outside his science, in spheres about which he knows nothing, he translates his ignorance into Greek and calls it agnosticism.

At all events, one thing seems clear; even if I was an agnostic, it is evident that I could not describe the conception of history sketched out in this little book as "historical agnosticism." Religious people would laugh at me, agnostics would indignantly ask, was I going to make fun of them? And thus I hope even British respectability will not be overshocked if I use, in English as well as in so many other languages, the term "historical materialism," to designate that view of the course of history which seeks the ultimate cause and the great moving power of all important historic events in the economic development of society, in the changes in the modes of production and exchange, in the consequent division of society into distinct classes, and in the struggles of these classes against one another.

This indulgence will perhaps be accorded to me all the sooner if I show that historical materialism may be of advantage even to British respectability. I have mentioned the fact that, about forty or fifty years ago, any cultivated foreigner settling in England was struck by what he was then bound to consider the religious bigotry and stupidity of the English respectable middle class. I am now going to prove that the respectable English middle class of that time was not quite as stupid as it looked to the intelligent foreigner. Its religious leanings can be explained.

When Europe emerged from the Middle Ages, the rising middle class of the towns constituted its revolutionary element. It had conquered a recognized position within mediaeval feudal organization, but this position, also, had become too narrow for its expansive power. The development of the middle class, the *bourgeoisie,* became incompatible with the maintenance of the feudal system; the feudal system, therefore, had to fall.

But the great international centre of feudalism was the Roman Catholic Church. It united the whole of feudalized Western Europe, in spite of all internal wars, into one grand political system, opposed as much to the schismatic Greeks as to the Mohammedan countries. It surrounded feudal institutions with the halo of divine consecration. It had organized its own hierarchy on the feudal model, and, lastly, it was itself by far the most powerful feudal lord, holding, as it did, fully one-third of the soil of the Catholic world. Before profane feudalism could be successfully attacked in each country and in detail, this, its sacred central organization, had to be destroyed.

Moreover, parallel with the rise of the middle class went on the great revival of science; astronomy, mechanics, physics, anatomy, physiology, were again cultivated. And the bourgeoisie, for the development of its industrial production, required a science which ascertained the physical properties of natural objects and the modes of action of the forces of nature. Now up to then science had but been the humble handmaid of the Church, had not been allowed to overstep the limits set by faith, and for that reason had been no science at all. Science rebelled against the Church;

the bourgeoisie could not do without science, and, therefore, had to join in the rebellion.

The above, though touching but two of the points where the rising middle class was bound to come into collision with the established religion, will be sufficient to show, first, that the class most directly interested in the struggle against the pretensions of the Roman Church was the bourgeoisie; and second, that every struggle against feudalism, at that time, had to take on a religious disguise, had to be directed against the Church in the first instance. But if the universities and the traders of the cities started the cry, it was sure to find, and did find, a strong echo in the masses of the country people, the peasants, who everywhere had to struggle for their very existence with their feudal lords, spiritual and temporal.

The long fight of the bourgeoisie against feudalism culminated in three great, decisive battles.

The first was what is called the Protestant Reformation in Germany. The war cry raised against the Church by Luther was responded to by two insurrections of a political nature: first, that of the lower nobility under Franz von Sickingen (1523), then the great Peasants' War, 1525. Both were defeated, chiefly in consequence of the indecision of the parties most interested, the burghers of the towns—an indecision into the causes of which we cannot here enter. From that moment the struggle degenerated into a fight between the local princes and the central power, and ended by blotting out Germany, for two hundred years, from the politically active nations of Europe. The Lutheran Reformation produced a new creed, indeed, a religion adapted to absolute monarchy. No sooner were the peasants of North-East Germany converted to Lutheranism than they were from freemen reduced to serfs.

But where Luther failed, Calvin won the day. Calvin's creed was one fit for the boldest of the bourgeoisie of his time. His predestination doctrine was the religious expression of the fact that in the commercial world of competition success or failure does not depend upon a man's activity or cleverness, but upon circumstances uncontrollable by him. It is not of him that willeth or of him that runneth, but of the mercy of unknown superior economic powers; and this was especially true at a period of economic revolution, when all old commercial routes and centres were replaced by new ones, when India and America were opened to the world, and when even the most sacred economic articles of faith—the value of gold and silver—began to totter and to break down. Calvin's church constitution was thoroughly democratic and republican; and where the kingdom of God was republicanized, could the kingdoms of this world remain subject to monarchs, bishops and lords? While German Lutheranism became a willing tool in the hands of princes, Calvinism founded a republic in Holland, and active republican parties in England, and, above all, Scotland.

In Calvinism, the second great bourgeois upheaval found its doctrine ready cut and dried. This upheaval took place in England. The middle-class of the towns brought it on, and the yeomanry of the country districts fought it out. Curiously enough, in all the three great bourgeois risings, the peasantry furnishes the army that has to do the fighting; and the peasantry is just the class that, the victory once gained, is most surely ruined by the economic consequences of that victory. A hundred years after Cromwell, the yeomanry of England had almost disappeared. Anyhow, had it not been for that yeomanry and for the *plebeian* element in the towns, the bourgeoisie alone would never have fought the matter out to the bitter end, and would never have brought Charles I to the scaffold. In order to secure even those conquests of the bourgeoisie that were ripe for gathering at the time, the revolution had to be carried considerably further—exactly as in 1793 in France and 1848 in Germany. This seems, in fact, to be one of the laws of evolution of bourgeois society.

Well, upon this excess of revolutionary activity there necessarily followed the inevitable reaction which in its turn went beyond the point where it might have maintained itself. After a series of oscillations, the new centre of gravity was at last attained and became a new starting-point. The grand period of English history, known to respectability under the name of "the Great Rebellion," and the struggles succeeding it, were brought to a close by the comparatively puny event entitled by Liberal historians "the Glorious Revolution."

The new starting-point was a compromise between the rising middle class and the ex-feudal landowners. The latter, though called, as now, the aristocracy, had been long since on the way which led them to become what Louis Philippe in France became at a much later period, "the first bourgeois of the kingdom." Fortunately for England, the old feudal barons had killed one another during the Wars of the Roses. Their successors, though mostly scions of the old families, had been so much out of the direct line of descent that they constituted quite a new body, with habits and tendencies far more bourgeois than feudal. They fully understood the value of money, and at once began to increase their rents by turning hundreds of small farmers out and replacing them by sheep. Henry VIII, while squandering the Church lands, created fresh bourgeois landlords by wholesale; the innumerable confiscations of estates, regranted to absolute or relative upstarts, and continued during the whole of the seventeenth century, had the same result. Consequently, ever since Henry VII, the English "aristocracy," far from counteracting the development of industrial production, had, on the contrary, sought to indirectly profit thereby; and there had always been a section of the great landowners willing, from economical or political reasons, to co-operate with the leading men of the financial and industrial bourgeoisie. The compromise of 1689 was, therefore, easily accomplished. The political spoils of "pelf and place" were left to the great landowning families, provided the economic interests of the financial, manufacturing and commercial middle class were sufficiently attended to. And these economic interests were at that time powerful enough to determine the general policy of the nation. There might be squabbles about matters of detail, but, on the whole, the aristocratic oligarchy knew too well that its own economic prosperity was irretrievably bound up with that of the industrial and commercial middle class.

From that time, the bourgeoisie was a humble, but still a recognized component of the ruling classes of England. With the rest of them, it had a common interest in keeping in subjection the great working mass of the nation. The merchant or manufacturer himself stood in the position of master, or, as it was until lately called, of "natural superior" to his clerks, his work-people, his domestic servants. His interest was to get as much and as good work out of them as he could; for this end they had to be trained to proper submission. He was himself religious; his religion had supplied the standard under which he had fought the king and the lords; he was not long in discovering the opportunities this same religion offered him for working upon the minds of his natural inferiors, and making them submissive to the behests of the masters it had pleased God to place over them. In short, the English bourgeoisie now had to take a part in keeping down the "lower orders," the great producing mass of the nation, and one of the means employed for that purpose was the influence of religion.

There was another fact that contributed to strengthen the religious leanings of the bourgeoisie. That was the rise of materialism in England. This new doctrine not only shocked the pious feelings of the middle class; it announced itself as a philosophy only fit for scholars and cultivated men of the world, in contrast to religion, which was good enough for the uneducated masses, including the bourgeoisie. With Hobbes it stepped on the stage as a defender of royal prerogative and omnipotence; it called upon absolute monarchy to keep down that *puer robustus sed malitiosus*,* to wit, the people. Similarly, with the successors of Hobbes, with Bolingbroke, Shaftesbury, etc., the new deistic form of materialism remained an aristocratic, esoteric doctrine, and, therefore, hateful to the middle class both for its religious heresy and for its anti-bourgeois political connections. Accordingly, in opposition to the materialism and deism of the aristocracy, those Protestant sects which had furnished the flag and the fighting contingent against the Stuarts continued to furnish the main strength of the progressive middle class, and form even to-day the backbone of "the Great Liberal Party."

In the meantime materialism passed from England to France, where it met and coalesced with another materialistic school of philosophers, a branch of Cartesianism. In France, too, it remained at first an exclusively aristocratic doctrine. But soon its revolutionary character asserted itself. The French materialists did not limit their criticism to matters of religious belief; they extended it to whatever scientific tradition or political institution they met with; and to prove the claim of their doctrine to universal application, they took the shortest cut, and boldly applied it to all subjects of knowledge in the giant work after which they were named—the *Encyclopédie*. Thus, in one or the

* Robust but malicious boy.—*Ed.*

other of its two forms—avowed materialism or deism—it became the creed of the whole cultured youth of France; so much so that, when the Great Revolution broke out, the doctrine hatched by English Royalists gave a theoretical flag to French Republicans and Terrorists, and furnished the text for the Declaration of the Rights of Man. The Great French Revolution was the third uprising of the bourgeoisie, but the first that had entirely cast off the religious cloak, and was fought out on undisguised political lines; it was the first, too, that was really fought out up to the destruction of one of the combatants, the aristocracy, and the complete triumph of the other, the bourgeoisie. In England the continuity of pre-revolutionary and post-revolutionary institutions, and the compromise between landlords and capitalists, found its expression in the continuity of judicial precedents and in the religious preservation of the feudal forms of the law. In France the Revolution constituted a complete breach with the traditions of the past; it cleared out the very last vestiges of feudalism, and created in the *Code Civil* a masterly adaptation of the old Roman law—that almost perfect expression of the juridical relations corresponding to the economic stage called by Marx the production of commodities—to modern capitalistic conditions; so masterly that this French revolutionary code still serves as a model for reforms of the law of property in all other countries, not excepting England. Let us, however, not forget that if English law continues to express the economic relations of capitalistic society in that barbarous feudal language which corresponds to the thing expressed, just as English spelling corresponds to English pronunciation—*vous écrivez Londres et vous prononcez Constantinople,* said a Frenchman—that same English law is the only one which has preserved through ages, and transmitted to America and the Colonies, the best part of that old Germanic personal freedom, local self-government and independence from all interference but that of the law courts which on the Continent has been lost during the period of absolute monarchy, and has nowhere been as yet fully recovered.

To return to our British bourgeois. The French Revolution gave him a splendid opportunity, with the help of the Continental monarchies, to destroy French maritime commerce, to annex French colonies, and to crush the last French pretensions to maritime rivalry. That was one reason why he fought it. Another was that the ways of this revolution went very much against his grain. Not only its "execrable" terrorism, but the very attempt to carry bourgeois rule to extremes. What should the British bourgeois do without his aristocracy, that taught him manners, such as they were, and invented fashions for him—that furnished officers of the army, which kept order at home, and the navy, which conquered colonial possessions and new markets abroad? There was indeed a progressive minority of the bourgeoisie, that minority whose interests were not so well attended to under the compromise; this section, composed chiefly of the less wealthy middle class, did sympathize with the Revolution but it was powerless in Parliament.

Thus, if materialism became the creed of the French Revolution, the God-fearing English bourgeois held all the faster to his religion. Had not the reign of terror in Paris proved what was the upshot, if the religious instincts of the masses were lost? The more materialism spread from France to neighbouring countries, and was reinforced by similar doctrinal currents, notably by German philosophy, the more, in fact, materialism and free thought generally became on the Continent, the necessary qualifications of a cultivated man, the more stubbornly the English middle class stuck to its manifold religious creeds. These creeds might differ from one another, but they were, all of them, distinctly religious, Christian creeds.

While the Revolution ensured the political triumph of the bourgeoisie in France, in England Watt, Arkwright, Cartwright, and others initiated an industrial revolution, which completely shifted the centre of gravity of economic power. The wealth of the bourgeoisie increased considerably faster than that of the landed aristocracy. Within the bourgeoisie itself, the financial aristocracy, the bankers, etc., were more and more pushed into the background by the manufacturers. The compromise of 1689, even after the gradual changes it had undergone in favour of the bourgeoisie, no longer corresponded to the relative position of the parties to it. The character of these parties, too, had changed; the bourgeoisie of 1830 was very different from that of the preceding century. The political power still left to the aristocracy, and used by them to resist the pretensions of the new industrial bourgeoisie, became incompatible with the new economic interests. A fresh struggle with the aristocracy was necessary; it could end only in a victory of the new economic power. First, the Reform Act was pushed through, in spite of all resistance, under the impulse of the French Revolution of 1830. It gave to the bourgeoisie a recognized and powerful place in Parliament. Then the Repeal of the Corn Laws, which settled, once for all, the supremacy of the bourgeoisie, and especially of its most active portion, the manufacturers, over the landed aristocracy. This was the greatest victory of the bourgeoisie; it was, however, also the last it gained in its own exclusive interest. Whatever triumphs it obtained later on, it had to share with a new social power, first its ally, but soon its rival.

The industrial revolution had created a class of large manufacturing capitalists, but also a class—and a far more numerous one—of manufacturing work-people. This class gradually increased in numbers, in proportion as the industrial revolution seized upon one branch of manufacture after another, and in the same proportion it increased in power. This power it proved as early as 1824, by forcing a reluctant Parliament to repeal the acts forbidding combinations of workmen. During the Reform agitation, the working-men constituted the Radical wing of the Reform party; the Act of 1832 having excluded them from the suffrage, they formulated their demands in the People's Charter, and constituted themselves, in oppostion to the great bourgeois Anti-Corn Law party, into an independent party, the Chartists, the first working-men's party of modern times.

Then came the Continental revolutions of February and March 1848, in which the working people played such a prominent part, and, at least in Paris, put forward demands which were certainly inadmissible from the point of view of capitalist society. And then came the general reaction. First the defeat of the Chartists on the 10th April, 1848, then the crushing of the Paris working-men's insurrection in June of the same year, then the disasters of 1849 in Italy, Hungary, South Germany, and at last the victory of Louis Bonaparte over Paris, 2nd December, 1851. For a time, at least, the bugbear of working-class pretensions was put down, but at what cost! If the British bourgeois had been convinced before of the necessity of maintaining the common people in a religious mood, how much more must he feel that necessity after all these experiences? Regardless of the sneers of his Continental compeers, he continued to spend thousands and tens of thousands, year after year, upon the evangelization of the lower orders; not content with his own native religious machinery, he appealed to Brother Jonathan,[95] the greatest organizer in existence of religion as a trade, and imported from America revivalism,[96] Moody and Sankey, and the like; and, finally, he accepted the dangerous aid of the Salvation Army, which revives the propaganda of early Christianity, appeals to the poor as the elect, fights capitalism in a religious way, and thus fosters an element of early Christian class antagonism, which one day may become troublesome to the well-to-do people who now find the ready money for it.

It seems a law of historical development that the bourgeoisie can in no European country get hold of political power—at least for any length of time—in the same exclusive way in which the feudal aristocracy kept hold of it during the Middle Ages. Even in France, where feudalism was completely extinguished, the bourgeoisie, as a whole, has held full possession of the government for very short periods only. During Louis Philippe's reign, 1830-48, a very small portion of the bourgeoisie ruled the kingdom; by far the larger part were excluded from the suffrage by the high qualification. Under the Second Republic, 1848-51, the whole bourgeoisie ruled, but for three years only; their incapacity brought on the Second Empire. It is only now, in the Third Republic, that the bourgeoisie as a whole have kept possession of the helm for more than twenty years; and they are already showing lively signs of decadence. A durable reign of the bourgeoisie has been possible only in countries like America, where feudalism was unknown, and society at the very beginning started from a bourgeois basis. And even in France and America, the successors of the bourgeoisie, the working people, are already knocking at the door.

In England, the bourgeoisie never held undivided sway. Even the victory of 1832 left the landed aristocracy in almost exclusive possession of all the leading government offices. The meekness with which the wealthy middle class submitted to this remained inconceivable to me until the great Liberal manufacturer, Mr. W. A. Forster, in a public speech implored the young men of Bradford to learn French, as a means to get on in the world, and quoted from his own experience how sheepish he looked when, as a Cabinet Minister, he had to move in society where French was, at least, as necessary as English! The fact was, the English middle class of that time were, as a rule, quite uneducated upstarts, and could not help leaving to the aristocracy those superior government places where other qualifications were required than mere insular narrowness and insular conceit, seasoned by business sharpness.* Even now the endless newspaper debates about middle-class education show that the English middle class does not yet consider itself good enough for the best education, and looks to something more modest. Thus, even after the

* And even in business matters, the conceit of national chauvinism is but a sorry adviser. Up to quite recently, the average English manufacturer considered it derogatory for an Englishman to speak any language but his own, and felt rather proud than otherwise of the fact that "poor devils" of foreigners settled in England and took off his hands the trouble of disposing of his products abroad. He never noticed that these foreigners, mostly Germans, thus got command of a very large part of British foreign trade, imports and exports, and that the direct foreign trade of Englishmen became limited, almost entirely, to the colonies, China, the United States and South America. Nor did he notice that these Germans traded with other Germans abroad, who gradually organized a complete network of commercial colonies all over the world. But when Germany, about forty years ago, seriously began manufacturing for export, this network served her admirably in her transformation, in so short a time, from a corn-exporting into a first-rate manufacturing country. Then, about ten years ago, the British manufacturer got frightened, and asked his ambassadors and consuls how it was that he could no longer keep his customers together. The unanimous answer was: (1) You don't learn your customer's language but expect him to speak your own; (2) You don't even try to suit your customer's wants, habits, and tastes, but expect him to conform to your English ones. [*Note by Engels.*]

repeal of the Corn Laws, it appeared a matter of course that the men who had carried the day, the Cobdens, Brights, Forsters, etc., should remain excluded from a share in the official government of the country, until twenty years afterwards a new Reform Act opened to them the door of the Cabinet. The English bourgeoisie are, up to the present day, so deeply penetrated by a sense of their social inferiority that they keep up, at their own expense and that of the nation, an ornamental caste of drones to represent the nation worthily at all state functions; and they consider themselves highly honoured whenever one of themselves is found worthy of admission into this select and privileged body, manufactured, after all, by themselves.

The industrial and commercial middle class had, therefore, not yet succeeded in driving the landed aristocracy completely from political power when another competitor, the working class, appeared on the stage. The reaction after the Chartist movement and the Continental revolutions, as well as the unparalleled extension of English trade from 1848-66 (ascribed vulgarly to Free Trade alone, but due far more to the colossal development of railways, ocean steamers and means of intercourse generally), had again driven the working class into the dependency of the Liberal party, of which they formed, as in pre-Chartist times, the Radical wing. Their claims to the franchise, however, gradually became irresistible; while the Whig leaders of the Liberals "funked," Disraeli showed his superiority by making the Tories seize the favourable moment and introduce household suffrage in the boroughs, along with a redistribution of seats. Then followed the ballot; then in 1884 the extension of household suffrage to the counties and a fresh redistribution of seats, by which electoral districts were to some extent equalized. All these measures considerably increased the electoral power of the working class, so much so that in at least 150 to 200 constituencies that class now furnishes the majority of voters. But parliamentary government is a capital school for teaching respect for tradition; if the middle class look with awe and veneration upon what Lord John Manners playfully called "our old nobility," the mass of the working-people then looked up with respect and deference to what used to be designated as "their betters," the middle class. Indeed, the British workman, some fifteen years ago, was the model workman, whose respectful regard for the position of his master, and whose self-restraining modesty in claiming rights for himself, consoled our German economists of the *Katheder-Socialist* school for the incurable communistic and revolutionary tendencies of their own working-men at home.

But the English middle class—good men of business as they are—saw farther than the German professors. They had shared their power but reluctantly with the working class. They had learnt, during the Chartist years, what that *puer robustus sed malitiosus*, the people, is capable of. And since that time, they had been compelled to incorporate the better part of the People's Charter in the Statutes of the United Kingdom. Now, if ever, the people must be kept in order by moral means, and the first and foremost of all moral means of action upon the masses is and remains—religion. Hence the parsons' majorities on the School Boards, hence the increasing self-taxation of the bourgeoisie for the support of all sorts of revivalism, from ritualism to the Salvation Army.

And now came the triumph of British respectability over the free thought and religious laxity of the Continental bourgeois. The workmen of France and Germany had become rebellious. They were thoroughly infected with socialism, and, for very good reasons, were not at all particular as to the legality of the means by which to secure their own ascendency. The *puer robustus,* here, turned from day to day more *malitiosus.* Nothing remained to the French and German bourgeoisie as a last resource but to silently drop their free thought, as a youngster, when seasickness creeps upon him, quietly drops the burning cigar he brought swaggeringly on board; one by one, the scoffers turned pious in outward behaviour, spoke with respect of the Church, its dogmas and rites, and even conformed with the latter as far as could not be helped. French bourgeois dined *maigre* on Fridays, and German ones sat out long Protestant sermons in their pews on Sundays. They had come to grief with materialism. "*Die Religion muss dem Volk erhalten werden,*"—religion must be kept alive for the people—that was the only and the last means to save society from utter ruin. Unfortunately for themselves, they did not find this out until they had done their level best to break up religion for ever. And now it was the turn of the British bourgeois to sneer and to say: "Why, you fools, I could have told you that two hundred years ago!"

However, I am afraid neither the religious stolidity of the British, nor the *post festum* conversion of the Continental bourgeois will stem the rising Proletarian tide. Tradition is a great retarding force, is the *vis inertiae* of history, but, being merely passive, is sure to be broken down; and thus religion will be no lasting safeguard to capitalist society. If our juridical, philosophical, and religious ideas are the more or less remote offshoots of the economical relations prevailing in a given society, such ideas cannot, in the long run, withstand the effects of a complete change in these relations. And, unless we believe in supernatural revelation, we must admit that no religious tenets will ever suffice to prop up a tottering society.

In fact, in England too, the working people have begun to move again. They are, no doubt, shackled by traditions of various kinds. Bourgeois traditions, such as the widespread belief that there can be but two parties, Conservatives and Liberals, and that the working class must work out its salvation by and through the Great Liberal Party. Working-men's traditions, inherited from their first tentative efforts at independent action, such as the exclusion, from ever so many old Trade Unions, of all applicants who have not gone through a regular apprenticeship; which means the breeding, by every such union, of its own blacklegs. But for all that the English working class is moving, as even Professor Brentano has sorrowfully had to report to his brother Katheder-Socialists. It moves, like all things in England, with a slow and measured step, with hesitation here, with more or less unfruitful, tentative attempts there; it moves now and then with an overcautious mistrust of the name of socialism, while it gradually absorbs the substance; and the movement spreads and seizes one layer of the workers after another. It has now shaken out of their torpor the unskilled labourers of the East End of London, and we all know what a splendid impulse these fresh forces have given it in return. And if the pace of the movement is not up to the impatience of some people, let them not forget that it is the working class which keeps alive the finest qualities of the English character, and that, if a step in advance is once gained in England, it is, as a rule, never lost afterwards. If the sons of the old Chartists, for reasons explained above, were not quite up to the mark, the grandsons bid fair to be worthy of their forefathers.

But the triumph of the European working class does not depend upon England alone. It can only be secured by the co-operation of, at least, England, France, and Germany. In both the latter countries the working-class movement is well ahead of England. In Germany it is even within measurable distance of success. The progress it has there made during the last twenty-five years is unparalleled. It advances with ever-increasing velocity. If the German middle class have shown themselves lamentably deficient in political capacity, discipline, courage, energy, and perseverance, the German working class have given ample proof of all these qualities. Four hundred years ago, Germany was the starting-point of the first upheaval of the European middle class; as things are now, is it outside the limits of possibility that Germany will be the scene, too, of the first great victory of the European proletariat?

F. Engels

April 20th, 1892

FREDERICK ENGELS

ON THE HISTORY OF EARLY CHRISTIANITY

I

The history of early Christianity has notable points of resemblance with the modern working-class movement. Like the latter, Christianity was originally a movement of oppressed people: it first appeared as the religion of slaves and emancipated slaves, of poor people deprived of all rights, of peoples subjugated or dispersed by Rome. Both Christianity and the workers' socialism preach forthcoming salvation from bondage and misery; Christianity places this salvation in a life beyond, after death, in heaven; socialism places it in this world, in a transformation of society. Both are persecuted and baited, their adherents are despised and made the objects of exclusive laws, the former as enemies of the human race, the latter as enemies of the state, enemies of religion, the family, social order. And in spite of all persecution, nay, even spurred on by it, they forge victoriously, irresistibly ahead. Three hundred years after its appearance Christianity was the recognized state religion in the Roman World Empire, and in barely sixty years socialism has won itself a position which makes its victory absolutely certain.

If, therefore, Prof. Anton Menger wonders in his *Right to the Full Product of Labour* why, with the enormous concentration of landownership under the Roman emperors and the boundless sufferings of the working class of the time, which was composed almost exclusively of slaves, "socialism did not follow the overthrow of the Roman Empire in the West," it is because he cannot see that this "socialism" did in fact, as far as it was possible at the time, exist and even became dominant—in Christianity. Only this Christianity, as was bound to be the case in the historic conditions, did not want to accomplish the social transformation in this world, but beyond it, in heaven, in eternal life after death, in the impending "millennium."

The parallel between the two historic phenomena forces itself upon our attention as early as the Middle Ages in the first risings of the oppressed peasants and particularly of the town plebeians. These risings, like all mass movements of the Middle Ages, were bound to wear the mask of religion and appeared as the restoration of early Christianity from spreading degeneration*; but behind the reli-

---

* A peculiar antithesis to this was the religious risings in the Mohammedan world, particularly in Africa. Islam is a religion adapted to Orientals, especially Arabs, i.e., on one hand to townsmen engaged in trade and industry, on the other to nomadic Bedouins. Therein lies, however, the embryo of a periodically recurring collision. The townspeople grow rich, luxurious and lax in the observation of the "law." The Bedouins, poor and hence of strict morals, contemplate with envy and covetousness these riches and pleasures. Then they unite under a prophet, a Mahdi, to chastise the apostates and restore the observation of the ritual and the true faith and to appropriate in recompense the treasures of the renegades. In a hundred years they are naturally in the same position as the renegades were: a new purge of the faith is required, a new Mahdi arises and the game starts again from the beginning. That is what happened from the conquest campaigns of the African Almoravids and Almohads in Spain to the last Mahdi of Khartoum[97] who so successfully thwarted the English. It happened in the same way or similarly with the risings in Persia and other Mohammedan countries. All these movements are clothed in religion but they have their source in economic causes; and yet, even when they are victorious, they allow the old economic conditions to persist untouched. So the old situation remains unchanged and the collision recurs periodically. In the popular risings of the

gious exaltaton there was every time a very tangible worldly interest. This appeared most splendidly in the organization of the Bohemian Taborites under Jan Žižka, of glorious memory; but this trait pervades the whole of the Middle Ages until it gradually fades away after the German Peasant War to revive again with the workingmen Communists after 1830. The French revolutionary Communists, as also in particular Weitling and his supporters, referred to early Christianity long before Renan's words: "If I wanted to give you an idea of the early Christian communities I would tell you to look at a local section of the International Working Men's Association."

This French man of letters, who by mutilating German criticism of the Bible in a manner unprecedented even in modern journalism composed the novel on church history *Origines du Christianisme*, did not know himself how much truth there was in the words just quoted. I should like to see the old "International" who can read, for example, the so-called Second Epistle of Paul to the Corinthians without old wounds re-opening, at least in one respect. The whole epistle, from chapter eight onwards, echoes the eternal, and oh! so well-known complaint: *les cotisations ne rentrent pas*—contributions are not coming in! How many of the most zealous propagandists of the sixties would sympathizingly squeeze the hand of the author of that epistle, whoever he may be, and whisper: "So it was like that with you too!" We too—Corinthians were legion in our Association—can sing a song about contributions not coming in but tantalizing us as they floated elusively before our eyes. They were the famous "millions of the International"!

Christian West, on the contrary, the religious disguise is only a flag and a mask for attacks on an economic order which is becoming antiquated. This is finally overthrown, a new one arises and the world progresses. [*Note by Engels.*]

One of our best sources on the first Christians is Lucian of Samosata, the Voltaire of classic antiquity, who was equally sceptic towards every kind of religious superstition and therefore had neither pagan-religious nor political grounds to treat the Christians otherwise than as some other kind of religious community. On the contrary, he mocked them all for their superstition, those who prayed to Jupiter no less than those who prayed to Christ; from his shallow rationalistic point of view one sort of superstition was as stupid as the other. This in any case impartial witness relates among other things the life-story of a certain adventurous Peregrinus, Proteus by name, from Parium in Hellespontus. When a youth, this Peregrinus made his *début* in Armenia by committing fornication. He was caught in the act and lynched according to the custom of the country. He was fortunate enough to escape and after strangling his father in Parium he had to flee.

"And so it happened"—I quote from Schott's translation—"that he also came to hear of the astonishing learning of the Christians, with whose priests and scribes he had cultivated intercourse in Palestine. He made such progress in a short time that his teachers were like children compared with him. He became a prophet, an elder, a master of the synagogue, in a word, all in everything. He interpreted their writings and himself wrote a great number of works, so that finally people saw in him a superior being, let him lay down laws for them and made him their overseer (bishop).... On that ground (i.e., because he was a Christian) Proteus was at length arrested by the authorities and thrown into prison.... As he thus lay in chains, the Christians, who saw in his capture a great misfortune, made all possible attempts to free him. But they did not succeed. Then they administered to him in all possible ways with the greatest solicitude. As early as daybreak one could see aged mothers, widows and young orphans crowding at the door of his prison; the most prominent among the Christians even bribed the warders and spent whole nights with him; they took their meals with them and read their holy books in his presence; briefly, the beloved Peregrinus" (he still went by that name) "was no less to them than a new Socrates. Envoys of Christian communities came to him even from towns in Asia Minor to lend him a helping hand, to console him and to testify in his favour in court. It is unbelievable how quick these people are to act whenever it is a question of their community; they immediately spare neither exertion nor expense. And thus from all sides money then poured in to Peregrinus so that his imprisonment became for him a source of great income. For the poor people persuaded themselves that they were immortal in body and in soul and that they would live for all eternity; that was why they scorned death and many of them even voluntarily sacrificed their lives. Then their most prominent lawgiver convinced them that they would all be brothers one to another once they were converted, i.e., renounced the Greek gods, professed faith in the crucified sophist and lived according to his prescriptions. That is why they despise all material goods without distinction and own them in common—doctrines which they have accepted in good faith, without demonstration or proof. And when a skilful imposter who knows how to make clever use of circumstances comes to them he can manage to get rich in a short time and laugh up his sleeve over these simpletons. For the rest, Peregrinus was set free by him who was then prefect of Syria."

Then, after a few more adventures,

"Our worthy set forth a second time" (from Parium) "on his peregrinations, the Christians' good disposition standing him in lieu of money for his journey: they administered to his needs everywhere and never let him suffer want. He was fed for a time in this way. But then, when he violated the laws of the Christians too—I think he was caught eating of some forbidden food—they excommunicated him from their community."

What memories of youth come to my mind as I read this passage from Lucian! First of all the "prophet Albrecht" who from about 1840 literally plundered the Weitling communist communities in Switzerland for several years—a tall powerful man with a long beard who wandered on foot through Switzerland and gathered audiences for his mysterious new Gospel of world emancipation, but who, after all, seems to have been a tolerably harmless hoaxer and soon died. Then his not so harmless successor, "the doctor" George Kuhlmann from Holstein, who put to profit the time when Weitling was in prison to convert the communities of French Switzerland to *his own* Gospel, and for a time with such success that he even caught August Becker, by far the cleverest but also the biggest ne'er-do-well among them. This Kuhlmann used to deliver lectures to them which were published in Geneva in 1845 under the title *The New World, or the Kingdom of the Spirit on Earth. Proclamation.* In the introduction, written by his supporters (probably August Becker) we read:

"What was needed was a man on whose lips all our sufferings and all our longings and hopes, in a word, all that affects our time most profoundly should find expression.... This man, whom our time was waiting for, has come. He is the doctor George Kuhlmann from Holstein. He has come forward with the doctrine of the new world or the kingdom of the spirit in reality."

I hardly need to add that this doctrine of the new world is nothing more than the most vulgar sentimental nonsense rendered in half-biblical expressions *à la Lamennais* and declaimed with prophet-like arrogance. But this did not prevent the good Weitlingers from carrying the swindler shoulder-high as the Asian Christians once did Peregrinus. They who were otherwise arch-democrats and extreme equalitarians to the extent of fostering ineradicable suspicion against any schoolmaster, journalist, and any man generally who was not a manual worker as being an "erudite" who was out to exploit them, let themselves be persuaded by the melodramatically arrayed Kuhlmann that in the "New World" it would be the wisest of all, *id est*, Kuhlmann, who would regulate the distribution of pleasures and that therefore, even then, in the Old World, the disciples ought to bring pleasures by the bushel to that same wisest of all while they themselves should be content with crumbs. So Peregrinus Kuhlmann lived a splendid life of pleasure at the expense of the community—as long as it lasted. It did not last very long, of course; the growing murmurs of doubters and unbelievers and the menace of persecution by the Vaudois Government put an end to the "Kingdom of the Spirit" in Lausanne—Kuhlmann disappeared.

Everybody who has known by experience the European working-class movement in its beginnings will remember dozens of similar examples. Today such extreme cases, at least in the large centres, have become impossible; but in remote districts where the movement has won new ground a small Peregrinus of this kind can still count on a temporary limited success. And just as all those who have nothing to look forward to from the official world or have come to the end of their tether with it—opponents of inoculation, supporters of abstemiousness, vegetarians, anti-vivisectionists, nature-healers, free-community preachers whose communities have fallen to pieces, authors of new theories on the origin of the universe, unsuccessful or unfortunate inventors, victims of real or imaginary injustice who are termed "good-for-nothing pettifoggers" by the bureaucracy, honest fools and dishonest swindlers—all throng to the working-class parties in all countries—so it was with the first Christians. All the elements which had been set free, i.e., at a loose end, by the dissolution of the old world came one after the other into the orbit of Christianity as the only element that resisted that process of dissolution—for the very reason that it was the necessary product of that process—and that therefore persisted and grew while the other elements were but ephemeral flies. There was no fanaticism, no foolishness, no scheming that did not flock to the young Christian communities and did not at least for a time and in isolated places find attentive ears and willing believers. And like our first communist workers' associations the early Christians too took with such unprecedented gullibility to anything which suited their purpose that we are not even sure that some fragment or other of the "great number of works" that Peregrinus wrote for Christianity did not find its way into our New Testament.

II

German criticism of the Bible, so far the only scientific basis of our knowledge of the history of early Christianity, followed a double tendency.

The first tendency was that of the *Tübingen school,* in which, in the broad sense, D. F. Strauss must also be included. In critical inquiry it goes as far as a *theological* school can go. It admits that the four Gospels are not eyewitness accounts but only later adaptations of writings that have been lost; that no more than four of the Epistles attributed to the apostle Paul are authentic, etc. It strikes out of the historical narrations all miracles and contradictions, considering them as unacceptable; but from the rest it tries "to save what can be saved" and then its nature, that of a theological school, is very evident. Thus it enabled Renan, who bases himself mostly on it, to "save" still more by applying the same method and, moreover, to try to impose upon us as historically authenticated many New Testament accounts that are more than doubtful and, besides, a multitude of other legends about martyrs. In any case, all that the Tübingen school rejects as unhistorical or apocryphal can be considered as finally eliminated for science.

The other tendency has but one representative—*Bruno Bauer*. His greatest service consists not merely in having given a pitiless criticism of the Gospels and the Epistles of the apostles, but in having for the first time seriously undertaken an inquiry into not only the Jewish and Greco-Alexandrian elements but the purely Greek and Greco-Roman elements that first opened for Christianity the career of a universal religion. The legend that Christianity arose ready and complete out of Judaism and, starting from Palestine, conquered the world with its dogma already defined in the main and its morals, has been untenable since Bruno Bauer; it can continue to vegetate only in the theological faculties and with people who wish "to keep religion alive for the people" even at the expense of science. The enormous influence which the Philonic school of Alexandria and Greco-Roman vulgar philosophy—Platonic and mainly Stoic—had on Christianity, which became the state religion under Constantine, is far from having been defined in detail, but its existence has been proved and that is primarily the achievement of Bruno Bauer: he laid the foundation of the proof that Christianity was not imported from outside—from Judea—into the Romano-Greek world and imposed on it, but that, at least in its world-religion form, it is that world's own product. Bauer, of course, like all those who are fighting against deep-rooted prejudices, overreached his aim in this work.

In order to define through literary sources too, Philo's and particularly Seneca's influence on emerging Christianity and to show up the authors of the New Testament formally as downright plagiarists of those philosophers he had to place the appearance of the new religion about half a century later, to reject the opposing accounts of Roman historians and take extensive liberties with historiography in general. According to him Christianity as such appears only under the Flavians, the literature of the New Testament only under Hadrian, Antonius and Marcus Aurelius. As a result the New Testament accounts of Jesus and his disciples are deprived for Bauer of any historical background: they are diluted in legends in which the phases of interior development and the moral struggles of the first communities are transferred to more or less fictitious persons. Not Galilee and Jerusalem, but Alexandria and Rome, according to Bauer, are the birthplaces of the new religion.

If, therefore, the Tübingen school presents to us in the remains of the New Testament stories and literature that it left untouched the extreme maximum of what science today can still accept as disputable, Bruno Bauer presents to us the maximum of what can be contested. The factual truth lies between these two limits. Whether that truth can be defined with the means at our disposal today is very doubtful. New discoveries, particularly in Rome, in the Orient, and above all in Egypt, will contribute more to this than any criticism.

But we have in the New Testament a single book the time of the writing of which can be defined within a few months, which must have been written between June 67 and January or April 68; a book, consequently, which belongs to the very beginning of the Christian era and reflects with the most naive fidelity and in the corresponding idiomatic language the ideas of the beginning of that era.

This book, therefore, in my opinion, is a far more important source from which to define what early Christianity really was than all the rest of the New Testament, which, in its present form, is of a far later date. This book is the so-called Revelation of John. And as this, apparently the most obscure book in the whole Bible, is moreover today, thanks to German criticism, the most comprehensible and the clearest, I shall give my readers an account of it.

One needs but to look into this book in order to be convinced of the state of great exaltation not only of the author, but also of the "surrounding medium" in which he moved. Our "Revelation" is not the only one of its kind and time. From the year 164 before our era, when the first which has reached us, the so-called Book of Daniel, was written, up to about 250 of our era, the approximate date of Commodian's *Carmen*,[98] Renan counted no fewer than fifteen extant classical "Apocalypses," not counting subsequent imitations. (I quote Renan because his book is also the best known by non-specialists and the most accessible.) That was a time when even in Rome and Greece and still more in Asia Minor, Syria and Egypt an absolutely uncritical mixture of the crassest superstitions of the most varying peoples was indiscriminately accepted and complemented by pious deception and downright charlatanism; a time in which miracles, ecstasies, visions, apparitions, divining, gold-making, cabbala[99] and other secret magic played a primary role. It was in that atmosphere, and, moreover, among a class of people who were more inclined than any other to listen to these supernatural fantasies, that Christianity arose. For did not the Christian gnostics[100] in Egypt during the second century of our era engage extensively in alchemy and introduce alchemistic notions into their teachings, as the Leyden papyrus documents, among others, prove. And the Chaldean and Judean *mathematici,* who, according to Tacitus, were twice expelled from Rome for magic, once under Claudius and again under Vitellius, practised no other kind of geometry than the kind we shall find at the basis of John's Revelation.

To this we must add another thing. All the apocalypses attribute to themselves the right to deceive their readers. Not only were they written as a rule by quite different people than their alleged authors, and mostly by people who lived much later, for example the Book of Daniel, the Book of Henoch, the Apocalypses of Ezra, Baruch, Juda, etc., and the Sibylline books, but, as far as their main content is concerned, they prophesy only things that had already happened long before and were quite well known to the real author. Thus in the year 164, shortly before the death of Antiochus Epiphanes, the author of the Book of Daniel makes Daniel, who is supposed to have lived in the time of Nebuchadnezzar, prophesy the rise and fall of the Persian and Macedonian empires and the beginning of the Roman Empire, in order by this proof of his gift of prophecy to prepare the reader to accept the final prophecy that the people of Israel will overcome all hardships and finally be victorious. If therefore John's Revelation were really the work of its alleged author it would be the only exception among all apocalyptic literature.

The John who claims to be the author was, in any case, a man of great distinction among the Christians of Asia Minor. This is borne out by the tone of the message to the seven churches. Possibly he was the apostle John, whose historical existence, however, is not completely authenticated but is very probable. If this apostle was really the author, so much the better for our point of view. That would be the best confirmation that the Christianity of this book is real genuine early Christianity. Let it be noted in passing that, apparently, the Revelation was not written by the same author as the Gospel or the three Epistles which are also attributed to John.

The Revelation consists of a series of visions. In the first Christ appears in the garb of a high priest, goes in the midst of seven candlesticks representing the seven churches of Asia and dictates to "John" messages to the seven "angles" of those churches. Here at the very beginning we see plainly the difference between *this* Christianity and Constantine's universal religion formulated by the Council of Nicaea. The Trinity is not only unknown, it is even impossible. Instead of the *one* Holy Ghost of later we here have the "*seven spirits of God*" construed by the Rabbis from Isaiah XI, 2. Christ is the son of God, the first and the last, the *alpha* and the *omega,* by no means God himself or equal to God, but on the contrary, "the beginning of the *creation* of God," hence an emanation of God, existing from all eternity but subordinate to God, like the above-mentioned seven spirits. In Chapter XV, 3, the martyrs in heaven sing "the song of Moses, the servant of God, and the song of the Lamb" glorifying God. Hence Christ here appears not only as subordinate to God but even, in a certain respect, on an equal footing with Moses. Christ is crucified in Jerusalem (XI, 8) but rises again (I, 5, 18); he is "the Lamb" that has been sacrificed for the sins of the world and with whose blood the faithful of all tongues and nations have been redeemed to God. Here we find the basic idea which enabled early Christianity to develop into a universal religion. All Semitic and European religions of that time shared the view that the gods offended by the actions of man could be propitiated by sacrifice; the first revolutionary basic idea (borrowed from the Philonic school) in Christianity was that by the one great voluntary sacrifice of a mediator the sins of all times and all men were atoned for once for all—in respect of the faithful. Thus the necessity of any further sacrifices was removed and with it the basis for a multitude of religious rites: but freedom from rites that made difficult or forbade intercourse with people of other confessions was the first condition of a universal religion. In spite of this the habit of sacrifice was so deeply rooted in the customs of peoples that Catholicism—which borrowed so much from paganism—found it appropriate to accommodate itself to this fact by the introduction of at least the symbolical sacrifice of the mass. On the other hand there is no trace whatever of the dogma of original sin in our book.

But the most characteristic in these messages, as in the whole book, is that it never and nowhere occurs to the author to refer to himself and his co-believers by any other name than that of *Jews*. He reproaches the members of the sects in Smyrna and Philadelphia against whom he fulminates with the fact that they "say they are Jews, and are not, but are the synagogue of Satan"; of those in Pergamos he says: they hold the doctrine of Balaam, who taught Balac to cast a stumbling-block *before the children of Israel,* to eat things sacrificed unto idols, and to commit fornication. Here it is therefore not a case of conscious Christians but of people who say they are Jews. Granted, their Judaism is a new stage of development of the earlier but for that very reason it is the only true one. Hence, when the saints appeared before the throne of God there came first 144,000 Jews, 12,000 from each tribe, and only after them the countless masses of heathens converted to this renovated Judaism. That was how little our author was aware in the year 69 of the Christian era that he represented quite a new phase in the development of a religion which was to become one of the most revolutionary elements in the history of the human mind.

We therefore see that the Christianity of that time, which was still unaware of itself, was as different as heaven from earth from the later dogmatically fixed universal religion of the Nicene Council; one cannot be recognized in the other. Here we have neither the dogma nor the morals of later Christianity but instead a feeling that one is struggling against the whole world and that the struggle will be a victorious one; an eagerness for the struggle and a certainty of victory which are totally lacking in Christians of today and which are to be found in our time only at the other pole of society, among the Socialists.

In fact, the struggle against a world that at the beginning was superior in force, and at the same time against the novators themselves, is common to the early Christians and the Socialists. Neither of these two great movements were made by leaders or prophets—although there are prophets enough among both of them—they are mass movements. And mass movements are bound to be confused at the beginning; confused because the thinking of the masses at first moves among contradictions, lack of clarity and lack of cohesion, and also because of the role that prophets still play in them at the beginning. This confusion is to be seen in the formation of numerous sects which fight against one another with at least the same zeal as against the common external enemy. So it was with early Christianity, so it was in the beginning of the socialist movement, no matter how much that worried the well-meaning worthies who preached unity where no unity was possible.

Was the International held together by a uniform dogma? On the contrary. There were Communists of the French pre-1848 tradition, among whom again were various shades: Communists of Weitling's school and others of the regenerated Communist League, Proudhonists dominating in France and Belgium, Blanquists, the German Workers' Party, and finally the Bakuninist anarchists, who for a while had the upper hand in Spain and Italy, to mention only the principal groups. It took a whole quarter of a century from the foundation of the International before the separation from the anarchists was final and complete everywhere and unity could be established at least in respect of most general economic viewpoints. And that with our means of communication—railways, telegraph, giant industrial cities, the press, organized people's assemblies.

There was among the early Christians the same division into countless sects, which was the very means by which discussion and thereby later unity was achieved. We already find it in this book, which is beyond doubt the oldest Christian document, and our author fights it with the same irreconcilable ardour as the great sinful world outside. There were first of all the Nicolaitans, in Ephesus and Pergamos; those that said they were Jews but were the synagogue of Satan, in Smyrna and Philadelphia; the supporters of Balaam, who is called a false prophet, in Pergamos; those who said they were apostles and were not, in Ephesus; and finally, in Thyatira, the supporters of the false prophetess who is described as a Jezebel. We are given no more details about these sects, it being only said about the followers of Balaam and Jezebel that they ate things sacrificed to idols and committed fornication. Attempts have been made to conceive these five sects as Pauline Christians and all the messages as directed against Paul, the false apostle, the alleged Balaam and "Nicolaos." Arguments to this effect, hardly tenable, are to be found collected in Renan's *Saint Paul* (Paris 1869, pp. 303-05 and 367-70). They all tend to explain the messages by the Acts of the Apostles and the so-called Epistles of Paul, writings which, at least in their present form, are no less than 60 years younger than the Revelation and the relevant factual data of which, therefore, are not only extremely doubtful but also totally contradictory. But the decisive thing is that it could not occur to the author to give five different names to one and the same sect and even two for Ephesus alone (false apostles and Nicolaitans) and two also for Pergamos (Balaamites and Nicolaitans), and to refer to them every time expressly as two different sects. At the same time one cannot deny the probability that there were also elements among these sects that would be termed Pauline today.

In both cases in which more details are given the accusation bears on eating meats offered to idols and on fornication, two points on which the Jews—the old ones as well as the Christian ones—were in continual dispute with converted heathens. The meat from heathen sacrifices was not only served at festal meals where refusal of the food offered would have seemed improper and could even have been dangerous; it was also sold on the public markets, where it was not always possible to ascertain whether it was pure in the eyes of the law. By fornication the Jews understood not only extra-nuptial sexual relations but also marriage within the degrees of relationship prohibited by the Jewish law or between a Jew and a gentile, and it is in this sense that the word is generally understood in the Acts of the Apostles XV, 20 and 29. But our John has his own views on the sexual relations allowed to orthodox Jews. He says, XIV, 4, of the 144,000 heavenly Jews: "These are they which were not defiled with women; for they are virgins." And in fact, in our John's heaven there is not a single woman. He therefore belongs to the trend, which also often appears in other early Christian writings, that considers sexual relations generally as sinful. And when we moreover take into consideration the fact that he calls Rome the Great Whore with whom the kings of the earth have committed fornication and have become drunk with the wine of fornication and the merchants of the earth have waxed rich through the abundance of her delicacies, it becomes impossible for us to take the word in the messages in the narrow sense that theological apologists would like to attribute to it in order thus to catch at some confirmation of other passages in the New Testament. On the contrary. These passages in the messages are an obvious indication of a phenomenon common to all times of great agitation, that the traditional bonds of sexual relations, like all other fetters, are shaken off. In the first centuries of Christianity, too, there appeared often enough, side by side with ascetics which mortified the flesh, the tendency to extend Christian freedom to a more or less unrestrained intercourse between man and woman. The same thing was observed in the modern socialist movement. What unspeakable horror was felt in the then "pious nursery" of Germany at Saint-Simon's a *réhabilitation de la chair* in the thirties, which was rendered in German as "*Wiedereinsetzung des Fleisches*" (reinstatement of the flesh)! And the most horrified of all were the then ruling distinguished estates (there were as yet no classes in our country) who could not live in Berlin any more than on their country estates without repeated reinstatement of their flesh! If only those good people had been able to know Fourier, who contemplated quite different pranks for the flesh! With the overcoming of utopianism these extravagances yielded to a more rational and in reality far more radical conception, and since Germany has grown out of Heine's pious nursery and developed into the centre of the Socialist movement the hypocritical indignation of the distinguished pious world is laughed at.

That is all the dogmatic content of the messages. The rest consists in exhorting the faithful to be zealous in propaganda, to courageous and proud confession of their faith in face of the foe, to unrelenting struggle against the enemy both within and without—and as far as this goes they could just as well have been written by one of the prophetically minded enthusiasts of the International.

III

The messages are but the introduction to the theme properly so-called of John's communication to the seven churches of Asia Minor and through them to the remaining reformed Judaism of the year 69, out of which Christianity later developed. And herewith we enter the innermost holy of holies of early Christianity.

What kind of people were the first Christians recruited from? Mainly from the "labouring and burdened," the members of the lowest strata of the people, as becomes a revolutionary element. And what did they consist of? In the towns of impoverished free men, all sorts of people, like the "mean whites" of the southern slave states and the European beachcombers and adventurers in colonial and Chinese seaports, then of emancipated slaves and, above all, actual slaves; on the large estates in Italy, Sicily, and Africa of slaves, and in the rural districts of the provinces of small peasants who had fallen more and more into bondage through debt. There was absolutely no common road to emancipation for all these elements. For all of them paradise lay lost behind them; for the ruined free men it was the former *polis*, the town and the state at the same time, of which their forefathers had been free citizens; for the war-captive slaves the time of freedom before their subjugation and captivity; for the small peasants the abolished gentile social system and communal landownership. All that had been smitten down by the levelling iron fist of conquering Rome. The largest social group that antiquity had attained was the tribe and the union of kindred tribes; among the barbarians grouping was based on alliances of families and among the town-founding Greeks and Italians on the *polis,* which consisted of one or more kindred tribes. Philip and Alexander gave the Hellenic peninsula political unity but that did not lead to the formation of a Greek nation. Nations became possible only through the downfall of Roman world domination. This domination had put an end once for all to the smaller unions; military might, Roman jurisdiction and the tax-collecting machinery completely dissolved the traditional inner organization. To the loss of independence and distinctive organization was added the forcible plunder by military and civil authorities who took the treasures of the subjugated away from them and then lent them back at usurious rates in order to extort still more out of them. The pressure of taxation and the need for money which it caused in regions dominated only or mainly by natural economy plunged the peasants into ever deeper bondage to the usurers, gave rise to great differences in fortune, making the rich richer and the poor completely destitute. Any resistance of isolated small tribes or towns to the gigantic Roman world power was hopeless. Where was the way out, salvation, for the enslaved, oppressed and impoverished, a way out common to all these groups of people whose interests were mutually alien or even opposed? And yet it had to be found if a great revolutionary movement was to embrace them all.

This way out was found. But not in this world. In the state in which things were it could only be a religious way out. Then a new world was disclosed. The continued life of the soul after the death of the body had gradually become a recognized article of faith throughout the Roman world. A kind of recompense or punishment of the deceased souls for their actions while on earth also received more and more general recognition. As far as recompense was concerned, admittedly, the prospects were not so good: antiquity was too spontaneously materialistic not to attribute infinitely greater value to life on earth than to life in the kingdom of shadows; to live on after death was considered by the Greeks rather as a misfortune. Then came Christianity, which took recompense and punishment in the world beyond seriously and created heaven and hell, and a way out was found which would lead the labouring and burdened from this vale of woe to eternal paradise. And in fact only with the prospect of a reward in the world beyond could the stoico-philonic renunciation of the world and ascetics be exalted to the basic moral principle of a new universal religion which would inspire the oppressed masses with enthusiasm.

But this heavenly paradise does not open to the faithful by the mere fact of their death. We shall see that the kingdom of God, the capital of which is the New Jerusalem, can only be conquered and opened after arduous struggles with the powers of hell. But in the imagination of the early Christians these struggles were immediately ahead. John describes his book at the very beginning as the revelation of "things which must *shortly* come to pass"; and immediately afterwards, I, 3, he declares "Blessed is he that readeth and they that hear the words of this prophecy . . . for *the time is at hand.*" To the church in Philadelphia Christ sends the message: "Behold, I come *quickly.*" And in the last chapter the angel says he has shown John "things which must *shortly* be done" and gives him the order: "Seal not the sayings of the prophecy of this book: for the time is *at hand.*" And Christ himself says twice (XXII, 12, 20) "I come *quickly.*" The sequel will show us how soon this coming was expected.

The visions of the Apocalypse, which the author now shows us, are copied throughout, and mostly literally, from earlier models, partly from the classical prophets of the

Old Testament, particularly Ezekiel, partly from later Jewish apocalypses written after the fashion of the Book of Daniel and in particular from the Book of Henoch which had already been written at least in part. Criticism has shown to the smallest details where our John got every picture, every menacing sign, every plague sent to unbelieving humanity, in a word, the whole of the material for his book; so that he not only shows great poverty of mind but even himself proves that he never experienced even in imagination the alleged ecstasies and visions which he describes.

The order of these visions is briefly as follows: First John sees God sitting on his throne holding in his hand a book with seven seals and before him the Lamb that has been slain and has risen from the dead (Christ) and is found worthy to open the seals of the book. The opening of the seals is followed by all sorts of miraculous menacing signs. When the fifth seal is opened John sees under the altar of God the souls of the martyrs of Christ that were slain for the word of God and who cry with a loud voice saying: "How long, O Lord, dost Thou not judge and avenge our blood on them that dwell on the earth?" And then white robes are given to them and they are told that they must rest for a little while yet, for more martyrs must be slain.

So here it is not yet a question of a "religion of love," of "Love your enemies, bless them that curse you," etc. Here undiluted revenge is preached, sound, honest revenge on the persecutors of the Christians. So it is in the whole of the book. The nearer the crisis comes, the heavier the plagues and punishments rain from the heavens and with all the more satisfaction John announces that the mass of humanity will not atone for their sins, that new scourges of God must lash them, that Christ must rule them with a rod of iron and tread the wine-press of the fierceness and wrath of Almighty God, but that the impious still remain obdurate in their hearts. It is the natural feeling, free of all hypocrisy, that a fight is going on and that—*à la guerre comme à la guerre.*

When the seventh seal is opened there come seven angels with seven trumpets and each time one of them sounds his trumpet new horrors occur. After the seventh blast seven more angels come on to the scene with the seven vials of the wrath of God which they pour out upon the earth; still more plagues and punishments, mainly boring repetitions of what has already happened several times. Then comes the woman, Babylon the Great Whore, sitting arrayed in scarlet over the waters, drunk with the blood of the saints and the martyrs of Jesus, the great city of the seven hills that rules over all the kings of the earth. She is sitting on a beast with seven heads and ten horns. The seven heads represent the seven hills, and also seven "kings." Of those kings five are fallen, one is, and the other is not yet come, and after him comes again one of the first five; he was wounded to death but was healed. He will reign over the world for 42 months or $3^1/_2$ years (half of a week of seven years) and will persecute the faithful to death and bring the rule of godlessness. But then follows the great final fight, the saints and the martyrs are avenged by the destruction of the Great Whore Babylon and all her followers, i.e., the main mass of mankind; the devil is cast into the bottomless pit and shut up there for a thousand years during which Christ reigns with the martyrs risen from the dead. But after a thousand years the devil is freed again and there is another great battle of the spirits in which he is finally defeated. Then follows the second resurrection, when the other dead also arise and appear before the throne of judgment of God (not of Christ, be it noted) and the faithful will enter a new heaven, a new earth, and a new Jerusalem for life eternal.

As this whole monument is made up of exclusively pre-Christian Jewish material it presents almost exclusively Jewish ideas. Since things started to go badly in this world for the people of Israel, from the time of the tribute to the Assyrians and Babylonians, from the destruction of the two kingdoms of Israel and Juda to the bondage under Seleucis, that is from Isaiah to Daniel, in every dark period there were prophecies of a saviour. In Daniel, XII, 1-3, there is even a prophecy about Michael, the guardian angel of the Jews, coming down on earth to save them from great trouble; many dead will come to life again, there will be a kind of last judgment and the teachers who have taught the people justice will shine like stars for all eternity. The only Christian point is the great stress laid on the imminent reign of Christ and the glory of the faithful, particularly the martyrs who have risen from the dead.

For the interpretation of these prophecies, as far as they refer to events of that time, we are indebted to German criticism, particularly Ewald, Lücke and Ferdinand Benary. It has been made accessible to non-theologians by Renan. We have already seen that Babylon, the Great Whore, stands for Rome, the city of seven hills. We are told in Chapter XVII, 9-11, about the beast on which she sits that:

"The seven heads" of the beast "are seven mountains, on which the woman sitteth. And there are seven kings: five are fallen, and one is, and the other is not yet come; and when he cometh he must continue a short space. And the beast that was, and is not, even he is the eighth, and is of the seven, and goeth into perdition."

According to this the beast is Roman world domination, represented by seven caesars in succession, one of them having been mortally wounded and no longer reigning, but he will be healed and will return. It will be given unto him as the eighth to establish the kingdom of blasphemy and defiance of God. It will be given unto him

"to make war with the saints and to overcome them.... And all that dwell upon the earth shall worship him, whose names are not written in the book of life of the Lamb.... And he causeth all, both small and great, rich and poor, free and bond, to receive a mark in their right hand, or in their foreheads: and that no man might buy or sell, save he that had the mark, or the name of the beast, or the number of his name. Here is wisdom. Let him that hath understanding count the number of the beast, for it is the number of a man; and his number is Six hundred threescore and six." (XIII, 7-18.)

We merely note that boycott is mentioned here as one of the measures to be applied against the Christians by the Roman Empire—and is therefore patently an invention of the devil—and pass on to the question who this Roman emperor is who has reigned once before, was wounded to death and removed but will return as the eighth in the series in the role of Antichrist.

Taking Augustus as the first we have: 2. Tiberius, 3. Caligula, 4. Claudius, 5. Nero, 6. Galba. "Five are fallen, and one is." Hence, Nero is already fallen and Galba is. Galba ruled from June 9, 68 to January 15, 69. But immediately after he ascended the throne the legions of the Rhine revolted under Vitellius while other generals prepared military risings in other provinces. In Rome itself the praetorians rose, killed Galba and proclaimed Otho emperor.

From this we see that our Revelation was written under Galba. Probably towards the end of his rule. Or, at the latest, during the three months (up to April 15, 69) of the rule of Otho, "the seventh." But who is the eighth, who was and is not? That we learn from the number 666.

Among the Semites—Chaldeans and Jews—there was at the time a kind of magic based on the double meaning of letters. As about 300 years before our era Hebrew letters were also used as symbols for numbers: a=1, b=2, g=3, d=4, etc. The cabbala diviners added up the value of each letter of a name and sought from the sum to prophesy the future of the one who bore the name, e.g., by forming words or combinations of words of equal value. Secret words and the like were also expressed in this language of numbers. This art was given the Greek name *gematriah*, geometry; the Chaldeans, who pursued this as a business and were called *mathematici* by Tacitus, were later expelled from Rome under Claudius and again under Vitellius, presumably for "serious disorders."

It was by means of this mathematics that our number 666 appeared. It is a disguise for the name of one of the first five caesars. But besides the number 666, Irenaeus, at the end of the second century, knew another reading—616, which, at all events, appeared at a time when the number puzzle was still widely known. The proof of the solution will be if it holds good for both numbers.

This solution was given by Ferdinand Benary of Berlin. The name is Nero. The number is based on נרון קסר Neron Kesar, the Hebrew spelling of the Greek Nerôn Kaisar, Emperor Nero, authenticated by means of the Talmud and Palmyrian inscriptions. This inscription was found on coins of Nero's time minted in the eastern half of the empire. And so—n (*nun*)=50; r (*resh*)=200; v (*vau*) for o=6; n (*nun*)=50; k (*kaph*)=100; s (*samech*)=60; r (*resh*)=200. Total 666. If we take as a basis the Latin spelling *Nero Caesar* the second *nun*=50 disappears and we get 666—50=616, which is Irenaeus's reading.

In fact the whole Roman Empire suddenly broke into confusion in Galba's time. Galba himself marched on Rome at the head of the Spanish and Gallic legions to overthrow Nero, who fled and ordered an emancipated slave to kill him. But not only the praetorians in Rome plotted against Galba, the supreme commanders in the provinces did too; new pretendants to the throne appeared everywhere and prepared to march on Rome with their legions. The empire seemed doomed to civil war, its dissolution appeared imminent. Over and above all this the rumour spread, especially in the East, that Nero had not been killed but only wounded, that he had fled to the Parthians and was about to advance with an army over the Euphrates to begin another and more bloody rule of terror. Achaia and Asia in particular were terrified by such reports. And at the very time at which the Revelation must have been written there appeared a false Nero who settled with a fairly considerable number of supporters not far from Patmos and Asia Minor on the island of Kytnos in the Aegean Sea (now called Thermia), until he was killed while Otho still reigned. What was there to be astonished at in the fact that among the Christians, against whom Nero had begun the first great persecution, the view spread that he would return as the Antichrist and that his return and the intensified attempt at a bloody suppression of the new sect that it would involve would be the sign and prelude of the return of Christ, of the great victorious struggle against the powers of hell, of the thousand year kingdom "shortly" to be established, the confident expectation of which inspired the martyrs to go joyfully to death?

Christian and Christian-influenced literature in the first two centuries gives sufficient indication that the secret of the number 666 was then known to many. Irenaeus no longer knew it, but on the other hand he and many others up to the end of the third century also knew that the returning Nero was meant by the beast of the Apocalypse. This trace is then lost and the work which interests us is fantastically interpreted by religious-minded future-tellers; I myself as a child knew old people who, following the example of old Johann Albrecht Bengel, expected the end of the world and the last judgment in the year 1836. The prophecy was fulfilled, and to the very year. The victim of the last judgment, however, was not the sinful world, but the pious interpreters of the Revelation themselves. For in 1836 F. Benary provided the key to the number 666 and thus put a torturous end to all the prophetical calculations, that new *gematriah.*

Our John can only give a superficial description of the kingdom of heaven that is reserved for the faithful. The new Jerusalem is laid out on a fairly large scale, at least according to the conceptions of the time: it is 12,000 furlongs or 2,227 square kilometres, so that its area is about five million square kilometres, more than half the size of the United States of America. And it is built of gold and all manner of precious stones. There God lives with his people, lightening them instead of the sun, and there shall be no more death, neither sorrow, neither shall there be any more pain. And a pure river of water of life flows through the city, and on either side of the river are trees of life, bearing twelve manner of fruits and yielding fruit every month; and the leaves of the tree "serve for the healing of the nations." (A kind of medicinal beverage, Renan thinks—*L'Antechrist*, p. 542.) Here the saints shall live for ever.

Such, as far as we know, was Christianity in Asia Minor, its main seat, about the year 68. No trace of any Trinity but, on the contrary, the old one and indivisible Jehovah of later Judaism which had exalted him from the national god of the Jews to the one and supreme God of heaven and earth, where he claims to rule over all nations, promising mercy to those who are converted and mercilessly smiting down the obdurate in accordance with the ancient *parcere subjectis ac debellare superbos.** Hence, this God, in person, not Christ as in the later accounts of the Gospels and the Epistles, will judge at the last judgment. According to the Persian doctrine of emanation which was current in later Judaism, Christ the Lamb proceeds eternally from him as do also, but on a lower footing, the "seven spirits of God" who owe their existence to a misunderstanding of a poetical passage (Isaiah, XI, 2). All of them are subordinate to God, not God themselves or equal to him. The Lamb sacrifices itself to atone for the sins of the world and for that it is considerably promoted in heaven, for its voluntary death is credited as an extraordinary feat throughout the book, not as something which proceeds necessarily from its intrinsic nature. Naturally the whole heavenly court of elders, cherubim, angels and saints is there. In order to become a religion monotheism has ever had to make concessions to polytheism—since the time of the Zend-Avesta.[101] With the Jews the decline to the sensuous gods of the heathens continued chronically until, after the exile, the heavenly court according to the Persian model adapted religion somewhat better to the people's fantasy, and Christianity itself, even after it had replaced the eternally self-equal immutable god of the Jews by the mysterious self-differentiating god of the Trinity, could find nothing to supplant the worship of the old gods but that of the saints; thus, according to Fallmerayer, the worship of Jupiter in Peloponnesus, Maina and Arcadia died out only about the ninth century. (*Geschichte der Halbinsel Morea*, I, p. 227.) Only the modern bourgeois period and its Protestantism did away with the saints again and at last took differentiated monotheism seriously.

---

* Pardon the humble and make war on the proud.—*Ed.*

In the book there is just as little mention of original sin and justification by faith. The faith of these early militant communities is quite different from that of the later victorious church: side by side with the sacrifice of the Lamb, the imminent return of Christ and the thousand-year kingdom which is shortly to dawn form its essential content; this faith survives only through active propaganda, unrelenting struggle against the internal and external enemy, the proud profession of the revolutionary standpoint before the heathen judges and martyrdom, confident in victory.

We have seen that the author is not yet aware that he is something else than a Jew. Accordingly there is no mention of baptism in the whole book, just as many more facts indicate that baptism was instituted in the second period of Christianity. The 144,000 believing Jews are "sealed," not baptized. It is said of the saints in heaven and the faithful upon earth that they had washed themselves of their sins and washed their robes and made them white in the blood of the Lamb; there is no mention of the water of baptism. The two prophets who precede the coming of the Antichrist in Chapter XI do not baptize; and according to XIX, 10, the testimony of Jesus is not baptism but the spirit of prophecy. Baptism should naturally have been mentioned in all these cases if it had already been in vigour; we may therefore conclude with almost absolute certainty that the author did not know of it, that it first appeared when the Christians finally separated from the Jews.

Neither does our author know any more about the second sacrament, the Eucharist. If in the Lutheran text Christ promises all the Thyatirans that remain firm in the faith to come *das Abendmahl halten* with them, this creates a false impression. The Greek text has *deipnêsô*—I shall eat supper (with him), and the English bible translates this correctly: I shall *sup* with him. There is no question here of the Eucharist even as a mere commemoration meal.

There can be no doubt that this book, with its date so originally authenticated as the year 68 or 69, is the oldest of all Christian literature. No other is written in such barbaric language, so full of Hebraisms, impossible constructions and mistakes in grammar. Chapter I, verse 4, for example, says literally: "Grace be unto you . . . from he that is being and that was and that is coming." Only professional theologians and other historians who have a stake in it now deny that the Gospels and the Acts of the Apostles are but later adaptations of writings which are now lost and whose feeble historical core is now unrecognizable in the maze of legend, that even the few Epistles supposed by Bruno Bauer to be "authentic" are either writings of a later date or at best adaptations of old works of unknown authors altered by additions and insertions. It is all the more important since we are here in possession of a book whose date of writing has been determined to the nearest month, a book that displays to us Christianity in its undeveloped form. This form stands in the same relation to the fourth century state religion with its fully evolved dogma and mythology as Tacitus's still unstable mythology of the Germans to the developed teaching of the gods of Edda as influenced by Christian and antique elements. The core of the universal religion is there, but it includes without any discrimination the thousand possibilities of development which became realities in the countless subsequent sects. And the reason why this oldest writing of the time when Christianity was coming into being is especially valuable for us is that it shows without any dilution what Judaism, strongly influenced by Alexandria, contributed to Christianity. All that comes later is western, Greco-Roman addition. It was only by the intermediary of the monotheistic Jewish religion that the cultured monotheism of later Greek vulgar philosophy could clothe itself in the religious form in which alone it could grip the masses. But once this intermediary found, it could become a universal religion only in the Greco-Roman world, and that by further development in and merging with the thought material that world had achieved.

NOTES

[1] *Petri Gassendi Animadversiones in decimum librum Diogenis Laertii, qui est de Vita, Moribus, Placitisque Epicuri.* (Pierre Gassendi, *Observations on the Tenth Book of Diogenes Laertius on the Life, Morals and Opinions of Epicurus*) Lyons, 1649. *p. 13*

[2] Seven notebooks written by Marx in 1839 on the history of Epicurean, Stoic and Sceptic philosophy, some of which he made use of for his thesis, have been kept to this day. *p. 14*

[3] David Hume, *A Treatise on Human Nature*, Vol. I, London, 1874, p. 532. *p. 14*

[4] *Kölnische Zeitung*, daily newspaper published in Cologne from 1802. In the 30's and the early 40's it supported the Catholic Church against Protestantism which was prevalent in Prussia. In 1842 its political editor was Karl Heinrich Hermes, a secret agent of the Prussian Government. It was a bitter opponent of *Rheinische Zeitung*, the editor of which was Marx. *p. 16*

[5] Marx quotes Lucian from the German *Griechische Prosaiker in neuen Übersetzungen.* Fünftes Bändchen. Stuttgart, 1827, p. 176. *p. 17*

[6] *Fetishism*—the worship of certain inanimate objects to which supernatural powers are attributed; remnants of it may be observed in modern religions. *p. 22*

[7] *The stoics*—adherents of a philosophical trend which arose in Greece in the 3rd century before our era and persisted until the 6th century of our era. They wavered between materialism and idealism. In its early period (ancient and middle Stoa) they devoted their attention mainly to the study of the laws of nature and the theory of cognition, mainly from the materialistic standpoint. In the Roman Empire period the New Stoa showed particular interest in problems of morals, treating them in a religious and idealistic spirit and defending the extra-corporeal existence of the soul, the cult of submission of man to fate, non-resistance to evil, self-denial, ascetics, the seeking of God, etc. All this influenced the formation of the Christian religion. *p. 23*

[8] *The sceptics*—adherents of a philosophical trend at the time of the decay of the slave system in Greece and Rome. They doubted the possibility of reliable knowledge of objective truth and consequently of the development of scientific thought. The teaching of the old sceptics, who were the mouthpiece of the subjective idealistic tendency, already bore traces of the degeneration of the once powerful philosophical thought of antiquity. *p. 23*

[9] *The Vedas*—ancient Indian collections of hymns, prayers and liturgical formulas which are the foundation of Vedio literature and religion, written over a number of centuries not later than the 6th century before our era. *p. 25*

[10] *Charte Constitutionelle,* adopted after the French Revolution of 1830. It was the basis of the July Monarchy. *p. 26*

[11] *Rheinische Zeitung für Politik, Handel und Gewerbe, (Rhine Gazette for Politics, Trade and Industry*), a daily newspaper published in Cologne from January 1, 1842 to March 31, 1843. It was founded by representatives of the Rhine bourgeoisie who opposed Prussian absolutism. Some Young Hegelians (Left Hegelians) contributed to it. Marx was a contributor from April 1842 and a member of the editorial board from October 1842. A number of articles by Engels were published in it. Under Marx's editorship it became more and more revolutionary-democratic and the government subjected it to strict censorship and finally suppressed it. *p. 30*

[12] Allusion to Hermes, editor of *Kölnische Zeitung*, having taken part in the German students' opposition movement in his youth. *p. 30*

[13] *Corybantes*—priests of the goddess Cybele; *Cabiri*, priests of the ancient Greek gods of the same name. The Corybantes and Cabiri were identified in Asia Minor with the *curetes* of Crete, priests of the goddess Rhea, mother of Zeus. According to the myth, the *curetes* drowned the voice of the new-born Zeus by striking their shields with their swords. *p. 31*

[14] Allusion to the fierce polemic of the German reactionary press against philosophical criticism of religion which began with D. F. Strauss's book *Das Leben Jesu*, Vol. I, 1835, Vol. II, 1836. *p. 32*

[15] *Berliner politisches Wochenblatt*—an extremely reactionary paper which appeared from 1831 to 1841 with contributions from K. Haller, Leo and Raumer. It had the support and protection of Crown Prince Frederick-William (Frederick-William IV from 1840). *p. 32*

[16] *Hamburger Correspondent*—abridged title of *Staats und Gelehrte Zeitung des Hamburgischen unparteiischen Korrespondenten (State and Scientific Gazette of the Hamburg Independent Correspondent)*. It appeared daily in the 40's and was reactionary and monarchist. *p. 32*

[17] *Deutsche Jahrbücher*—abridged title of the literary and philosophical journal of Young Hegelians *Deutsche Jahrbücher für Wissenschaft und Kunst (German Yearbook of Science and Art)*. Published in Leipzig and edited by A. Ruge from July 1841 to January 1843. *p. 32*

[18] *Saint Bartholomew's Night*—massacre of the Huguenots by the Catholics in Paris during the night before the feast of St. Bartholomew, August 24, 1572, ordered by the French court at the instigation of the Catholic clergy. It continued for three days and several thousands of Huguenots were killed. Similar massacres were organized throughout France. *p. 33*

[19] *Huguenots*—Calvinist Protestants in France in the 16th and 17th centuries. At the beginning of the movement they were mainly bourgeois and craftsmen but later the nobility, in the south of France and a section of the feudal lords, dissatisfied with the policy of centralizing the monarchy, dominated the movement. The development of the movement led to civil war between the Catholics and the Huguenots which began in 1562, intensified after St. Bartholomew's Night and lasted intermittently up to 1594. The Huguenots were granted freedom of religious profession by the Edict of Nantes in 1598 but they continued to be persecuted by the government and the Catholic Church. *p. 36*

[20] *Königsberger Zeitung*—abridged title of the daily *Königlich-Preussische Staats-Kriegs- und Friedens-Zeitung (Royal Prussian State, War and Peace Gazette)* published in Königsberg from 1752 to 1850. In the 40's of the 19th century it was a progressive bourgeois paper. *p. 38*

[21] *The Historical School of Right*—a reactionary trend in historical and juridical science which arose in Germany at the end of the 18th century. *p. 43*

[22] Marx here alludes to Anacharsis, a Scythian by birth, whom the Greeks, according to Diogenes Laertius, listed among the seven Greek sages. *p. 47*

[23] *The September Laws*—reactionary laws enacted by the French Government in September 1835 limiting trial by jury and introducing

severe measures against the press. The latter included increased money deposits for periodicals and imprisonment and large fines for attacks on private property and the existing state system. p. 53

24 *Metaphysics*—anti-dialectic method in thought and cognition which considers things and phenomena as complete, immutable, independent of one another and free from internal contradiction.

In this passage it is a question of metaphysics in the conception prevalent up to the 19th century as a part of philosophy treating speculatively of questions not falling within the pale of experience, e.g., the origins of being, the substance of the world, God, the soul, free will, etc. By the metaphysicians of the 17th century Marx means the rationalists, who considered reason as the only source of true knowledge and discarded sensuous experience as unreliable. While this tendency played a progressive role in the 17th century by maintaining the all-powerfulness of reason in the struggle against the religious dogmatic trend, in the 18th century it became an obstacle to the development of materialistic philosophy and of science. p. 60

25 The *Jansenists*, named after the Dutch theologian Jansenius, representatives of the oppositional trend among the French Catholics in the 17th and early 18th centuries voicing the discontentment of a part of the French bourgeoisie with the feudal ideology of official Catholicism. p. 61

26 *Nominalism*, from the Latin *nomen*, name, a trend in medieval philosophy which held that the general concepts are only names designating analogous objects. In other words, they recognized objects as primary and concepts as secondary. In this sense nominalism was the first manifestation of materialism in the Middle Ages. p. 63

27 *Theistic*, pertaining to *theism*, a philosophical and theological doctrine maintaining the existence of one personal god, creator of the universe. p. 65

28 *Deism*—a trend in philosophy and theology which rejected the idea of a personal god, holding god to be the impersonal primary cause of the world. Under the domination of the feudal and clerical world outlook deism often was a disguised form of materialism and atheism. Subsequently, deism served the bourgeois ideologists to preserve and justify religion of which they only discarded the more absurd and discredited dogmas and rites. p. 65

29 *Rheinischer Beobachter*—conservative daily newspaper published in Cologne from 1844 to the beginning of 1848. p. 82

30 From Schiller's *Das Lied von der Glocke*. p. 90

[31] An allusion to Daumer's *Der Feuer- und Molochdienst der alten Hebräer (Fire and Moloch Worship with the Ancient Hebrews)*. Brunswick, 1842, and *Die Geheimnisse des christlichen Alterthums (The Mysteries of Christian Antiquity)*. Hamburg, 1847. *p. 92*

[32] Ironical allusion to Daumer's *Mahomed und sein Werk*, Hamburg, 1848. *p. 93*

[33] Allusion to Knigge's *Ueber den Umgang mit Menschen* (*On Intercourse with Men*). Hanover, 1804. *p. 94*

[34] Allusion to Goethe's *Wilhelm Meisters Lehrjahre*. *p. 96*

[35] *Waldenses*—a religious sect which appeared among the lower urban classes in Southern France in the late 12th century. It is said to have been founded by Peter Wald, a Lyons merchant. The Waldenses advocated abolition of property, condemned the accumulation of wealth by the Catholic Church and called for a return to the customs of early Christianity. The heresies of the Waldenses spread particularly among the rural population of the mountainous regions in Southern Switzerland and Savoy where they supported survivals of the primitive communal system and patriarchal relations. *p. 99*

[36] *Albigenses*—a religious sect widespread in the towns of Southern France and Northern Italy in the 12th and 13th centuries. Its centre was Albi, in the south of France. The Albigenses opposed the pompous ritual and the hierarchy of the Catholic Church and expressed in a religious form the protest of the tradesmen and handicraftsmen in the towns of the South against feudalism. They were joined by the nobility of the South of France who wanted the secularization of church lands. In 1209 Pope Innocent III organized a crusade against them and the movement was suppressed after a long war and fierce repressions. *p. 99*

[37] One of the leaders of the Peasants' ("shepherds") Revolt in France in 1251. *p. 99*

[38] *Calixtines and Taborites*—trends in the Hussite national-liberation and Reformation movement against the German nobility, the German Empire and the Catholic Church in Bohemia in the first half of the 15th century. The *Calixtines* maintained that the laity should receive the cup as well as the bread in the Eucharist. They were supported by Bohemian nobility and burghers and sought no more than a moderate church reform and the secularization of church lands. The *Taborites*, so called from the town of Tabor, the centre of the movement, were the revolutionary-democratic wing of the Hussites. Their demands reflected the desire of the peasantry and lower urban

classes for the abolition of feudal oppression. Feudal reactionaries made use of the treachery of the Calixtines towards the Taborites in order to suppress the Hussite movement. *p. 100*

[39] The *Flagellants*—an ascetic sect widespread in Europe from the 13th to the 15th centuries. They professed self-castigation as a means of expiating sin. The *Lollards*—a religious sect, particularly widespread in England from the 14th century, which bitterly opposed the Catholic Church. They were followers of the English reformist Wycliffe and drew the most radical conclusions from his teachings. They adopted a religious and mystical stand against feudal privileges. Many of them took part in Wat Tyler's Rebellion in 1381. They were cruelly persecuted from the end of the 14th century. *p. 102*

[40] *Chiliasm*, from the Greek *chiliasmos*, derived from *chilias*, a thousand, a mystical doctrine teaching a second advent of Christ to usher in a thousand years of justice, equality and prosperity. Chiliasm arose during the decay of slave society owing to the unbearable oppression and sufferings of the working people who sought an escape in fantastic visions of deliverance. These beliefs were widespread in early Christianity and were later continually revived in the doctrines of the various medieval sects. *p. 102*

[41] *The Augsburg Confession*—a statement of the Lutheran doctrine read to the Emperor Charles V at the Imperial Diet in Augsburg in 1530; it was an adaptation to the interests of the princes of the burgher ideals of a "cheap church"—abolition of pompous rites, simplification of church hierarchy, etc. It was rejected by the Emperor. The war waged against him by the princes who adopted the Lutheran Reformation ended in 1555 with the religious peace of Augsburg. This empowered the princes to determine the faith of their subjects at their own discretion. *p. 105*

[42] Allusion to a parliament of representatives of the German states included in the German Union set up by Prussia. It met in Erfurt from March 20 to April 29, 1850 and drew up plans for the unification of Germany under the hegemony of reactionary monarchist Prussia. The plans were a failure and the Erfurt Parliament ended with the dissolution of the German Union. *p. 106*

[43] This was the title of a malignant pamphlet against the peasant movement published by Luther in May 1525, when the Peasant War was at its fiercest. *p. 107*

[44] Engels here refers to the views of the German idealist philosopher Strauss and of Feuerbach, who adopted a pantheistic approach to religious questions in his early writings. *p. 111*

[45] W. Zimmermann, *Allgemeine Geschichte des grossen Bauernkrieges (General History of the Great Peasant War)*, Vol. II, Stuttgart, 1842, p. 75. *p. 114*

[46] Engels alludes to Münzer's pamphlet *Ausgedrückte Entblossung des falschen Glaubens der ungetreuen Welt durchs Zeugnis des Evangelions Lucae, vorgetragen der elenden erbärmlichen Christenheit zur Erinnerung ihres Irrsals (Explicit Refutal of the False Belief of the Unorthodox World by the Testimony of the Gospel of Luke, Presented to Miserable and Unhappy Christianity as a Reminder of its Erring)*, published in Mühlhausen in 1524. *p. 114*

[47] According to more precise data, Münzer first went to the imperial town of Mühlhausen, from which he was banished in September 1524 for taking part in disturbances of the city poor. He then went to Nuremberg. *p. 117*

[48] Münzer's printed reply to Luther in 1524 was entitled: *Hoch verursachte Schutzrede und Antwort wider das geistlose, sanftlebende Fleisch zu Wittenberg, welches mit verkehrter Weise durch den Diebstahl der heiligen Schrift die erbärmliche Christenheit also ganz jämmerlich besudelt hat. (Well-Grounded Defence and Reply to Godless, Easy-Living Flesh in Wittenberg, which has Pitifully Sullied Unhappy Christianity through Shameless Distortions of the Holy Scripture.)* *p. 117*

[49] These extracts from the first book of *Capital* (Moscow, 1954) are from Chapter 1, pp. 79-81 and from Marx's notes to Chapter XIII (Note 3, pp. 372-73) and to Chapter XXIII (Note 2, pp. 616-18). *p. 135*

[50] *Kulturkampf*—Bismarck's struggle in the 70's against the German Catholic Party, the party of the "centre," by police repressions against Catholics. *p. 143*

[51] See *Anti-Dühring*, by F. Engels. Moscow, 1954, pp. 144-45, 436-440, 476-477, 480. *p. 145*

[52] Laws enacted by Bismarck during the *Kulturkampf* against the Catholic Church in May 1873. See note 50. *p. 149*

[52] Allusion to Copernicus's book *De Revolutionibus orbium coelestium (On the Revolutions of Heavenly Bodies)*, 1543, expounding the theory of helio-centricity. According to this theory the centre of our planetary system is not the earth, as was formerly held, but the sun. The earth revolves round the sun, at the same time rotating on its own axis. *p. 155*

[54] Euclid—the great mathematician of Ancient Greece, wrote the *Elements of Geometry*, the first systematization of the whole of geometry based on firmly established axioms. Euclid's *Elements* were for a long time the only authority on geometry in the world. *p. 155*

[55] According to what is known as the geocentric theory of the Greek astronomer Ptolemeus the earth was held to be the centre of the universe. This theory was the basis of the religious outlook on the universe. It remained in recognition until the discoveries of Copernicus. *p. 155*

[56] Allusion to a theory dominating in the 17th and 18th centuries which held that the process of combustion depended on the presence in bodies of a particular substance called phlogiston. Research carried out by Lomonosov and Lavoisier proved the inconsistency of this theory. *p. 156*

[57] The hypothesis according to which celestial bodies have their origin in burning nebular masses. *p. 160*

[58] *Amphioxus* (the lancelet)—a fish-like animal about 5 cm. long which breeds in the Indian Ocean, the Pacific Ocean, off the shores of the Malayan Archipelago and Japan, the Mediterranean and Black seas and other places. It is a transitional form between invertebrates and vertebrates. *Lepidosiren*, an Amazon mud-fish, belongs to the order of the lung fishes or Dipnoi, having both lungs and gills. It is found in South America and a number of other places. *p. 163*

[59] *Ceratodus* (barramunda)—a Dipnoi breeding in Australia. *Archaeopteryx*, an extinct animal, was the most ancient representative of the bird class and at the same time had features of the reptiles. *p. 163*

[60] Engels is probably referring to Haeckel's assertion that the simplest living beings he had investigated, and which he called Monera, were completely structureless particles of protein nevertheless carrying out all the essential functions of life. See Haeckel, *Generelle Morphologie der Organismen* (*General Morphology of Organisms*), Vol. I, Berlin, 1866, pp. 133-36. *p. 167*

[61] *Eozoon canadense*—a fossil found in pre-Cambrian excavations in Canada and considered as the remains of ancient primitive organisms. This view of the organic origin of this fossil was refuted by Möbius in 1878. *p. 167*

[62] "*Alles was entsteht, ist wert, dass es zugrunde geht.*" Mephistopheles in Goethe's *Faust*, Part I, Sc. 3. *pp. 169-70*

[63] Engels here quotes the words of the Italian astronomer A. Secchi in his book *Die Sonne (The Sun)*, German edition, Brunswick, 1872. *p. 170*

[64] *Barataria* (from the Spanish *barato*, cheap), name given by Cervantes in his *Don Quixote* to a non-existent island of which Sancho Panza was governor. *p. 177*

[65] *Thallium* was discovered by Crookes in 1861. The *radiometer*, designed by Crookes in 1874, is an instrument for measuring the intensity of radiations. *p. 181*

[66] Allusion to the "Commission for the Investigation of Spiritualist Phenomena" set up by the Physical Society at St. Petersburg University on May 6, 1875; it completed its work on March 21, 1876. It proposed to those disseminating spiritualism in Russia—Aksakov, Butlerov and others—that they provide information on "genuine" spiritualist phenomena. Among the members of the Commission were the scientists, Mendeleyev, Bobylyov and Krayevich. It came to the conclusion that "spiritualist phenomena arise from unconscious movements or deliberate deception and the spiritualist doctrine is superstition." Its conclusions were published in the newspaper *Golos* (*The Voice*), No. 85, March 25, 1876. Mendeleyev published the materials of the Commission under the title: *Materials for a Judgment on Spiritualism*, St. Petersburg, 1876. *p. 184*

[67] From the libretto of Mozart's opera *The Magic Flute*. Act I. Sc. 18. *p. 186*

[68] Engels hints at the reactionary attacks against Darwinism in Germany, particularly after the Paris Commune, 1871. Even an important scientist like Virchow, who had previously supported Darwinism, suggested in 1877 that the teaching of Darwinism be prohibited, asserting that it was closely connected with the socialist movement and therefore dangerous for the existing social system. *p. 186*

[69] The dogma of the Infallibility of the Pope was defined by the Council of the Vatican on July 18, 1870. The German Catholic theologian Döllinger rejected this dogma. Bishop Ketteler of Mainz was also against it at first but he soon reconciled himself to it and became one of its zealous defenders. *p. 187*

[70] The words are quoted from the letter written by the biologist Thomas Huxley to the London Dialectical Society, which had invited him to take part in the work of a committee to study spiritualist phenomena. Huxley declined and made a number of ironical remarks

about spiritualism. His letter, dated January 29, 1869, was printed in *The Daily News* on October 17, 1871. It is also given on page 389 of Davies's book *Mystic London*, mentioned above. *p. 187*

71 The notes and fragments included here are from Engels's *Dialectics of Nature*, Moscow 1954, pp. 259-62 and 268-69. The heading was supplied by the Institute of Marxism-Leninism. *p. 189*

72 See Note 53. *p. 190*

73 "*Sire, je n'avais pas besoin de cette hypothèse*" (Sire, I did not need that hypothesis) was Laplace's answer to Napoleon's question why he made no mention of God in his work on celestial mechanics. *p. 192*

74 Engels is here alluding to Tyndall's speech at a meeting of the British Association for the Advancement of Science held in Belfast on August 19, 1874 (published in *Nature* of August 20, 1874). *p. 193*

75 *Ignorantia non est argumentum*: Spinoza speaks in the appendix to the first part of his *Ethics* of the appeal to ignorance as being the sole argument used by representatives of the clerical-theological outlook on nature. *p. 193*

76 Reference to Heine's *Apollgott*. *p. 196*

77 *The Tübingen School*—school of biblical research and critique founded by F. Bauer in the first half of the 19th century. The rationalistic criticism of the Gospel by its adherents is notable for its inconsistency in desiring to maintain certain propositions of the Bible as historically reliable. Without wishing to do so this school greatly contributed by its criticism to undermine the authority of the Bible as a reliable historical source. *p. 205*

78 Cf. *German Ideology* by Karl Marx and Frederick Engels. *p. 213*

79 Engels has in mind Heine's remarks on the "German revolution in philosophy" in his essay *Zur Geschichte der Religion und Philosophie in Deutschland* (*On the History of Religion and Philosophy in Germany*), written in 1833. *p. 216*

80 Allusion to Max Stirner's *Der Einzige und sein Eigenthum* (*The Ego and His Own*), published in Leipzig in 1845. *p. 224*

81 Feuerbach's *Das Wesen des Christenthums* (*The Essence of Christianity*) was published in Leipzig in 1841. *p. 224*

82 Neptune, discovered in 1846 by Johann Galle, a German astronomer. *p. 229*

[83] Allusion to Robespierre's attempt to set up a worship of the "Supreme Being." *p. 240*

[84] *The schoolmaster of Sadowa*—an expression used currently by German publicists after the Prussian victory at Sadowa in the Austro-Prussian War of 1866. The implication was that the Prussian victory was due to the superiority of the Prussian public education system. *p. 245*

[85] *Rhadamanthus*—symbol of the inflexible judge in Greek mythology. *p. 245*

[86] *Albigenses*, see Note 36. *p. 264*

[87] This term is applied to the German Empire (excluding Austria) established in 1871 under the hegemony of Prussia. *p. 267*

[88] Reference to Engels's *Origin of the Family, Private Property and the State.* *p. 273*

[89] See Karl Marx, *Capital*, Book I, Moscow 1954, Ch. X, pp. 231-302. *p. 285*

[90] Reference to P. Barth's book *Die Geschichtsphilosophie Hegels und der Hegelianer bis auf Marx und Hartmann* (*The Philosophy of History of Hegel and the Hegelians down to Marx and Hartmann*), Leipzig, 1890. *p. 286*

[91] *Vorwärts*—central organ of German Social-Democracy after the Gotha Unification Congress. Published in Leipzig, 1876-78. *p. 288*

[92] *Mark*—old German community. Engels wrote a brief outline on the history of German peasantry since ancient times under the title "Mark" as a supplement to the first German edition of his work *Socialism: Utopian and Scientific.* *p. 289*

[93] *Agnosticism*, from the Greek prefix *a*, not, and *gnosis*, knowledge. It admits the existence of material things but considers them unknowable. *p. 291*

[94] See pp. 63-66 of this collection. *p. 293*

[95] *Brother Jonathan*—earlier equivalent of Uncle Sam. *p. 308*

[96] *Revivalism*—a religious movement to revive the declining influence of religion. *p. 308*

[97] *Almoravids*—a Berber feudal dynasty in North Africa and Southern Spain in the 11th and 12th centuries. *Almohads*—a Berber feudal dynasty which superseded the Almoravids and reigned in the

12th and 13th centuries. *The Mahdi of Khartoum*, Mohammed Ahmed (c. 1844-1885) leader of the national rising of peasants and nomads in the Eastern Sudan (1881-1885), directed against English and other European colonists. It resulted in their expulsion until 1898. *p. 317*

[98] Reference to Commodian's *Carmen apologeticum adversus Judaeos et gentes (Apologetic Song against the Jews and Gentiles.)* *p. 326*

[99] *Cabbala*—a mystic religious doctrine connected with magic and widespread among the Jews. *p. 326*

[100] *Gnostics*—a religious mystic trend of early Christianity; a reactionary eclectic trend in philosophy. *p. 326*

[101] *Zend-Avesta*—a collection of "sacred books" of the Zoroastrian religion which spread over Ancient Persia, Azerbaijan and Central Asia: it is assumed to have been compiled between the 9th century before our era and the 3rd century of our era. *p. 344*

NAME INDEX

C

E

F

G

I

M

T

Z

INDEX of Biblical and Mythological Names

SHORT SUBJECT INDEX